FIDEL CASTRO
and the Quest for a

10/05

FIDEL CASTRO

and the Quest for a Revolutionary Culture in CUBA

Julie Marie Bunck

The Pennsylvania State University Press
University Park, Pennsylvania

Library of Congress Cataloging-in-Publication Data

Bunck, Julie Marie, 1960–
    Fidel Castro and the quest for a revolutionary culture in Cuba / Julie Marie
Bunck.
        p.   cm.
    Includes bibliographical references and index.
    ISBN 0-271-01086-X (cloth: alk. paper)—ISBN 0-271-01087-8 (paper: alk.
paper): $13.95
    1. Cuba—Politics and government—1959– 2. Cuba—History—Revolu-
tion, 1959—Social aspects. 3. Social values—Cuba. 4. Political culture—Cuba.   I. Title.
F1788.B79   1994
972.9106'4—dc20   93-13387
                                                                                        CIP

Published by The Pennsylvania State University Press, Barbara Building, Suite
C, University Park, PA 16802-1003

It is the policy of The Pennsylvania State University Press to use acid-free paper
for the first printing of all clothbound books. Publications on uncoated stock
satisfy the minimum requirements of American National Standard for Information Sciences—Permanence of Paper for Printed Library Materials, ANSI Z39.48–
1984.

Dedicated to my parents,
John and Betty Bunck
on the fortieth anniversary of
their wedding
April 11, 1993

Contents

Abbreviations   ix

Preface   xi

1. Fidel Castro and the Quest for a Revolutionary Culture   1

2. Castro and the Children: The Struggle for Cuba's
   Young Minds   21

3. Castro and the Goal of Sexual Equality   87

4. The Revolutionary Battle to Transform Attitudes
   Toward Labor   125

5. Revolutionary Sports: A Genuine Success   185

6. The Successes and Failures of the Quest for a
   Revolutionary Culture   215

Bibliography   223

Index   231

Abbreviations

AJR	Association of Rebel Youth
ANAP	National Association of Small Farmers
CDRs	Committees for the Defense of the Revolution
CTC	Cuban Confederation of Labor
CVDs	Voluntary Sports Councils
EIDEs	Schools for Basic Training in Sports
EIRs	Schools of Revolutionary Instruction
EJT	Army of Working Youth
ESPRAs	Schools for Advanced Training of Athletes
FAR	Revolutionary Armed Forces
FEEM	Federation of Secondary School Students
FEU	Federation of University Students
FMC	Federation of Cuban Women
INDER	National Institute of Sports, Physical Education, and Recreation
INRA	National Institute of Agrarian Reform
ISPJAE	José Antonio Echeverría Higher Polytechnical Institute
JUCEPLAN	Central Planning Board
NSPAC	National Social Prevention and Attention Commission
PCs	People's Councils
PNR	National Revolutionary Police
SEPMI	Society for Patriotic Military Education
SNTEC	Trade Union of Education and Scientific Workers
TTM	Territorial Troop Militia
UJC	Union of Young Communists
UMAP	Military Units to Aid Production
UPC	Union of Pioneers in Cuba

Preface

The revolutionary government of Fidel Castro has long attempted to change traditional Cuban culture. This book analyzes the efforts to bring about cultural change and the responses of the Cuban people to those efforts. By culture I mean the fundamental beliefs, opinions, and values of a given society, all of which are products of that society's specific historical experience. This study explores a series of cardinal questions about the attempts by the Cuban government, over the last several decades, to transform culture, to create the proper *conciencia,* indeed, in the words of the Castro leadership, to mold a "new man."[1] What particular aspects of pre-revolutionary culture did the leaders target? What strategies did they employ to bring about cultural change? How did the leadership's goals and strategies vary over time? In what ways did Cuban citizens resist the government's pressures? In what respects did the Castro government succeed in transforming traditional culture? In what respects did traditional culture remain constant?

Although the revolutionary onslaught directed against Cuban institutions, including businesses, banks, and labor unions, has been widely analyzed, scholars have less frequently recognized that transforming Cuban culture amounted to one of Castro's leading revolutionary goals. Many works on revolutionary Cuba have wholly failed to address the question of cultural change. The single most important work to date on the subject is Richard Fagen's *The Transformation of Political Culture in Cuba,* which

1. For all their revolutionary zeal in other areas of Cuban life, Fidel Castro and his government officials did not attempt to revolutionize the Spanish language by creating a term that would explicitly encompass both men and women. Rather, the Castro government typically characterized its efforts as an attempt to create a "Nuevo Hombre" ("new man"). Of course, traditionally, Spanish speakers use the masculine terms "he" or "man" to refer to both men and women.

appeared in 1969, a decade after Castro came to power.[2] Fagen argued that cultural change in Cuban society would come about quickly and readily. However, when Fagen examined cultural change, too little time had elapsed since the Revolution for its effects on society to be accurately assessed. In my view Fagen seriously overestimated the prospects for cultural transformation.[3]

The question of cultural change in Cuba has perhaps been often overlooked because of the scarcity of accessible and legitimate sources. Although the Cuban Revolution presents to scholars an intriguing case study of a government's attempt to manipulate culture and society's efforts to resist the leadership's policies, the Cuban government has effectively closed the country to an inquiring world. For more than thirty years Cuba has remained isolated and generally inaccessible to scholarly research. The government has frowned particularly on independent, critical studies of cultural change. Hence, while the Revolution has raised many significant issues, the revolutionary leaders carefully planted a thicket of difficulties that have severely obstructed independent attempts to pursue questions about cultural change on the island.

Ideally, one would study cultural change by probing the views, sentiments, attitudes, and values of the citizens themselves. In open societies formal and informal survey research can be employed toward this end. However, Cuba's revolutionary government, like that of other closed Marxist societies, has not allowed foreign scholars to carry out such research. And, given the leadership's intolerance for dissent, one must question the validity of the few survey-research projects that have been carried out to date by Cuban academics, sympathetic foreign scholars, or the Cuban government itself.

Yet it is precisely the nature of Cuban society—closed, mysterious, re-

2. Richard Fagen, *The Transformation of Political Culture in Cuba* (Stanford: Stanford University Press, 1969).

3. Tzvi Medin's more recent work on cultural change in Cuba presents a valuable study of the government's methods of projecting revolutionary messages to the masses. Tzvi Medin, *Cuba: The Shaping of Revolutionary Consciousness* (Boulder: Lynne Rienner Publishers, 1990). Medin's work examines the various avenues—theater, art, poetry, cinema, music, fiction, and the media—through which the government sent revolutionary messages in its efforts to transform Cuban culture. His book, however, neither discusses what specific aspects of culture the Castro leadership targeted nor analyzes the results of the state's efforts to transform Cuban culture. A few other scholars have briefly or indirectly touched on the subject of cultural change. Jorge Domínguez, for example, devoted a chapter to cultural change in his *Cuba: Order and Revolution* (Cambridge: Harvard University Press, 1978). Luis Salas, likewise, touched on the subject of cultural change in his fascinating, yet now dated, work on juvenile delinquency in revolutionary Cuba. See Luis Salas, *Social Control and Deviance in Cuba* (New York: Praeger, 1979).

pressed—that makes it a particularly attractive subject for research. If the Castro government were more moderate, Cuban society would likely be more open and scholars more free to canvass popular opinions. Moreover, a more moderate government's attempt to transform culture would likely have been considerably less remarkable. Consequently, the study of cultural change in revolutionary Cuba would be less important and much less interesting. The case of revolutionary Cuba thus attracts as well as frustrates those who wish to study cultural change.

This book is premised on the belief that the questions addressed are sufficiently important that answering them as accurately as possible by probing imperfect sources is preferable to not attempting to answer them at all. In an effort to appraise cultural change in revolutionary Cuba in an independent manner, I have relied upon a range of available sources.

First, I have considered carefully what Cuban leaders said and did. Since leaders often respond to the behavior and attitudes of citizens, the words and actions of Fidel Castro and his colleagues provide a useful source of information about citizens as well as leaders. For example, if Castro spent a good deal of time discussing vagrancy in his speeches, and if the government passed a number of increasingly harsh antivagrancy laws, one can assume with some confidence that vagrancy remained a problem in Cuban society.

In an effort to catch glimpses of popular attitudes and values, I have also scavenged through Cuban newspapers, magazines, government reports, and other public and private publications. I have drawn as well on a range of surveys, studies, and statistical charts authored by the Cuban government and scholars from Cuba and other countries. In addition, I have relied on a wide variety of newspapers from the United States and Latin America, the United States *Foreign Broadcast Information Service* daily reports, and the *Latin America Weekly Reports,* a British publication. I have thus drawn on an array of sources of information on revolutionary Cuba, some sympathetic to the Castro government and some opposed to it.

Whatever sources one relies upon, detecting and explaining cultural change can be a tricky business. That a society's citizens begin to behave differently does not necessarily indicate cultural change. While culture can influence behavior, it is not the sole determinant of behavior. Although behavioral changes may indeed reflect a genuine, newly acquired revolutionary *conciencia,* other factors may also influence the way in which citizens act. Behavioral change among citizens may reflect a surrender to government-imposed rules of social conduct. State coercion can force citizens to abandon or temporarily modify behavior that reflects their authentic values and beliefs.

Hence, behavior that is rooted in a society's culture should be differentiated from behavior that merely responds to coercion, or the threat of coercion, and would cease absent the coercion.[4] For example, a government might effectively compel people to participate in a revolutionary campaign through punishing or threatening those who fail to participate. Since such behavior would not necessarily reflect strongly held values and beliefs, it could not accurately be viewed as rooted in that society's culture.

The Cuban leadership has not been alone in tinkering with society's traditional values, attitudes, and beliefs. While this study examines only Fidel Castro's revolutionary project to transform culture, the questions it raises may well pertain to the efforts of various other twentieth-century governments that have struggled, with varying degrees of enthusiasm and constancy, to create a revolutionary culture.[5]

Today, amidst the debris of the collapse of communism within the Soviet Union and Eastern Europe, what can we observe about the efforts of these governments to destroy traditional values and to create radically new ones? What is the relationship between cultural and institutional change in revolutionary societies? To what extent have communist leaders been able to manipulate society and transform traditional culture? In what respects have citizens resisted and frustrated the leadership's programs to bring about cultural change? How and under what circumstances are governments able to change culture? To what extent do communist leaders ultimately rely on coercion to attempt to impose on their people changes in behavior or actual changes in culture?

The purpose of this book is to provoke discussion and encourage fur-

---

4. Here I am taking a stand on the controversial question of whether to view culture as a system of beliefs or to adopt an anthropologically oriented definition that includes objective phenomena such as actions and behavior. I have opted for the former, and in doing so I have joined Gabriel Almond, Sidney Verba, and Lucian W. Pye, among others. Richard Fagen, Robert Tucker, Clifford Geertz, and Kenneth Jowitt are among the scholars who have adopted a more behavioral and anthropological definition of culture. For references see Fagen; Gabriel Almond, "Communism and Political Culture Theory," *Comparative Politics* 15, no. 2 (January 1983): 127–138; Robert C. Tucker, "Communism and Political Culture," *Newsletter on Comparative Studies on Communism* 4, no. 3 (May 1971): 3–12, and "Culture, Political Culture, and Communist Society," *Political Science Quarterly* 78, no. 2 (June 1973): 173–190; Kenneth Jowitt, "An Organizational Approach to the Study of Political Culture," *American Political Science Review* 68, no. 3 (September 1974): 1171–1191; Clifford Geertz, "A Study of National Character," *Economic Development and Cultural Change* 12 (January 1964): 207–208, and *The Interpretation of Cultures: Selected Essays* (New York: Basic Books, 1973).

5. David Paul's work on communist Czechoslovakia offers perhaps the most interesting study of a government's attempt to change culture. David Paul, *The Cultural Limits of Revolutionary Politics: Change and Continuity in Socialist Czechoslovakia* (New York: Columbia University Press, 1979).

ther research on the subject of political culture. If it does not offer all readers definitive answers, I trust it does raise certain pertinent questions. I hope it will stimulate further study on cultural change in Cuba and other societies.

I began the preliminary research for this book eight years ago as a dissertation. In that initial stage of this project, Professor Jorge Domínguez at Harvard University and professors Jim Ceaser and Inis Claude at the University of Virginia provided constant intellectual guidance and cheerful support. Over the past years, in the course of expanding the core study into this book, I received much additional, fruitful advice from numerous friends, colleagues, and mentors. I would especially like to thank Professor Martha Derthick at the University of Virginia and Professor Donald Seekins at the University of the Ryukyus in Okinawa, Japan, for their valuable comments on the framework of my study. I also profited immensely from the extensive comments offered by Professor Edward González at the University of California at Los Angeles and Professor Irving Louis Horowitz at Rutgers University. I am grateful as well to various individuals who helped to prepare the manuscript for publication, including most notably Sandy Thatcher, Director of Penn State Press, and his wife Cathy who assisted this project over many months and, often, over very great distances. I would also like to extend special thanks to Inis Claude for his continuing support in this study. Without his insights and advice over many years this work would be of a much lesser quality. Finally, I extend my deepest thanks to my husband, Michael Fowler, who served as my most enthusiastic supporter as well as my most rigorous critic, my most fluent editor as well as my most trusted adviser and partner. To all who participated in matters large and small, I express my profound appreciation. Any errors that remain are mine alone.

1

Fidel Castro and
the Quest for
a Revolutionary Culture

> Socialism is based fundamentally on *conciencia.*
> —Fidel Castro, 1987

A society in the throes of a revolution undergoes considerable change in political, economic, and social institutions, including banks, churches, businesses, the media, the government, and organized labor. A revolution, by its very nature, transforms many such institutions. Certain kinds of revolutionaries, however, seek to change a society's culture as well. After seizing power, Marxist-Leninist leaders in particular have often attempted to replace the traditional culture—which they view as an exploitative product of capitalism—with an egalitarian, socialist culture more appropriate to meeting revolutionary objectives.

A culture is normally quite complex. It reflects a country's identity, which is firmly rooted only after a long and at times difficult period of growth. As Seymour Martin Lipset wrote, "Countries, like people, are not handed identities at birth but acquire them through the arduous process of 'growing' up."[1] Since the rules and norms of a culture often guide the action of citizens, culture can play the role of social conscience. It is, in essence, a society's collective "frame of mind."

Culture influences people as to what is right and wrong, true and false, and valuable and worthless in society. It can instruct citizens on matters as diverse as marrying and worshiping, working and playing, selecting leaders and raising children. In nonrevolutionary societies culture generally reflects and, to some degree, maintains established social and economic institutions.[2] Indeed, culture, one might say, mirrors society's view and understanding of itself.

1. Seymour Martin Lipset, *The First New Nation* (Garden City, N.Y.: Anchor Books, 1967), p. 18.
2. See discussion of culture and consciousness in John McMurtry, *The Structure of Marx's World-View* (Princeton: Princeton University Press, 1978), pp. 148, 156.

The process of cultural change, usually evolutionary rather than abrupt, is never wholly complete. Yet while culture continues to change over time, it is not readily transformed. Revolutionaries often discover that altering political and economic institutions is decidedly simpler than radically transforming culture. Embedded in every society, it seems, are subtle yet powerful human forces that tend to resist and condition efforts to change culture to suit revolutionary objectives.

REVOLUTIONARY CUBA: OFFICIAL EFFORTS TO TRANSFORM CULTURE

In 1959 Cuba's revolutionary leader, Fidel Castro, and his comrade from Argentina, Ernesto "Che" Guevara, moved swiftly to create different political and economic institutions. Indeed, change became the Revolution's overarching theme.[3] The revolutionary government appropriated the communications media, most businesses, and all banks. To try to eliminate the influence of the Catholic Church, the Marxist-Leninist leaders closed Catholic schools and harried many priests and nuns into exile. The leadership then established an education system to instruct Marxist-Leninist principles and objectives. To protect the Revolution from internal and external enemies, the leaders also formed a domestic intelligence organization based on "defense committees" that placed communities under the watchful eyes of Party activists.

Although many of their initial efforts were directed toward changing prerevolutionary institutions, the Cuban communist leaders viewed cultural change as the most important goal of the Revolution. Thus, after the preliminary assault on institutions, the leaders immediately turned their full attention toward eliminating and replacing certain aspects of prerevolutionary culture. Over the ensuing years the leaders expended astounding amounts of energy and resources in their efforts to bring about extensive cultural change.

Because of the immediacy and vigor with which its leadership attempted to transform prerevolutionary attitudes and values, Cuba presents a particularly useful case study of a government's efforts to bring about rapid and sweeping cultural change. While other twentieth-century revolutionary governments have periodically attempted to transform culture, most of these regimes never viewed cultural change as the chief goal

3. For a discussion of early revolutionary goals and policies, see Richard Fagen, *The Transformation of Political Culture in Cuba* (Stanford: Stanford University Press, 1969), p. 3.

of their revolutionary projects. The Soviet Union and the Eastern bloc countries, for example, placed less emphasis on developing a revolutionary consciousness and more on establishing a firm economic footing, what Marx referred to as the "objective conditions" necessary for a revolution to succeed. The leaders of these regimes generally believed that transforming institutions, creating cooperatives, and laying the economic foundation for their revolutionary societies were their foremost objectives. Compared with the perspective held by Castro and his subordinates, such views were closely aligned with orthodox Marxist theory.

The Cuban communist leaders took cultural change to be their transcendent goal. In ignoring the doctrinaire notion that cultural change must follow construction of a secure economic foundation, the Cuban approach sought to build socialism and communism simultaneously. In Marxist terms the Castro government tried at the same time to develop an appropriate "subjective consciousness" and to construct a solid material base. Cuban leaders believed that transforming the country's institutions would not automatically, nor necessarily, nor even eventually, transform Cuban culture. Instead, the Castro government opted to focus directly upon changing culture as an independent objective of vital importance.

THE REVOLUTIONARY ASSAULT ON TRADITIONAL CUBAN CULTURE

The revolutionary government plainly viewed prerevolutionary Cuban culture through the prism of its Marxist-Leninist ideology. Cultural ills such as *machismo* and racism, materialism and laziness, elitism and greed were seen as direct consequences of an exploitative mode of production and of neighboring American imperialism. Fidel Castro and his assistants believed that many of society's most pervasive attitudes, particularly those toward race, women, capitalism, individualism, manual labor, and nascent, liberal democratic values, could be traced to Cuba's historical experience. The Castro leadership thus sought to replace these attitudes, wholly incompatible with a Marxist-Leninist society, with a more appropriate set of beliefs and values.

The revolutionary leaders did not, however, attempt to destroy every aspect of traditional Cuban culture. In fact, to advance revolutionary causes, the leadership relied on and preserved many prerevolutionary attitudes. For example, Castro plainly used Cuba's Hispanic tradition of a strong, highly centralized, authoritarian government to legitimize his communist government. The revolutionary leaders also frequently drew on Cuban society's military values and its general acceptance of, or passivity toward, a political role for the military. In addition, the government clearly recognized the traditional importance of charisma and oratory as bases of legitimacy in Cuban politics. Equally important, on repeated occasions Castro garnered support and enthusiasm for his revolutionary movement by effectively exploiting the historic strand of anti-American attitudes within Cuban society.

Consonant with Marxist doctrine, while the Castro government cultivated and preserved aspects of traditional culture that the leaders viewed as useful and beneficial, it aimed to reform dramatically certain other Cuban beliefs, opinions, and values that seemed to undermine revolutionary goals. The leaders ventured to create a society that would adopt values and attitudes different from, and even diametrically opposed to, those of the old order. The Castro government sought a new "*conciencia,*" a Spanish term employed by the Cuban communist leaders to denote a proper set of revolutionary values, beliefs, and attitudes, such as dedication, selflessness, sacrifice, and loyalty. The traditional Cuban, burdened with an unacceptable false consciousness and with capitalist-imperialist views of state and society, had to be transformed into a new individual. Much like Lenin's model of the ideal citizen, Castro's so-called "new man" would be imbued with a communist *conciencia.*

What would constitute the characteristics of a citizen who had appropriate revolutionary *conciencia?* In general terms the Castro government urged the Cuban people to adopt as their model someone who was selfless and cooperative, obedient and hardworking, gender-blind, incorruptible, and nonmaterialistic. Ideally, the loyalty of the new citizen to the Communist Party and the government would be unassailable. The leaders believed that, as Marx had predicted, the political order would eventually wither away and a homogeneous society would live under a rule of absolute benevolence.[4] Indeed, the leaders believed that once the government had successfully inculcated the masses with this revolutionary *conciencia,* Cuba would witness spectacular economic progress.

In this effort the government created party-dominated mass organizations on all levels of society and for all ages, including labor organizations, youth leagues, and women's groups. These vanguard organizations set out to foster a revolutionary conscience among Cuban citizens in everyday life: in schools, the home, and the workplace. In addition, the Castro government attempted to redirect loyalties from the Cuban family, the Cath-

---

4. See Joseph Cropsey, "Karl Marx," in *History of Political Philosophy,* ed. Leo Strauss and Joseph Cropsey (Chicago: University of Chicago Press, 1987), pp. 824–825.

olic Church, and various African religions to the Cuban nation and the Communist Party. It rewarded ideological and revolutionary support and conformity. And it searched out and penalized dissent and nonconformity. Most important, the leadership implemented a broad spectrum of policies in a vigorous effort to create a dramatically different, radically egalitarian set of values and attitudes that would support and strengthen Cuba's new revolutionary institutions.

MARX AND LENIN ON THE TRANSFORMATION OF CULTURE

This chief goal of the Cuban Revolution, creating a "new man," was no mere whim of Fidel Castro's. Indeed, the objective of transforming culture is clearly derived from Marxist ideology. Karl Marx believed that capitalism destroyed man. The capitalist political economy estranged and alienated citizens and fomented human greed and selfishness. Marx contended that man in capitalist society became "at odds with his species" and developed a "false consciousness," which reflected self-interest and unnecessary materialist desires.[5] Capitalism, Marx argued in *Capital*, establishes an "accumulation of misery, agony of toil, slavery, ignorance, brutality, and mental degradation."[6] This condition, he believed, prevented people from recognizing reality, from finding and knowing truth, from understanding that whims and foolish wants had mastered their oppressive and disorderly lives.[7]

According to Marx, the individual is "modified in each historical epoch."[8] All history, he contended, "is nothing but the transformation of human nature."[9] The revolutionary overthrow of capitalism and the creation of socialism would liberate mankind. Thereafter, each socialist regime would have to reeducate its people so they could fully understand their new society and be released from the chains of greed. In this way a true communist consciousness would replace man's false consciousness.

5. For a discussion of Marx's view of capitalism, see Cropsey, p. 809. See also Erich Fromm, *Marx's Concept of Man* (New York: Frederick Ungar, 1961), pp. 20–21, 25, 63.

6. Quoted in Cropsey, p. 821.

7. Karl Marx, "Economic and Philosophical Manuscripts," quoted in Fromm, p. 151.

8. Karl Marx, *Capital*, ed. Frederick Engels and trans. Samuel Moore and Edward Aveling, 2 vols. (Moscow: Progress Publishers, 1965), 1:609. See a valuable discussion of the Marxian view of man in McMurtry, p. 20. See also Fromm, p. 25.

9. Karl Marx, *The Poverty of Philosophy*, ed. Frederick Engels (Moscow: Progress Publishers, 1966), p. 128. This passage is quoted in McMurtry, p. 37.

Socialism's principal goal, then, was to instruct citizens to avoid illusions and recognize and realize their true needs.

Who was to instruct and educate socialist citizens? Marx believed that thoroughly transformed economic institutions would foster the development of a socialist culture. Lenin, however, rejected this view. In his 1902 essay "What is to be Done?" Lenin argued that only the rigorous efforts of professional revolutionaries could transform a capitalist culture into a socialist one. He contended that radical intellectuals who formed small, secretive, dedicated, disciplined, and highly organized communist groups were capable of molding the consciousness of the masses.[10] As part of this effort to bring about a new consciousness, Lenin instructed revolutionary leaders to seize control of all publications, to target the masses with "systematic, persistent, and regular propaganda," to create and control mass organizations, to indoctrinate people at all levels of society, and to eradicate all factions and dissidents.[11] These communist leaders were to teach citizens about the rules and principles of their revolutionary society and instruct them on how to live under these novel conditions in a newly created socialist state. Lenin's vision of the good society thus depended directly on the revolutionary leadership's ability to change traditional prerevolutionary culture. In this regard the efforts of the Cuban government to transform culture were more Leninist than Marxist.

Both Marx and Lenin believed that once the people were seized with the proper revolutionary consciousness, socialist society could develop under the ruling principle of "from each according to his ability, to each according to his needs." One scholar described this view:

> This is a maxim fit to serve as the fundamental law among loyal, wise, and incorruptible friends, devoted to one another with an absolutely unselfish benevolence. . . . Marxian society would be a society of billions of friends warmly joined in the rarest and most sensitive union of amity. . . . Marx dreamed of that human condition in which good ends would be sought by good men using only good means and responding to (because possessing) only good motives.[12]

The creation of a Marxist utopia thus depended upon the revolutionary government's success in molding a socialist conscience among its citizens.

10. See John G. Gurley, *Challengers to Capitalism: Marx, Lenin, Stalin, and Mao* (New York: Norton, 1979), pp. 72–74.

11. V. I. Lenin, "Blueprints for World Conquest as Outlined by the Communist International" (Washington, 1946), pp. 65–72; reprinted in Sidney Hook, *Marx and the Marxists: The Ambiguous Legacy* (Malabar, Fl.: Robert E. Krieger, 1982), pp. 187–190.

12. Explanation of the Marxist view by Cropsey, pp. 822–824.

Since I could not explore every attitude and value that the Castro government aimed to change, I chose to investigate several of the revolutionary leaders' most important targets. First, I decided to examine the government's remarkable efforts to mold Cuban youth. While the leaders understood that the views of more mature citizens would be difficult to alter, they saw children as having open, malleable minds. In its effort to transform culture, the Castro government may have expended the greatest amount of time, energy, and resources on changing the views of the next generation of Cubans.

To complement my analysis of Castro's effort to transform the minds of young Cubans, I selected two aspects of culture that the leadership viewed as particularly significant targets for change: popular attitudes toward women and toward manual labor. I chose these two readily identifiable and widely projected attitudes because the government openly, indeed incessantly, insisted that they conflicted directly with the egalitarian and labor-oriented objectives of the Marxist-Leninist Revolution. The leaders themselves often claimed that these two attitudes were among the most offensive and antirevolutionary of the Cuban people. Consequently, the government went to extraordinary lengths to eliminate and replace these troublesome aspects of traditional Cuban culture.

Finally, Fidel Castro's goal to create new, revolutionary attitudes toward sports has received widespread international recognition. The government introduced an astounding array of programs aimed at changing popular attitudes toward sports and encouraging all Cubans to participate in athletic events. I devote the final chapter to examining the Cuban leadership's attempts to discredit prerevolutionary attitudes toward sports as elitist and capitalist and to create a new sports culture.

FIDEL CASTRO'S VARYING STRATEGIES TO TRANSFORM CULTURE

In the course of the first three decades of the Revolution, the Cuban leadership experimented with a wide variety of measures, from moral persuasion to coercion, from humiliation tactics to material rewards, in an attempt to realize its supreme goal of cultural transformation. This chapter provides an overview of the strategies employed by Fidel Castro and his subordinates in their efforts to transform Cuban culture. The following chapters examine those strategies in detail, as they pertain to youth, women, labor, and sports.

Throughout the early years of the Revolution the Castro government relied primarily on noncoercive measures, such as moral suasion and public praise, to influence the culture and behavior of Cuban citizens. As the Revolution progressed, however, the state increasingly turned to two particular methods of coercion. At times the government used its superior force to control citizens directly. Some methods of direct coercion remained mild, such as public admonishments and humiliation tactics or obligatory parent-training programs. Other methods were decidedly harsher. Those who failed to bend to the leadership's dictates received undesirable work assignments or suffered separation from their families, or even incarceration in labor camps or jails.

Cuban leaders also compelled cultural change through "indirect" coercion or behind-the-scene manipulation, that is, by employing subtle, "hidden," and often quite mild sanctions to penalize nonconformity. Methods of indirect coercion included separating children from their families through "voluntary" organizations and labor brigades as well as obligatory boarding schools. Similarly, increasing military authority indirectly coerced Cuban citizens to accept cultural change. Encouraging peer pressure and neighborhood vigilance through the Committees for the Defense of the Revolution (CDRs) also helped to ensure conformity. At the same time the Castro leadership influenced the actions of its people by selectively rewarding some citizens and depriving others of benefits. In Cuba, a society subject to extreme central control, leaders could and did distribute and withhold resources in order to compel behavioral change by rewarding the cooperative and denying goods to the recalcitrant.

THE FOUR PHASES OF THE CUBAN REVOLUTION: AN OVERVIEW

The Cuban government strategically employed three different methods of attempting to bring about cultural change: the noncoercive, the indirectly coercive, and the directly coercive. That is, in different periods the leadership selected varying methods of attempting to bring about cultural change. During the first thirty years of the Revolution, the government's policies aimed at transforming culture generally evolved through four distinct phases. These four phases, briefly outlined in the following pages, provide a historical framework upon which the subsequent chapters are based.

Phase One

The Cuban Revolution triumphed on the first of January 1959, and the new government immediately set out to bring about sweeping institutional change. During this early period, in order to abolish class disparities, the leaders confiscated and redistributed privately owned properties. Thus, the government quickly expropriated land for agrarian reform and housing for urban reform. It nationalized all foreign and many domestic enterprises and institutions, from centers of education to banks. The government also seized control of the media and religious institutions. To create a more egalitarian society, and also to quell dissent, Castro took care to follow each of these abrupt changes with efforts to slash the cost of housing and electricity, to increase salaries and provide wage benefits to Cuban workers, and to distribute free public services, such as medical care, recreation, and education.

After 1961, once Fidel Castro revealed his Marxist-Leninist faith, cultural transformation took on an even more vital role than institutional transformation. Yet while the government acted quickly and confidently to transform social institutions, the revolutionary leaders were less sure of the proper strategy to develop a new *conciencia* among the citizens. Confusion existed on the precise characteristics of the citizen they intended to mold. Consequently, during the first phase the leadership experimented with different blueprints, different foundations, and different specifications for their ambitious project.

In retrospect, the government's initial policies to bring about cultural change appear eclectic. Castro primarily turned to tactics of moral suasion, mass ideological education, and some indirect coercion. The government established the Committees for the Defense of the Revolution as a system to mobilize and reeducate citizens, to publicize official goals and activities, to counter internal and external campaigns of aggression, and to promote and organize cooperatives, civil defense, and first-aid projects. To complement this initiative, the government strongly encouraged citizens to participate in revolutionary organizations, voluntary labor programs, and the literacy campaign. It also attempted to transform Cuban culture by creating scholarship programs and opening boarding schools for youth and day-care centers for working mothers.

Typically, the leadership did not choose to impose these measures by force; instead, it simply encouraged voluntarism and widely promoted the heralded revolutionary concept of *conciencia*. Indeed, during these early years, the vast majority of citizens who chose to remain in Cuba accepted, indeed enthusiastically supported, these revolutionary goals and the measures used to attain them. They saw great potential in the Revolution and

had high expectations for its leaders and policies. Those early noncon-
formists who did exist found themselves silenced and overwhelmed by
the government's energetic program and its early popularity. Many thus
chose to emigrate.

Even in this early period, however, Cuban leaders experimented with
other more coercive policies designed to promote the development of new
values and attitudes among less supportive and more skeptical and com-
placent citizens. These policies included public admonishments, the military draft, economic sanctions, and rehabilitation centers for uncooperative adults and "problem" youth. The government also implemented
various measures to control and discipline unruly and troublesome university students and professors.

Phase Two

In early 1968, shortly after Che Guevara's death, the Castro government
dramatically intensified the policies of the first eight years of the Revolution by launching the "Revolutionary Offensive." As part of the Offensive
the leaders further centralized economic and political power by taking
over the remaining privately owned businesses that were still operating
in Cuba. In one swift stroke the government announced the immediate
socialization of some fifty-seven thousand small enterprises, from vending
stands to restaurants to electrical repair shops. These pockets of the "petty
bourgeoisie," Fidel Castro claimed, represented the capitalism and crass
materialism that the Revolution sought to eradicate. Almost overnight the
government eliminated the remaining vestiges of small-scale urban capitalism, and Cuba became the most socialized economy in the world.[13]

The revolutionary leaders also wholly rejected the use of material incentives as the primary means to stimulate production. The Castro government focused upon consumerism, selfishness, and other troublesome, capitalist attitudes among the masses. The leadership moved vigorously to
uproot the suspected source of these attitudes: material incentives. Perhaps even more important, the leaders chose to deemphasize material incentives for practical reasons. With its economy faltering, the government
could no longer supply workers with the tangible rewards offered earlier.
Hence, Castro increasingly substituted moral incentives.

As part of the Offensive the Cuban government markedly increased its
use of moral suasion and mass ideological education to transform popular

13. Juan M. del Aguila, *Cuba: Dilemmas of a Revolution* (Boulder: Westview Press,
1984), p. 91.

attitudes. The leadership established the experimental youth society on the Isle of Pines and opened voluntary work-study schools in the countryside for children. The government began an "exemplary student" program, advocated increased voluntary labor, and continued to proselytize in favor of ideologically appropriate mores. In addition, during this relatively brief second phase, the Castro government used the coercive power of the state to ensure that citizens conformed. Simultaneously, the role of the military slowly, steadily, and perhaps insidiously permeated many aspects of Cuban society.

Despite these concerted efforts, by the end of the first decade the leadership's optimism regarding an emerging socialist *conciencia* had substantially waned. Indeed, Castro could not help but be disillusioned by popular behavior. Workers, students, even soldiers resisted government programs in a subtle, yet perplexing and irritating, manner. Rates of truancy, vagrancy, prostitution, and crime surged. Theft by juveniles stood as a particular problem. The lottery, which officials generally viewed as a prerevolutionary capitalist institution, flourished. The government's guaranteed wage for workers led not to increased *conciencia* and higher levels of productivity but to more workers absent from their jobs. By the end of the 1960s labor absenteeism had reached a record high. In addition, since the legal market had been abolished, Cubans increasingly turned to the illegal black market to acquire desired goods. Traditional and officially unacceptable Cuban attitudes and values stubbornly persisted in the face of widespread government pressure.

The Castro government soon recognized these signs of noncompliance, materialism, lack of discipline, and individualism. At the same time Cuban leaders had to confront a troubled economy, which, after years of neglect, had plummeted disastrously. The 1970 sugar harvest fell far short of the official goal. Economic and political crises fed upon one another and brought about a substantial psychological breakdown within society. The average Cuban citizen began to question, and often reject, the leadership's demands for sacrifice, discipline, self-denial, voluntarism, and optimism. By 1969 the deprivation of goods in Cuba had become an inescapable fact of life. Strict rationing and severe shortages forced mass austerity.

Many citizens, tired, frustrated, and disappointed, resisted the government's constant pushing and harassing. Mass support and cooperation dwindled. Moral incentives simply failed to motivate Cubans to work hard and comply with the government's requirements. Citizens expected material rewards for their efforts. They demonstrated their lack of enthusiasm for the leadership's policies by performing their jobs negligently and carelessly, thus causing production levels to fall. Others began to leave the workplace early. Still others failed to go to work each day. Indeed, many citizens displayed their disenchantment in far more overt and extreme forms: the number of suicides skyrocketed. Despite the government's rhetorical campaign, Cuban society had slipped into a period of despair and disillusionment.

Phase Three

In an attempt to avert impending social collapse, by the early 1970s Cuban leaders abandoned their former policies and adopted radical measures. In an attempt to control more effectively unacceptable social behavior, the Cuban government introduced a "carrot and stick" approach. First, the leadership unveiled a spectrum of more coercive policies. For example, Castro militarized the polytechnical institutes and the country's largest revolutionary children's organization, the Young Pioneers. The government purged the universities, abolished the lottery, and mandated labor cards and dossiers for all workers. It compelled all secondary students to engage in work-study education. It expanded the role of the CDRs to include neighborhood vigilance. And it established requisite parent-training programs imposed through a system of formal and informal sanctions. The government also created mandatory work brigades and opened "rehabilitation" centers.

At the same time, to revitalize the severely weakened economy and to raise productivity, Castro deemphasized all the rhetoric and policies employing moral suasion and reintroduced material incentives. The leadership thus accommodated the materialistic desires of Cuban citizens. If the government wanted Cubans to work hard and support the leadership, it would garner that support by rewarding proper behavior with bonuses, salary increases, and luxury items. In essence, the Cuban government recast its policies and introduced positive incentives to encourage voluntary compliance and improve performance among the island's workers.

Thus, by the early 1970s the official "carrot and stick" approach sought to raise productivity and to diminish or eliminate the irksome foot-dragging and nonconformist behavior of the masses. Castro used his unrivaled control over society's resources to distribute rewards to cooperative citizens and to deprive the unworthy of various goods. In doing so the government deemphasized its original goal of changing the traditional values and attitudes of Cuban culture. Instead, the government found itself forced to accept the orthodox Soviet-style objective of focusing on influencing behavior rather than on changing attitudes. In this way, setting aside the earlier preeminent concern for cultural change, Cuban leaders tried to raise productivity while ensuring compliance and obedience.

Certainly, the Cuban revolutionary government preserved its highest rewards for those few who were willing and able to fulfill, and preferably exceed, official cultural expectations. The leadership expected every citizen to cooperate. It did not hesitate to coerce those who overtly resisted and openly refused to meet minimal requirements. However, the Cuban leaders generally chose not to employ methods of direct coercion against citizens who willingly did the minimum but continued to oppose policies and perform various quiet acts of noncompliance. Rather, the government penalized these foot-draggers with indirect coercion: it discreetly denied them certain basic goods and services. For instance, the government penalized negligent, careless workers who passively accomplished only the bare minimum by denying them opportunities for career advancement, political, economic, or social leadership positions, and scholarships for their children. These punishments, although relatively subtle compared to more overt abuses of human rights, amounted to unmistakable and significant penalties in a society that strictly rationed nearly all goods.

Clearly, if a citizen wanted to live securely and comfortably in Castro's Cuba, doing the minimum did not suffice. Those who wished more from life were required to go further to please Cuban officials. Such citizens, either as a result of a genuine change in attitude or a desire for goods and bonuses, supplied their labor, participated in revolutionary programs, and cooperated with the CDRs. To reward their support, the government provided material favors such as clothing, food, and housing as well as improved career opportunities and various educational benefits for their children.

This group of moderately supportive citizens, however, did not typically earn higher rewards, such as membership in the Party or coveted leadership positions. Such benefits required even greater levels of dedication, commitment, and support. Those loyal comrades who sought to participate in the power structure and Party membership had to lead labor armies, organize political rallies, volunteer time and energy to production, attend schools of Marxist instruction, and campaign wholeheartedly for official policies and programs. Through material benefits, powerful positions, and access to unusual opportunities, the government rewarded those who demonstrated unfaltering dedication and loyalty to revolutionary goals and ideology. Thus, during this third phase of cultural change in revolutionary Cuba, the leaders did not uniformly lower their expectations for all citizens. The loyal communist could still achieve much so long as he was willing to work long hours to promote official objectives.

Throughout the 1970s, as the Cuban economy grew stronger, Fidel Castro and his colleagues continued to pursue economic efficiency and growth by offering material incentives. While leaders appealed to economic aspirations in order to motivate workers to build the material foundation of their communist society, the goal of developing mass *conciencia* continued to recede in importance. In the early 1980s, during the effort to enhance economic efficiency further, the leadership implemented these policies with renewed vigor. The Cuban government linked individual productivity and salary ever more closely. Indeed, to augment further Cuba's gross national product, the government moved to decentralize political power and economic decision making and to permit market-type activities. In 1980 Castro allowed the opening of local markets, where peasants could sell their produce at market rates. The government also legalized private home rentals, permitted private construction, and allowed a private service sector to operate. Cuban citizens could again go into private business to carry out tailoring, plumbing, gardening, hairdressing, and repairing autos and appliances. By the same token, when material incentives failed and citizens resisted official policy in an unacceptable fashion, the government did not hesitate to coerce its people in order to ensure conformity and compliance with revolutionary goals.

In contrast to Castro's repeated disappointments at official efforts to transform culture, the economic policies of this period appeared to bring encouraging results. The 1970s and early 1980s witnessed an impressive growth rate. Sugar harvests were generally good. Construction increased. Soviet economic aid flowed freely. Between 1981 and 1985 Cuban officials painted a rosy economic picture: the economy reportedly grew at an average of 7 percent a year.[14] Yet even this encouraging economic performance concealed several grave problems.

First and most important, toward the end of this period startling changes occurred in the Soviet Union. In March 1985 Mikhail Gorbachev took power as General Secretary of the Soviet Communist Party. Shortly thereafter Gorbachev embarked on his historic effort to alter the very foundations of Soviet socialism. The new Soviet leader introduced two sweeping programs that threatened the economic and political security of the Cuban government. The first, Gorbachev's policy of *perestroika* or "restructuring," clearly retreated from traditional Marxist principles and objectives. *Perestroika* sought to carry out wholly unprecedented domestic economic reforms to allow private ownership, decentralize the economic system, and provide a spectrum of market incentives. In trying to revitalize and restructure the faltering Soviet economy, Gorbachev sought to integrate his country into the international capitalist system. Gorba-

14. Susan Eckstein, "The Rectification of Errors Or the Errors of the Rectification Process in Cuba?" *Cuban Studies* 20, no. 1 (Fall/Winter 1990): 73. This is an official Cuban government statistic that appeared in *Granma Weekly Review* (*GWR*), August 27, 1989, p. 12.

chev's second program, *glasnost,* appeared even more heretical to doctrinaire Marxist-Leninists. *Glasnost* sought to "open" Soviet society by calling upon the government to tolerate a more vocal press, to allow increasing numbers of dissidents to emigrate, and to permit historically repressed peoples and groups to organize and voice protests.

These economic and political reforms extended to international relations as well. After 1986 Soviet foreign policy shifted away from a focus on Cold War tensions and expensive, Third World revolutionary commitments. As part of this trend the Soviet Union steadily diminished its political support for former allies, including Cuba. Perhaps most troublesome, the Soviets sent unmistakable signals to Fidel Castro that economic support would be substantially curbed. Given the economic and political climate of the late 1980s, the Castro government perceived *glasnost* and *perestroika* in a menacing light.

For decades Cuba had struggled to garner sufficient hard currency to pay its debts to Western creditors, to import additional products from capitalist countries, and to attract desperately needed investment capital. However, to nurture the alliance with Castro, the Soviets had quietly supported a lopsided economic arrangement. Soviet leaders had patiently tolerated Havana's unwise use of hard currency, mismanagement of economic aid, and failure to meet sugar-export contracts between the two countries. To retain a strategically valuable ally, the Soviets continued to provide economic aid and "sweetheart" exchanges of oil and sugar.

By the early 1980s the Castro government depended heavily upon Eastern European and Soviet aid to maintain Cuban investment and consumption levels. By late 1984, however, attitudes toward Cuba in Moscow had changed sufficiently to prompt the Soviet leadership to pressure Castro to fulfill contractual commitments. And in both 1984 and 1985 the Castro government reluctantly used scarce hard currency to buy sugar on the world market for export to the Soviets and other allies. In addition, Soviet policymakers and the Soviet press repeatedly called on the Cuban leadership to increase efficiency and productivity, to diversify trading partners, and to attain a more responsible position in the Soviet-Cuban economic alliance. The Soviets also encouraged the Cubans to carry out *perestroika*-type reforms.[15] Meanwhile, as the Eastern bloc itself began to splinter, trading links with former Soviet satellites started to disintegrate.[16]

15. See, for example, Ramón Orozco, "Fidel Holds Out against Reform," *World Press Review* (May 1990): 32; Jorge I. Domínguez, *To Make a World Safe for Revolution* (Cambridge: Harvard University Press, 1989), p. 110; Susan Kaufman Purcell, "Cuba's Cloudy Future," *Foreign Affairs* 69 (Summer 1990): 116; K. W. Ellisen, "Succeeding Castro," *The Atlantic* 265 (June 1990): 38.

16. See *New York Times,* March 16, 1988, p. A13.

For the Cuban leadership these extraordinary changes in international politics raised distressing political concerns and placed the country on a precarious economic footing. In the mid-1980s more than 90 percent of Cuban trade involved the Soviet-led trading bloc, Comecon.[17] The Cuban economy, traditionally quite vulnerable to international developments, had become tightly bound to political and economic policies in Eastern Europe and the Soviet Union. Cuban leaders thus immediately felt the effects of this new Soviet approach to domestic and international economic and political affairs.

A second and related crisis soon arose. The Cuban government faced a rapidly growing debt to its Western trading partners. Cuba's economic expansion during the prior decade had depended in part upon imports, many from Western countries. In the mid-1980s, however, hard-currency exports did not keep pace with imports. Moreover, the cost of servicing money previously borrowed from Western sources rose sharply. Cuba's economic strategy thus triggered a sudden rise in the government's hard-currency trade deficit and its foreign debt.

To make matters worse for the Cubans, in late 1985 world oil prices plunged. During the early 1980s the Castro government had earned nearly 40 percent of its foreign-exchange revenues each year by reexporting surplus Soviet oil. But by 1985 world oil prices had fallen precipitously. The Soviets continued to allow Cuba to procure Soviet oil without using up hard currency; however, on account of the low international market price, Cuba's hard-currency earnings from sales of surplus oil dropped drastically. In addition, the level of exports to Western trading partners decreased as a result of low sugar and oil prices on the world market. Moreover, with the fall of the dollar the value of the island's Western debt spiraled. The consequence of these economic setbacks was quite troubling. Cuba moved from having one of the lowest hard-currency debt/export ratios in Latin America in the mid-1970s to having one of the highest by 1985.[18] By May 1986 Cuba could no longer service its debt and had to suspend debt payments.[19]

These political and economic difficulties triggered a third crisis: widespread apathy, noncompliance, and resistance among Cuban citizens. The Cuban people neither behaved nor thought as the leaders required. By the mid-1980s the prior official emphasis on profit and material incentives, coupled with the deteriorating economy, brought on unprecedented levels of popular speculation, profiteering, and "petty bourgeois attitudes."

17. Comecon was the Council for Mutual Economic Assistance. See Purcell, p. 114.
18. Eckstein, pp. 73–74.
19. *GWR,* May 17, 1986, p. 1.

Moreover, some problems that seemed under control in the 1960s and 1970s, such as prostitution, reappeared with a vengeance. The unacceptable behavior of workers, from apathy and lack of discipline to vagrancy, negligence, and absenteeism, plagued the agricultural sector and brought on dismal levels of productivity. In addition, judicial neglect, increasing crime, open disregard for Fidel Castro and the Communist Party, and disinterest and apathy among the country's youth greatly troubled the leadership.

These problems prompted Fidel Castro once again to rethink and readjust his political and economic policies. During this third period the overall shift in official tactics reveals both serious economic defeats and the impotence of Cuban efforts to bring about substantial cultural change. In short, the government's policies had utterly failed to mold Che's "new man." Although certain changes in culture did occur, most cultural evolution did not progress as the leadership had envisioned. Cubans were not thinking and acting as right-minded Marxist-Leninist citizens. Ultimately, the daily acts of noncompliance forced the Cuban government, once again, to modify its expectations and reorient its tactics. During the third phase citizens had not generally supported official measures to transform Cuban culture.

Phase Four

In 1986 various difficulties—most prominently the fiscal crises, the deficient *conciencia,* and the increasing alienation from past communist allies—prompted Fidel Castro to launch his most sweeping program to date: the Rectification Campaign. Rectification centered on three principal objectives. First, to deal with the economic crisis, the government implemented an austerity program, which Castro labeled "an economic war of all the people."[20] Throughout the late 1980s, as the Soviet Union and the Eastern bloc curbed exports of grain, flour, technology, spare parts, and manufactured goods, and as Cuba's hard-currency reserves dwindled, the Castro government increasingly moved to cut consumption, minimize imports, and tighten daily rations.[21]

Second, the Rectification reversed the prior domestic trend toward individual market practices and material incentives. The Rectification bluntly and contemptuously rejected the Soviet Union's "betrayal of Marxism-

20. Ibid., January 12, 1986, p. 3.

21. Purcell, p. 118; see also Gillian Gunn, "Will Castro Fall?" *Foreign Policy* 79 (Summer 1990): 133.

Leninism" and its move toward market-oriented economic policies and a more open society. Castro insisted that the Cuban citizen would not adopt "any methods that reek of capitalism."[22] The government moved to ban private construction and enterprises, to close down the local farmer markets, to prohibit private manufacturing and street vending, and to assume greater control over sales and rentals.

Curiously, however, while Castro denied Cuban citizens the opportunity to engage in market activities, he did not hesitate to court foreign firms to invest in Cuban enterprises. The government tried to attract capital, particularly in the tourism sector, without endorsing capitalism.[23] In fact, in July 1992 the leadership went so far as to amend the 1976 Constitution to ease restrictions on trade with capitalist foreign investors.[24] This, it was hoped, would provide desperately needed hard currency. Ignoring years of venomous anticapitalist rhetoric, the leadership suddenly invited foreign capitalists to bring their money and energy to the island to invest in joint ventures with the Cuban state.[25]

Throughout this fourth phase Cuban officials argued that the market experiments of the 1970s not only weakened the economy but also severely undermined the official effort to transform culture. Misguided policies had led to selfishness and illicit money making, inequalities in earnings, excessive emphasis on material rewards, and inefficient use of labor. The government attacked middlemen and peasants for abusing their economic opportunities and prospering at the consumer's expense. Fidel Castro lamented that these experiments had "created a class of newly rich who are doing as they please."[26] These market-type experiments, he insisted, had bolstered traditional "capitalist" attitudes of laziness, selfishness, and materialism.[27]

Finally, and most important, the Rectification sought to reinvigorate mass *conciencia,* to purify the population ideologically, to eradicate increasing problems of social attitudes and behavior, and to mobilize the masses to volunteer their labor and energy in yet another period of crisis. At the December 1986 Third Party Congress, Castro declared that the leadership must confront, correct, and struggle against problems related to the attitudes and behavior of party members, workers, youth, and

---

22. Fidel Castro speech, quoted in *Topeka Capital-Journal,* December 25, 1988, p. 8F.

23. See Susan Kaufman Purcell, "Collapsing Cuba," *Foreign Affairs* 71 (1992): 134. See also *Washington Post,* July 12, 1992, p. A20.

24. *Washington Post,* July 12, 1992, pp. A20, A29; *Daily Yomiuri* (Tokyo, Japan), August 12, 1992, p. 11.

25. *Washington Post,* July 12, 1992, p. A20.

26. *GWR,* July 13, 1986, p. 9; see also ibid., May 25, 1986, p. 1.

27. U.S. *Foreign Broadcast Information Service,* December 5, 1986, p. Q11.

women.[28] Castro called on the nation to revitalize Che's aspiration to create in Cuba a new citizen. "What are we rectifying?" Fidel Castro asked in 1987 at the ceremony marking the twentieth anniversary of the death of Che Guevara:

> We're rectifying all those things . . . and there are many . . . that strayed from the revolutionary spirit, from revolutionary work, revolutionary virtue, revolutionary effort, revolutionary responsibility; all those things that strayed from the spirit of solidarity among people. We're rectifying all the shoddiness and mediocrity that is precisely the negation of Che's ideas.[29]

The Cuban leader called for a rebirth of "consciousness, a communist spirit, a revolutionary will." These, he insisted, "will always be a thousand times more powerful than money."[30]

To attain high productivity, an authentic socialist economy, and a pure *conciencia,* the government fashioned a three-pronged strategy. First, during this era of severe economic crises and scarce goods, the government moved away from, but did not wholly abandon, monetary rewards as incentives. Cuban leaders attempted to reinvigorate Che Guevara's "pure" socialist wage policies of the late 1960s. In banning certain material incentives and select private enterprises, these economic policies called for centralized planning, Party domination of the economy, and moral incentives in the workplace.[31] Just as Che had counselled, Cuban leaders during the Rectification opted to use moral stimuli and constant mass political education as the means to bring about higher productivity as well as changes in attitudes. Citizens were to work and sacrifice not for material bonuses but for patriotic and moral reasons. Underlying the philosophical desire to return to Che's strategy lay a pragmatic motive: Cuba simply no longer had the goods to offer its loyal citizens. Hence, while the leaders spoke of resurrecting moral incentives, revitalizing *conciencia* and revolutionary loyalty, and eradicating materialism and incipient capitalism, the Rectification program might also cut consumption and ensure economic austerity. Plainly, this economic objective weighed heavily among Cuban leaders.

Furthermore, in an effort to control the troublesome everyday behavior of Cuban citizens, the Castro government immediately introduced more coercive policies, including forced labor of Cuban workers, increased mili-

28. Ibid., p. Q1.
29. *GWR,* October 18, 1987, p. 4.
30. Ibid., Special Report, December 7, 1986, p. 2.
31. See, for example, Fidel Castro speech in ibid., October 18, 1987, pp. 5–6.

tarization, and harsher legal punishments for defiance. Finally, the leadership increased remarkably the Party's role in economic and political supervision.[32] These principal tactics—the deemphasis of material incentives and reemphasis of moral incentives, the renewal of coercive policies, and the substantial increase in the role of the Communist Party in society— have marked the fourth and ongoing phase of the Castro government's efforts to transform Cuban society.

CONCLUSION

Dividing the revolutionary history of Cuba into the four phases outlined above is designed to provide a general introductory overview of the Castro government's fundamental policy initiatives. In practice, however, those who craft policy often proceed incrementally—by fits and starts, one might say—and not through wholly consistent "Grand Designs." Moreover, even a highly centralized authoritarian regime can experience the problem that distinct bureaucratic groups often take quite different policy initiatives. In government the right hand and the left hand are rarely perfectly coordinated.

In the chapters that follow, the efforts of the revolutionary leadership to transform Cuban cultural attitudes toward youth, women, labor, and sports will at times follow quite closely the four general phases outlined above. At other times Cuban policy in one field, such as women, will diverge to some extent from policy in another area, such as labor. Nevertheless, keeping the four broad phases of Cuban policy in mind should help the reader to understand how the details of policy initiatives in any particular field parallel or differ from the broader trends of that era.

32. Ibid.

2

Castro and the Children
The Struggle for Cuba's Young Minds

First we tell tales to children. . . . And surely they
are, as a whole false. . . . Then shall we . . . let the
children hear just any tales fashioned by just
anyone? . . . First . . . we must supervise the makers
of tales; and if they make a fine tale, it must be
approved, but if it's not, it must be rejected. . . .
Many of these they now tell must be thrown out.
—Socrates, *The Republic of Plato*
Book 2, 377a–377c

The destiny of the fatherland and the Revolution
will greatly depend on your participation. . . . You
have enormous responsibility.
—Fidel Castro to youth, 1991

Since more than 40 percent of Cuban citizens today are younger than
forty years old, assessing the role of youth in the Revolution is an integral
part of analyzing the Cuban government's attempt to transform culture.
Fidel Castro and his revolutionary associates believed that Cuba's children
would eventually determine whether a new socialist man would be created
and whether the Revolution would succeed. From the beginning of the
Revolution the leaders targeted the nascent minds of Cuba's youth for
cultural change. Although many adults continued to hold prerevolutionary values and attitudes, the leadership hoped that the children's "virgin"
minds, as Castro called them, would be open and malleable. In the early
1960s the leaders predicted that the next generation, thoroughly imbued
with an appropriate communist mentality, would confidently lead the
country from socialism to communism. As prerevolutionary generations
passed away, outdated "bourgeois" mores would die with them. A flourishing new Cuban culture would then emerge.
Fidel Castro believed that concentrating on molding Cuba's youth
would have far-reaching advantages. In seizing upon the energy, enthusi-

asm, curiosity, and innocence of children, Cuban leaders could garner support for the government as well as promote a sense of common purpose, mass participation, and revolutionary spirit among the next generation. Moreover, through the children the leadership could instruct parents and grandparents in the new ideology. Finally, by gaining control over children's education and daily activities, the government could help to transfer individual loyalties from the family to the state.

YOUTH AND EDUCATION IN PREREVOLUTIONARY CUBA

Although Cuba's prerevolutionary private educational institutions, predominantly Catholic, were among the best schools in Latin America, the vast majority of citizens had no access to them. The public schools, often corrupt and inefficient, educated most children. Throughout the public-school system teachers tended to be poorly trained. Worst of all, rural education remained grossly neglected. At the time of the Revolution only twenty-one public secondary schools were scattered about the countryside. The prerevolutionary disarray of the Cuban public-school system led to unfortunate consequences. The 1953 census indicated that approximately 25 percent of all individuals ten years or older had never been to school at all; in addition, more than 50 percent had dropped out before completing the sixth grade.[1]

During the 1950s Cuban public education remained abysmal. Between 1950 and 1958 the population grew at 2 percent a year, but primary public-school enrollment increased only 1 percent a year. On the eve of the Revolution fewer than 50 percent of the children between the ages of seven and fourteen attended school. Indeed, only about 12.8 percent of Cuba's 6.4 million citizens had received an education. Given the poor quality of the schools, students who did attend generally received an inadequate education. In the 1950s three out of four Cubans who had "completed" their schooling were either illiterate or at best semi-educated.[2] In 1958 Cuban illiteracy stood at about 24 percent.

1. Richard Jolly, "The Educational Aims and Program of the Revolutionary Government," in *Cuba: The Economic and Social Revolution,* ed. Dudley Seers (Chapel Hill: University of North Carolina Press, 1964), p. 164.

2. Richard Fagen, *The Transformation of Political Culture in Cuba* (Stanford: Stanford University Press, 1969), p. 35; see also Jolly, pp. 164–167; Jules Dubois, *Fidel Castro: Rebel Liberator or Dictator?* (Indianapolis: Bobbs-Merrill, 1959), pp. 166–172.

PHASE ONE

Basic Education and Literacy

Immediately after taking power, the Cuban government boldly transformed the prerevolutionary educational system.[3] During the first half-decade Fidel Castro's two cardinal goals were literacy and ideological education. Even prior to the Revolution he had claimed that literacy should be a government priority. As early as 1953, when Castro stood trial for commanding an attack on the Moncada Army Barracks, he declared that literacy was critical to a successful revolution and to subsequent economic, political, and social progress. In 1955 Castro promised that "a revolutionary government would undertake the integral reform of the educational system."[4] Two years later in his Sierra Maestra Manifesto, Castro called for an "intense campaign against illiteracy."[5]

Upon taking power, the revolutionary leadership confronted a stagnant public-education system. Adult education scarcely existed. Graft and corruption flourished. On October 13, 1959, the revolutionary government, intent on carrying out its promise to transform Cuba's educational institutions, passed Article 149 of the Cuban Constitution. Designed to revamp education in the country, this article authorized the government to regulate completely the educational system, to abolish all private schools, and to dictate school curricula. At a very early date Castro thus seized the total control necessary to reform Cuban education.[6]

The Literacy Campaign

On September 26, 1960, Castro announced before the United Nations General Assembly:

---

3. In Chapter One I outlined the four phases through which the Castro government's policies passed during the first three decades of the Revolution. The leadership's policies toward youth and education can best be described in five phases instead of four. Therefore, for clarity, this chapter will divide the first phase into two stages.

4. Herbert L. Matthews, *Revolution in Cuba* (New York: Charles Scribner's Sons, 1975), p. 181.

5. Hugh S. Thomas, Georges A. Fauriol, and Juan Carlos Weiss, *The Cuban Revolution: Twenty-Five Years Later* (Boulder: Westview Press, 1984), p. 40; see also Jolly, p. 173; Fagen, pp. 33–36; Leo Huberman and Paul M. Sweezy, *Socialism in Cuba* (New York: Monthly Review Press, 1969), p. 24.

6. Sam Dolgoff, *The Cuban Revolution: A Critical Perspective* (Montreal: Black Rose Books, 1976), p. 179.

Next year our people propose to launch an all-out offensive against illiteracy, with the ambitious goal of teaching every illiterate person to read and write. Organizations of teachers, students, and workers—the entire population—are preparing themselves for an intensive campaign; and within a few months Cuba will be the first country in the Americas to be able to claim that it has not a single illiterate inhabitant.[7]

"Death to illiteracy will be the number one goal of 1961," declared Cuba's First Congress of the Municipal Councils of Education in October 1960. The following month Cuban officials launched a special census to locate illiterates. Then, in the following ringing terms Fidel Castro announced that 1961 would be the "Year of Education":

[W]e shall be able to proclaim to the entire world that in our country there remains not one person who is unable to read and write. . . . [W]e shall terminate the school year early and mobilize all the students from the sixth grade up. . . . [W]e shall organize an army of teachers and send them to every corner of the country.[8]

Following through on its promises the Cuban government then recruited and trained literacy workers for teaching responsibilities. On January 28, 1961, Castro announced that on April 15 all secondary and preuniversity schools would close. Officials would then recruit "an army of one hundred thousand literacy workers" selected from students who had completed at least the sixth grade and were at least thirteen years old. Castro reminded the students that to live and work, to serve and assist, to teach and learn with the poor, humble rural masses would be a privilege as well as a duty. At this time the government also formed a volunteer group called the "Conrado Benito Brigades," which consisted of youngsters (*brigadistas*) who were to be sent to the most remote corners of Cuba to teach and "revolutionize" the illiterates. The excitement and image of such an adventure, of such an all-encompassing national effort, captured the energy, dedication, and enthusiasm of most Cubans. For the young, especially, the literacy campaign was an exciting event, laden with hope and anticipation. The sense of a new and promising beginning pervaded the Cuban people.[9]

7. Fidel Castro quoted in Fagen, pp. 33–34; see United Nations Official Records of the General Assembly, 15th sess., pt. 1, Plenary Meetings, vol. 1, Verbatim Record (New York: September 20 to October 17, 1960), p. 126.
8. Fagen, pp. 38, 41.
9. Ibid., pp. 24–43; see also Huberman and Sweezy, p. 24.

By the end of the summer the leadership had fully trained and equipped, mobilized and deployed its "literacy army." The "final offensive" against the "entrenched fears of ignorance" was under way. Children, relieved of their school work, were put into uniforms, supplied with hammocks and blankets, and sent to the countryside to "alphabetize" the illiterates.[10] In fact, during the literacy campaign the Cuban government transported more than a quarter of a million students to locations across the length of the island. It supplied them with three million books and more than one hundred thousand paraffin lamps. For the next six months students lived with rural families and battled illiteracy.[11]

Although the speeches, billboards, and newspaper articles promoting literacy were not particularly ideological in content, the textbooks took on clear political overtones. The Ministry of Education prepared two texts for the campaign, called *Let's Alphabetize* and *We Shall Triumph*. Although the books did not explicitly mention socialism, communism, or Marx, each consisted of twenty-four "themes of revolutionary orientation" that covered such topics as imperialism and nationalization, racial discrimination and anti-Americanism.[12]

As the end of the literacy campaign neared, the government planned a "victory" celebration. Fidel Castro invited the participants to Havana for a week of fun: sports, recreation, cultural activities, a big parade, and a speech by Castro himself.[13] On December 15, 1961, the crowds of youth began to arrive. One scholar described the occasion as follows:

> Dressed in the remnants of their uniforms, often wearing peasant hats and beads, and carrying their knapsacks and lanterns, the *brigadistas* swarmed into the capital, singing and laughing and exchanging stories of their experiences. The similarities between the joyous return of the literacy army and the triumphal entry of the guerrilla troops only three years earlier were not lost on the population. It was one of the Revolution's finest hours.[14]

All Havana turned out for a spectacular festival culminating in Castro's speech. The revolutionary government claimed that virtually all Cubans could now read and write. While perhaps not as successful as the Revolu-

10. Matthews, p. 182.

11. Jolly, p. 192; see also Matthews, p. 182; Rolland G. Paulston, "Education," in *Revolutionary Change in Cuba*, ed. Carmelo Mesa-Lago (Pittsburgh: University of Pittsburgh Press, 1971), p. 387.

12. Fagen, pp. 39–40.

13. Issues of *Revolución*, December 18–23, 1961.

14. Fagen, p. 53.

tion's leaders boasted, the campaign did increase literacy significantly throughout the country. The campaign stood as an important early triumph for the government and the nation. The leadership had taken an initial, highly successful measure aimed at transforming Cuban culture.

The literacy campaign, involving more than one and a quarter million Cubans, also mobilized the masses in impressive fashion. As the campaign progressed, it reached a scope, duration, and intensity that states usually attain only on a war footing. The leadership's rhetoric charged the movement with the dramatic imagery of national emergency, revolutionary battle, and heroic victory. The literacy campaign thus revealed the militaristic style of the revolutionary leaders. It set a precedent of militarism that would steadily intensify over the next thirty years. Castro and his assistants conceptualized the literacy campaign, as they did nearly all national efforts, as a military exercise: as a "war," a "battle," or a "struggle." Over time this militaristic mentality came to dominate policy making concerned with cultural change.

Cuban leaders further enhanced revolutionary enthusiasm by vigorously praising and applauding supportive citizens. The leadership commended teachers and students alike for their displays of national pride and accomplishments. The literacy campaign allowed those who had formerly only observed the new government's actions to contribute actively to a cause that virtually all the people supported. The campaign thus effectively motivated the masses to participate in and support the Revolution. In fact, the literacy crusade formed a wholly unprecedented experience for every Cuban. It stood as a positive challenge to the people. It symbolized a government undertaking that would indisputably benefit the country. Consequently, most citizens wanted to be involved, whether from a sense of idealism or adventure, humanitarianism or curiosity, patriotism or altruism.

The literacy campaign also had a lasting impact because for nearly six months it consumed every participant's life. The intimacy of the activity pulled Cubans together in a single patriotic and noble effort, thereby strengthening the feelings of common purpose, mutual support, and nationalism. The leadership could logically conclude that, since voluntarism underlay the literacy campaign, Cubans emerged from the "battle" with a stronger sense of revolutionary determination. Authorities praised all the participants as selfless revolutionary "soldiers" and "heroes."

Equally important, perhaps, the literacy campaign provided the leadership with a vital sense of momentum in its efforts to reconstruct Cuban society.[15] Predictably, once Castro declared the socialist character of his

15. Matthews, p. 182; see also Fagen, pp. 52–63; Jolly, pp. 201–202.

Revolution in April 1961 and then announced his Marxist-Leninist faith the following December, the government's educational policies took on a stronger ideological flavor. Once the revolutionary leadership had abolished private and religious schools, the education of young Cubans became a powerful tool to mold the island's culture and create the new Cuban citizen.

Ideological Education

As early as mid-1960 Cuban leaders had already started to emphasize Marxist ideology within the education system. In April 1960 the government established the *Instituto Superior de Educación* to prepare school teachers for their role in the new school system by teaching them Marxist-Leninist precepts.[16] In late 1961 the government sent seventeen hundred students to study in Soviet-bloc countries. In July 1961 the National Institute of Agrarian Reform (INRA) sent another one thousand students to Eastern Europe to study for a year. In August and September 1962, two thousand more students joined them. In addition, about fifty older students attended universities in the foreign communist countries.[17]

In January 1961 the leadership perceived a particularly pressing need for ideological specialists, people who "would be the builders and loyal supporters of the 'new society,' who understood the basis of Marxism-Leninism and could influence its development in Cuba."[18] Shortly thereafter the government formed the Schools of Revolutionary Instruction ("EIRs," or *Escuelas de Instrucción Revolucionaria*), designed to develop revolutionaries for leadership positions. On December 20, 1961, Castro explained: "[T]he task of the schools . . . is the ideological formation of revolutionaries, and then, by means of the revolutionaries, the ideological formation of the rest of the people."[19] The government carefully selected students for the schools. To be chosen, one had to demonstrate not just basic intelligence but a keen understanding of proper revolutionary attitudes as well.

The Cuban leadership opened twelve regional EIRs and one national "finishing" EIR. For an intensive three months, more than seven hundred students attended the schools full time; they then completed their term by studying another three months at the national school. By the beginning of 1962 more than ten thousand students—all at least fourteen years old—had attended the EIRs and had absorbed carefully planned political and

16. Dolgoff, p. 179.
17. Jolly, pp. 250–251.
18. Ibid., pp. 206–207.
19. *Cuba Socialista* 3 (February 1964), Havana: 63.

ideological education. By late 1963 nine national schools existed, along with seven provincial schools, and two hundred local EIRs.[20]

In early 1962 Castro opened boarding schools (*internados*), "where life [was] rugged, work [was] hard and disciplined,"[21] and began awarding the scholarships, or *becas*, promised the *brigadistas* during the literacy campaign. Once again, officials selected recipients based on their revolutionary participation and that of their parents. By mid-1962, seventy thousand children had received a free opportunity to attend boarding school. Most students traveled to Havana and lived all week in "scholarship hostels," the abandoned houses of Miami-bound Cubans, before returning home on Saturday night.

The *becados* studied specific topics. The first year, for example, approximately 401 started training to be nurses, 1,743 learned to fish in Varadero, 125 studied agricultural accounting, 70 attended the national school of sugar cooperatives, and 300 took classes on the artificial insemination of livestock.[22] The leadership gave the students uniforms, books, board, and lodging. By 1965 Havana alone housed 80,000 *becados*, most of whom spent only one day a week with their parents.[23] On May Day 1966, Castro announced that more than 150,000 youngsters were living in boarding schools and receiving an education at the state's expense.[24]

These scholarship programs[25] stand out for several reasons. Perhaps most important, they offered to students of all socioeconomic levels the opportunity to receive an education that was free, but at the price of a significant degree of ideological conformity. During these early years, the numbers attending school increased quickly. The programs also marked the beginning of a steady expansion in the centralized control of education. Government officials selected the participants, chose their field of study, housed them comfortably, and fed them well. By separating children from parents and carefully supervising them, the government could use the scholarship programs to influence the upbringing and discipline, socialization and ideological training of youth.

On December 13, 1961, at a conference on revolutionary ideology and objectives, Gaspar Jorge García, the Secretary-General of the Trade Union

20. Fagen, pp. 105–114.

21. Huberman and Sweezy, p. 34.

22. Jolly, p. 240.

23. Peter Schmid, "Letter from Havana," *Commentary* 40, no. 3 (September 1965): 60.

24. Fidel Castro, speech on May Day 1966, quoted in *Fidel Castro Speaks*, ed. Martin Kenner and James Petras (New York: Grove Press, 1969), p. 207.

25. The Cuban government also provided scholarships for primary age children. Here again the leadership paired academic topics with extensive Marxist-Leninist instruction. See Karen Wald, *Children of Che: Childcare and Education in Cuba* (Palo Alto: Ramparts Press, 1978), p. 49; see also Matthews, p. 182.

of Education and Scientific Workers (SNTEC), explained the goals of the revamped educational system: "The society in which the children will live . . . will be Communist when they are adults. Communist! . . . What is proposed is to train active and conscientious builders of the Communist society. . . . [I]t will be achieved to the degree that old educators are re-educated and a new mentality is created, a new socialist mentality."[26]

The system of rewards and deprivation that underlay the scholarship program allowed the government to encourage Cuban citizens to cooper-ate with official revolutionary programs. The leadership rewarded compli-ant citizens who had strong records of revolutionary participation with educational opportunities for their children. It denied unsupportive citi-zens such benefits. To attain the government's most coveted educational rewards, a family had to show unflagging support for the government's programs. By rewarding ideological conformity, rather than intelligence alone, the Castro leadership succeeded in strengthening its grip on Cuban society, though it sacrificed the benefits of providing the most education to the best and brightest students.

Training Teachers for Revolutionary Education

In the quest to transform the culture of Cuban youth, school teachers stood out as one notable target group. Since teachers can exert much in-fluence over children, the government wanted to prepare its teachers, in-tellectually and ideologically, to mold the "new men." In 1961, after con-sulting with Soviet and Czechoslovakian officials, Cuban leaders designed a project to improve teacher quality.[27] Shortly thereafter, the Cuban Minis-try of Education opened the first teacher-training school in Minas del Frio. Although voluntary, the school actively recruited many students and had a substantial effect on the education of Cuban youth.

Minas del Frio, a mountain town in the Sierra Maestra, conveys the tough romanticism of the guerrilla struggle that led to Castro's victory. Indeed, Cuban officials designed the school to provide teachers with a "revolutionary" as well as an educational experience. The leadership hoped that, in preparing students to take on rural instruction, the Minas del Frio school would inculcate professional dedication, a revolutionary conscience, and doctrinaire Marxism-Leninism. In January 1962, three thousand students started classes at the school. By August more than one-third had become discouraged and left. One year later the leadership re-

26. Gerald H. Read, "The Revolutionary Offensive in Education," in *Fidel Castro's Personal Revolution in Cuba: 1959-1973*, ed. James Nelson Goodsell (New York: Knopf, 1975), pp. 211–212.

27. Dolgoff, p. 181.

warded those committed students who had remained through the rigorous program, transferring them to a luxurious school at Topes de Collantes.[28] Thereafter, many of these students, as well as those from other teaching-preparatory schools, demonstrated their loyalty to the Cuban government by joining the "Frank País Brigade." Students pledged to teach wherever the leadership sent them, and Castro assured ample rewards.

For loyal teachers who worked in the countryside, the leadership built a center at La Plata. While relaxing on weekends, teachers could exchange ideas, participate in group activities and games, and revive their spirit and enthusiasm for attaining revolutionary objectives. In addition, a lavish resort at Varadero served as an exclusive summer vacation spot for rural school teachers. To attract vacationing teachers, the government significantly subsidized rates. Perhaps it had to. Upon arrival the teachers found themselves required to take "refresher courses" in revolutionary teaching techniques.

During the early 1960s, to complement the official initiatives focused on teachers, the content of Cuban education underwent major changes as well. On all levels the leadership reformed syllabi and course materials and refocused their ideological orientation. A Cuban emigré has described the changes she observed during her elementary school years in the early 1960s as follows: "[A] curriculum was implemented which stressed political awareness. . . . Every story read, game played, or assignment given seemed designed to develop within us a . . . sense of moral obligation to the state."[29] During this period the authorities abolished the independence of each Cuban school. They rooted out the major differences and even the lesser distinctions that had long characterized various schools.[30]

Youth Organizations

To influence children to accept the idea of a revolutionary "new Cuban man," the Castro government invented and established various youth organizations. On May 10, 1960, the government introduced the Association of Rebel Youth (AJR). This group, created by the Army's Department of Education and tutored and supervised by professional cadres, sought to mobilize young people between the ages of fourteen and twenty-seven.[31] The AJR, later renamed the Union of Young Communists (UJC), quickly

28. Ibid.
29. Marcia del Mar, *A Cuban Story* (Winston-Salem: John F. Blair, 1979), p. 23.
30. Jolly, p. 223.
31. Jorge I. Domínguez, *Cuba: Order and Revolution* (Cambridge: Harvard University Press, 1978), p. 209.

evolved from the original idea of a mass association to a highly exclusive Party organization.[32]

The revolutionary government also created another important group known first as the Union of Rebel Pioneers, then as the Union of Pioneers in Cuba (UPC). Officials organized its members to engage in acts of solidarity, recreation, and community service, such as campaigns to collect bottles, newspapers, and trash. In addition, the state employed the UPC, similar to the Boy Scouts in the United States, to teach children revolutionary goals and requirements. Since the more elite UJC often selected its members from the Pioneers, the UPC served as a training ground for young revolutionaries.[33] The UPC selected its members based on the child's behavior, attitudes, school grades, and attendance, as well as the degree to which the child's parents participated in government-sponsored activities. By occupying children's spare time, the UPC organization furthered their political education in Cuba's revolutionary society. Once again the Young Communists and the Pioneers demonstrated the government's increasing use of a selective system that rewarded loyal "revolutionaries" and took away benefits from passive or dissenting citizens.

By late 1961 the CDRs had started to recruit children into special youth CDRs (CDR *infantiles*). In these organizations young Cubans took on the same types of vigilance and social-service activities that the adult CDRs performed.[34] A central purpose was to encourage youngsters to identify more closely with the Cuban state. To further this goal, the government organized special activities for children, such as games, a national children's day, revolutionary poetry readings, and special celebrations on national holidays.[35]

Day-Care Centers

In 1961 the leadership announced the opening of *círculos infantiles* (day-care centers), the first of which opened on July 26, 1961. With the government's guidance and support, the Federation of Cuban Women (FMC) organized the program and opened thirty-seven day-care centers by the end of 1961. Although the day-care centers were primarily designed to encourage female entry into the labor force, they also targeted young chil-

32. Ibid., pp. 279, 321–322.
33. Wald, p. 185; see also Domínguez, p. 279; *Hoy*, May 29, 1960 and October 28, 1960; Andrés Suárez, *Cuba: Castroism and Communism, 1959–1966* (Cambridge: M.I.T. Press, 1967), p. 127.
34. Fagen, p. 85; see also *Revolución*, October 26, 1961, p. 14; *Con la Guardia en Alto*, September 1964, pp. 15–17.
35. Fagen, p. 89.

dren for early revolutionary education. Given the importance of the early years of childhood development in influencing later attitudes and values, the government seized the opportunity to use the centers to attempt to mold revolutionary beliefs among Cuba's toddlers.

The FMC also established schools to train girls over fourteen to work in the day-care centers. These schools taught revolutionary ideology as well as child care, productive work methods, and educational skills.[36] In order to attend, students had to be active revolutionaries and FMC members. As one revolutionary said, "We cannot have anyone lacking revolutionary conviction involved in the formation of the new generation."[37]

Militarizing Youth

Despite these various programs aimed at Cuban children, as early as 1963 the country's youth were not thinking and behaving as the government had anticipated. In the initial years of the Revolution, Cuban society witnessed a steadily rising rate of juvenile delinquency. To reverse this trend, the leadership enacted a law that required three years of military service for all fifteen- to seventeen-year-old "delinquents."[38] Castro justified this measure by stating that the government would discipline defiant, "problem" youngsters: "We know of many cases of young men who were a headache to their fathers, who were incorrigible, who misbehaved, who stayed away from their classes."[39] This November 1963 law also took in "uneducated, ignorant, [or] . . . parasitical" adolescents who had dropped out of secondary school.

Relying on a broad construction of this vague law, the Cuban government found many youths in need of military service. For these young men, service in the Armed Forces often entailed spending a large part of the year cutting cane or picking coffee beans for the state. The government openly divided the Army into two classes: those who would and those who would not be permitted to bear arms. Raúl Castro, head of the Revolutionary Armed Forces (FAR), justified a three-year service period by claiming that it would enable the Army to increase production substantially. Thus, compulsory military service supplied the Cuban state with a cheap, yet organized, disciplined, and militarized labor corps. In fact, the

36. Wald, p. 122.
37. Marvin Leiner, *Children Are the Revolution: Day Care in Cuba* (New York: Viking Press, 1974), pp. 37–39.
38. Dolgoff, p. 182.
39. Theodore Draper, *Castroism: Theory and Practice* (New York: Praeger, 1965), p. 177.

delinquents law succeeded not only in supplementing the "volunteer" labor system but in reversing rising delinquency rates, at least for a time.[40]

What home and school failed to teach these youngsters, the FAR would teach, albeit with a somewhat different approach. Castro declared, "[W]hen life is too easy, when things come too easily, it isn't good."[41] In praising the military as the highest form of education and discipline, Castro proposed on November 13, 1964, that *all* youth serve time in the military. The Cuban leader argued that otherwise a large percentage of youngsters would develop "without discipline, without training, without being organized and without that conditioning which military instruction provides."[42] After implying that only military training can create a genuine revolutionary spirit, Castro suggested combining school and military training by establishing military centers of technological instruction.[43]

Curbing University Autonomy

Along with juvenile delinquency, the universities posed a troublesome problem for the revolutionary government. The University of Havana, like most Latin American universities, had traditionally enjoyed almost complete autonomy from the state. Upon taking power, Castro immediately began to pressure the university to conform to official ideology. Cuban leaders quickly replaced the university's elected governing council with their own state-controlled body. After gaining administrative control of the Federation of University Students (FEU), the leadership then forced the opposition candidate in the FEU presidential election to withdraw from the race. Although the FEU continued to contain students with divergent political viewpoints, the Castro government had secured its control over the administrative board and the office of the president. These political power plays notably curbed the autonomy of university student organizations.

Shortly thereafter, in keeping with its goal of militarizing youth, the Cuban government created the University Student Militias within the FEU. Before long this organization provoked a conflict that marked

40. Ibid., pp. 174–177.

41. Ibid., p. 178.

42. Ibid.

43. Ironically, five years earlier Castro went on record speaking out strongly against military compulsion. In January 1959 Castro explained that "we will not establish military service because it is not right to force a man to put on a uniform and a helmet, to give him a rifle and force him to march." Cited in *Revolución*, January 14, 1959. Four months later, on May 12, 1959, Fidel assured his listeners: "I wish to say one thing about what I think of compulsory military service. It should not be compulsory to be a soldier." Somewhere along the way Castro either changed his mind or revealed the truth.

the end of university autonomy. For some time the government tried to convince students that their "heroic mission" was to wear the "uniform of a militia member." Predictably, perhaps, students rebelled against this official pressure. In fact, fewer than three hundred out of twenty thousand students joined the Militias. Then, in February 1960 some students protested the diplomatic visit of the Soviet Union's Minister of Foreign Trade, Anastas Mikoyan. When Mikoyan placed a wreath on the statue of Cuba's revered hero, José Martí, these students became outraged that a representative of what was perceived to be an authoritarian regime would be "invited to insult the memory of Martí." They marched carrying signs that read "Down with Communism." Furious, Castro immediately replaced a substantial percentage of the university's faculty and textbooks and expelled hundreds of "counterrevolutionary students."[44] Once again the leadership subordinated scholarly excellence to ideological conformity.

By early 1962 Cuban leaders had enacted sweeping university reforms. The government changed standards for entry into the universities by establishing political criteria. To gain entry into the universities or remain at them, students had to demonstrate revolutionary enthusiasm and support. The state required all admitted students to take courses in dialectical and historical materialism for three semesters, comprising approximately 12 percent of a student's total education. In fact, the government required that all students in the University of Havana's Department of Political Science be members of either the UJC or the Communist Party.[45] In July 1965 Minister of Education Armando Hart declared: "[W]e must orientate education according to Marxism-Leninism. Marx's *Capital* must . . . be studied in all primary grades. . . . [T]he teachings of Marxism-Leninism in the universities is obligatory."[46]

By the end of 1965 the university's faculty and staff members began complaining to the government about the quality of professors and students. Absenteeism concerned officials. Class attendance, by professors as well as students, had dropped precipitously. Some protested the government's newly acquired control of the university by openly shunning classes. Others were simply too busy with other matters to attend. Outside activities, from militia duty to voluntary labor to participation in mass organizations, occupied increasing time and energy. As a consequence, students paid little attention to homework. One official complained that "often students do not complete more than 18 of 30 weeks' work."[47] The

44. Dolgoff, pp. 108–110. This is an account by Andrés Valdespino, a faculty member at the University of Havana, of the government takeover of the university.
45. Domínguez, p. 396.
46. Dolgoff, p. 108.
47. Jolly, pp. 260–261.

university administration responded to these complaints by enacting stricter requirements: unless a student maintained 80 percent attendance, he or she was ineligible for the final examination.[48]

In addition, in May 1964 the government introduced polytechnical programs modelled after those in the Soviet Union. In 1961 Minister of Education Armando Hart had traveled to the Soviet Union to study its polytechnical educational system. The Cuban version of those programs eventually aimed to immerse students in practical, productive work. These objectives quite clearly reflected Castro's distaste for educational institutions that nurtured in students what he called an intellectual, or "bookish," outlook on life.[49]

During the first five years of the Revolution, the leadership thus cast about, trying to find the proper role for education in the revolutionary society. The leadership shifted its policies during these early years from emphasizing basic literacy to promoting political and ideological socialization. Leading Cuban officials increasingly viewed education as a means through which a revolutionary conscience could be fostered and elitism abolished. The government thus expanded substantially its role in Cuban education. Initially, Castro and his colleagues had faith in the willingness of Cuban citizens to support enthusiastically a new approach to education. Despite the early optimism, however, troublesome signs of defiance among the nation's younger generation soon developed. As the years went by, the recalcitrance of youth warranted continual concern and comment by government officials.

A New Direction

After the initial period of experimenting with different policies toward Cuban youth, by 1965 the Castro government was searching for a fresh approach to counter increasingly apparent difficulties. Che Guevara's powerful 1965 essay "Man and Socialism in Cuba," emphasizing the creation of the "new man" and the complete transformation of national culture, filled the intellectual void in policy making and rapidly became the guiding principle in Cuban educational endeavors.[50] In October 1965 the Castro government launched a revised educational "offensive." Minister of Education Armando Hart announced that the Revolution was entering

48. Ibid., p. 261.
49. Read, p. 215.
50. Read discusses this in some detail on pp. 212–213; see Che's writings on education during this period in *Venceremos! The Speeches and Writings of Ernesto Che Guevara*, ed. John Gerassi (New York: Macmillan, 1968), pp. 387–400.

an aggressive phase of educational development during which every Cuban would find his or her moral and ideological consciousness transformed. Political education would equal, and perhaps surpass, literacy in the Cuban government's priorities. Once again the leadership concentrated its education initiative primarily on youth.[51]

During the following two years the Castro government attempted to impose upon the educational system, and upon Cuban society, an explicit group of well-defined beliefs and values. As one scholar wrote, by late 1965 the aim for Cuban education had changed dramatically:

> [The aim] was no longer simply to raise the level of basic knowledge and skills, but to foster the creation of a new man; a socialist man, honest, selfless, devoted to the community, and freed from greedy and corrupt bourgeois inclinations. . . . The overall purpose of education at all levels is to produce better Communists, men and women, unconditionally loyal to the party and party leadership.[52]

The Steady Expansion of the Government's Role in Education

In 1965 the Castro leadership expelled another group of students, intellectuals, and artists from the University of Havana. On May 26, 1965, Jaime Crombet, the former president of the FEU, spoke at the University, instructing "the Union of Young Communists and the Federation of University Students [to] see to it that the curriculum follows the orientation of Fidel Castro."[53] In another university lecture three weeks later, Blas Roca, a member of the Central Committee, advocated creating Communist Party cells to "facilitate the campaigns of the University to eliminate counterrevolutionaries and homosexuals."[54]

This campaign to further official authority over Cuban education extended beyond the universities. In July 1966 the government took over administering the *círculos* from the Federation of Cuban Women. The leadership immediately changed the manner in which the day-care centers operated. Although originally operating five days a week, the *círculos* now expanded their schedules to include Saturday. Some centers even went so far as to offer twenty-four hour, sleep-in care for the children.[55]

Most important, the government redefined the objectives of day-care

51. Read, p. 212.
52. Thomas, Fauriol, and Weiss, p. 41.
53. Dolgoff, pp. 108–109.
54. Both speeches in *Este y Oeste*, Caracas, June 15, 1966.
55. Leiner, p. 54.

centers. An original aim had been to free mothers from the daily daytime care of their children, thus providing better opportunities to join the work force. By 1965, however, the government explicitly acknowledged that the centers were also designed to provide children with a collective environment in which to grow up and be instilled with revolutionary values. Clementina Serra, Director of the National Program of Childcare Centers and a member of the Central Committee, said "[T]he childcare program has two main objectives: to liberate women so they can become an active part of the productive work force, and to aid in the social development of the children. Both objectives are very important, but the formation of the child is primary."[56] The political education of Cuban children had joined sexual equality as a chief rationale for the child-care centers.[57]

Youth Organizations Take on a New and Important Role

In 1966 the Cuban leadership turned its attention to revolutionary youth organizations. The government saw these groups as a valuable means to occupy children's spare time, and it urged youngsters to join and participate.[58] Aside from providing a social forum for children, such organizations helped the government to educate and control Cuban youth, to curtail juvenile delinquency and the nascent "capitalist attitudes" that the Marxist-Leninist leaders so feared.[59]

To increase participation, the Cuban leaders opened to all children membership in the popular youth organization, the Young Pioneers. The government apparently viewed this group as an effective tool with which to involve every child in revolutionary activities. Ricardo García Pampin, an adult leader of the organization, explained that the Pioneers would become more than an extracurricular community service organization. It was to become "a vehicle for engaging in the ideological struggle."[60]

One underlying objective in opening up membership in the Young Pioneers may have been to pressure parents to take a stand on their attitude toward the government.[61] García Pampin elaborated: "We were in the process in which everyone had to define himself: they were either on the side

56. Quoted in Wald, p. 120.

57. Ibid., pp. 118–119.

58. Luis P. Salas, "Juvenile Delinquency in Postrevolutionary Cuba: Characteristics and Cuban Explanations," in *Cuban Communism*, ed. Irving Louis Horowitz, 4th ed. (New Brunswick, N.J.: Transaction, 1981), p. 263.

59. Luis P. Salas, *Social Control and Deviance in Cuba* (New York: Praeger, 1979), pp. 28–29.

60. Wald, p. 186.

61. García Pampin explained: "The participation of children in revolutionary activities at times aided in their parents' definition of their own roles" (ibid.).

of the Revolution or they were not." Through this tactic the leadership tried to expose adults who were not actively revolutionary. García Pampin explained that this youth group "forced" parents to decide whether they stood with Fidel Castro as "revolutionaries" or against him as "*gusanos.*" In fact, García Pampin stated baldly that the Pioneer adult directors encouraged children to practice loyalty to the Revolution before loyalty to family.[62] One Cuban emigré recalled her childhood activities in revolutionary Cuba: "The fact that the state was of greater importance than family, friendship, or religion was always emphasized."[63] García Pampin further explained:

> We could talk of many interesting experiences of children who have transformed the conduct of their parents. For instance, a doctor was planning to leave the country, and his son was a Pioneer. . . . Then the son, when it came time for them to leave, told his father that he was a Pioneer, and that Pioneers don't betray their country. The decision was made by the child; the father stayed.[64]

Whether such stories were true or apocryphal, professional cadres did tutor and supervise the Pioneers, teaching the youngsters to adhere to a strict code of conduct. Jesús Montane, one of the organization's adult leaders, explained that the cadres taught the Pioneers "to develop a sense of honor, modesty, courage, comradeship, love of both physical and intellectual work, respect for workers, and responsibility in caring for social property. . . . [and] a love for our Revolutionary Armed Forces and the Ministry of the Interior."[65]

After 1966 membership in the Young Pioneers increased markedly, and the organization became extremely active and visible among Cuban youth.[66] For instance, the Pioneers carried out school competitions for "exemplary student" status. Students earned official recognition by participating in productive activities and revolutionary events and maintaining respectful relations with teachers and other students. The government lauded those Young Pioneers who conducted themselves as dedicated revolutionaries by practicing cleanliness, self-analysis, punctuality, cooperation, obedience, good attendance, and disciplined study. The state rewarded such loyalty with a pin, flag, banner, or some other revolutionary symbol.[67] In the late 1960s the Pioneers also began to stage public

62. Ibid.
63. del Mar, p. 23.
64. Wald, pp. 186–187.
65. *Granma*, April 3, 1975; see also Domínguez, p. 279.
66. Domínguez, p. 279.
67. Wald, p. 190.

political debates on such issues as American imperialism, material incentives, and productivity. They also produced radio programs and presented plays that reenacted events in Cuba's revolutionary history such as the attack on the Moncada Barracks, the landing of the *Granma,* and the Bay of Pigs victory. The government also established summer camps at which Pioneers participated in revolutionary activities and took classes on ideology.[68]

Over the following five years the status of the UPC continued to grow as the leadership increased its emphasis on preparing children ideologically for eventual UJC membership. García Pampin explained why the Pioneer organization grew in significance in the late 1960s: "We are trying to form future communists. . . . [T]he schools alone can't satisfy all the objectives that we have set out for ourselves. . . . The Union of Pioneers is better structured than the schools for creating the kind of characteristics we want to see in our young people."[69] By the end of the Revolution's first decade the Pioneers had become a valuable tool in official efforts to mold youth attitudes.

Controlling Juvenile Delinquency

The government also implemented various measures to control juvenile delinquency and other forms of youth defiance. On October 3, 1965, Fidel Castro announced that the state had established military rehabilitation labor camps for recalcitrant youth. These camps provided Cuban officials with an additional phalanx of labor available to carry out civic work projects. In addition, the leadership formed several Youth Re-Education Centers for youngsters under sixteen who had been found guilty of minor offenses. These centers, too, combined agricultural labor and disciplined military training.[70]

As part of this continuing effort to diminish juvenile delinquency, in 1966 the government built a number of sports and recreational facilities for children.[71] The leadership also created the Federation of Secondary-School Students, an organization similar to the Young Pioneers, that promoted athletics, school attendance, vigilance activities, and an honor code to prevent cheating. In late 1965 the government introduced yet another educational idea: "School Goes to the Countryside." In seeking to combine education and productive work, this program sent to the rural areas to camp, study, and work tens of thousands of students, with their books

68. Ibid., pp. 196–197, 214.
69. Ibid., pp. 192–193.
70. Dolgoff, p. 184.
71. *Bohemia,* December 9, 1966; December 30, 1966.

and teachers, for forty-five days.[72] By the end of 1966, twenty thousand students were participating in this program.[73]

By the fall of 1966 the government had converted the Isle of Pines, an island off the coast of Cuba that had served for centuries as a penal colony, into a working community for young Cubans. The Isle of Youth, as it was renamed, formed a party-directed semipermanent residence with a Spartan atmosphere and a "pure communist" setting of egalitarianism and sacrifice. It lured young people who longed to escape from city life or from the rigors of their poor country dwellings. In this halcyon, bucolic environment, students grew citrus trees, raised cattle and other livestock, and produced vegetables. As one scholar described it, the Isle of Youth served as a "lab where young 'uncontaminated' [Cubans] go to live out the dream."[74]

Yet despite all these intensive, costly programs to fashion revolutionary young people, the problems of Cuban youth worsened. The leadership railed at youngsters and the adults who influenced them for not demonstrating a "revolutionary *conciencia*." In a December 1966 speech Castro assailed university students, reproaching them with the curious claim that they had less "revolutionary consciousness than middle-grade agronomists"! And on July 26, 1967, Castro warned, "It should not be forgotten that . . . the entire generation living in our country at the time of the revolution was completely educated under the influence of capitalist ideas, methods, and feelings."[75]

Always distrustful of intellectuals, Castro denounced the university's "wall of theory and abstractionism" and insisted that the government would establish new educational institutions that would promote a revolutionary labor conscience among all students:[76]

> [S]chools will not resemble those institutions of days gone by. . . . Our children today will learn the meaning of work from the earliest age. Even if they are just six, and in first grade, they will know how to grow lettuce. . . . Thus they will acquire a noble concept of

72. Paulston, p. 387; see also Huberman and Sweezy, p. 42; Read, pp. 216–217; Fagen, p. 149.

73. Fagen, p. 259.

74. Ibid., p. 149; see also Salas, *Social Control*, p. 21.

75. Speech by Fidel Castro, July 26, 1967, quoted in Lowry Nelson, *Cuba: The Measure of a Revolution* (Minneapolis: University of Minnesota Press, 1972), p. 134.

76. Hugh S. Thomas, *Cuba: The Pursuit of Freedom* (New York: Harper & Row, 1971), p. 1,429.

work, not the idea of work as something to be scorned, nor of work as a sacrifice, but rather as a pleasure.[77]

On August 18, 1968, Minister of Education José Llanusa addressed the Makarenko Pedagogical Institute. He instructed teachers to develop their "students as Communists, representative of generations that will be better" than their own. He continued: "You must be concerned . . . about . . . the ideological formation of those students."[78]

At this time Castro also took note of the high drop-out rate of Cuban elementary students. In 1966 only 21 percent of the students who had originally registered in first grade had completed and graduated from sixth grade. In 1967 only about 40 percent of Cuban first graders moved on with their schooling.[79] Indeed, more than 30 percent of Cuba's potential second graders were not enrolled in school at all. By 1969, of the 410,250 students who had entered first grade, only 46 percent finished sixth grade.[80] Thus, while the revolutionary government had instituted impressive educational reforms, after a decade of effort the system still struggled to retain half of its students between primary school and the sixth grade. This presented the Castro government with grave social and economic problems: students were being neither properly educated nor effectively socialized. The government expected them to be in school until age sixteen; thereafter, they were expected to serve in the Armed Forces or go to work. The many teenage drop-outs—idle, uninvolved in revolutionary activities, and in many cases participants in antigovernment campaigns— seriously concerned the Castro government. Instead of joining the vaunted "new men" of the Revolution, these children were existing on the margin of Cuban society.[81] "Many young people are neither working nor studying," Castro complained. "[No parent has the right] to permit his son to be an idler, a vagabond, a future delinquent." Castro continued:

> Perhaps it is not a crime under capitalism, but a society which aspires to satisfy human needs through work and the application of technology cannot be indifferent when [youth are permitted to be] ignorant and illiterate. . . . We shall have to have laws which severely

77. Nelson, pp. 133–134; see also complete text of speech in *Granma*, February 5, 1967; Matthews, p. 346.

78. Read, pp. 213–214.

79. Nelson, pp. 139–141.

80. Domínguez, p. 171.

81. For enlightening discussion of the early educational policies and successes, see ibid., pp. 165–173.

punish parents who do not comply with the elementary duty of sending their children to school.[82]

Indeed, the government reminded Cuban youth and their parents that it would simply not tolerate unrevolutionary behavior.

PHASE TWO

By 1965 coaching Cuban youth in correct ideological thinking already formed an official priority in education. By 1968, however, it had become the transcendent objective of the education system. Cuban leaders subordinated the prior emphasis on literacy to the new objective of transforming Cuban youth *conciencia*. In this period the Castro government initiated the "Revolutionary Offensive" to construct "pure" communism and create the so-called "new man."

Work-Study Programs

In early 1968 the leadership began to require secondary students to participate in work-study programs. The government had decided that the forty-five day, "School Goes to the Countryside" experience had worked so well that all rural schools would henceforth operate on a work-study basis. In these boarding schools, the first of which opened in 1969, children worked half of the day and studied the other half.[83] During the harvest season the schools closed for several weeks and students worked full time.

Many Cuban parents protested against this new program, which required their children to perform agricultural labor as part of their formal education.[84] As Max Figueros, General Director of Educational Development in the Ministry of Education, explained, the Cuban government anticipated these complaints: "We knew there might be problems with the new idea, so we tried it out first in our most provincial area, Camaguey. The students presented no difficulties. For them it was a holiday, with recreational activities, being away like at a camp, and a lot of fun. For the

82. Speech by Fidel Castro, September 28, 1967, quoted in Maurice Halperin, *The Taming of Fidel Castro* (Berkeley and Los Angeles: University of California Press, 1981), p. 229.

83. Joe Nicholson, Jr., *Inside Cuba* (New York: Sheed and Ward, 1974), p. 23.

84. Fred Ward, *Inside Cuba Today* (New York: Crown Publishers, 1978), p. 97.

parents, it was hard."[85] Over the course of the year, the permanent "School Goes to the Countryside" program expanded to include the vast majority of Cuban youngsters. This work-study program provided the government with ever-increasing influence over children living and working apart from their parents.

Another Assault on the Universities

In early 1968 the Castro government disciplined the universities once again. First, the leadership announced a strict dress and hair code. Then, in December 1967, to increase the influence of doctrinaire Marxist-Leninists over political thought, the government dissolved the FEU and assigned its organized activities to the UJC. Since the FEU had been a significantly more politically diverse organization than the UJC, and since less than 30 percent of FEU members belonged to the UJC, this policy cut the majority of university students out of most political activities.[86] Thereafter, university political activism became the business of a small and highly selective group of young communists.[87] "Revolutionary" students had been rewarded with virtually complete control over organized political activities in higher education. The leadership had stripped passive or dissenting students not just of leadership roles but of any chance to participate formally in political activities or organizations.[88]

Even these stern measures in higher education failed to satisfy the Cuban leadership. In December 1968 Castro bitterly criticized the universities once again and declared that he would eventually abolish them altogether, "since most activities in Cuban society did not require higher education."[89] To increase his authority, Castro then created a Higher Council of Universities, headed by the Ministry of Education, designed to govern the universities with some assistance from the UJC.

85. Ibid., pp. 97–98.

86. Shortly thereafter, the UJC established the Centennial Youth Column, which called for volunteers to perform agricultural labor in Camaguey for three years. While working, these young men and women took courses and studied. For young males it served as an alternative to military service. Domínguez, pp. 322, 485–487.

87. *Granma Weekly Review* (*GWR*), March 21, 1971; May 30, 1971; August 1, 1971; see also Domínguez, p. 280.

88. Union membership displayed excessive elitism. The vast majority of union members were white-collar professionals, scientists, and teachers. Membership included very few blue-collar workers and agricultural and industrial workers. For a complete discussion of this, see Domínguez, p. 322.

89. Dolgoff, p. 181.

Youth Resistance Increases

Just as Castro experienced continuing problems at the universities, requiring ever stricter countermeasures, so he found that Cuban children were not as malleable and easily controlled as he had hoped. Despite the many innovative measures during the Revolutionary Offensive targeted at further influencing and educating children, the Cuban leadership remained largely disillusioned with the results.

In fact, the rate of juvenile delinquency in Cuba did not decrease. In 1967 minors committed 41 percent of all crimes in Cuba, a figure slightly above 1958 statistics. In 1968 children under sixteen years of age committed well over one-fourth of all minor thefts (involving items such as radios, rings, cigarettes, and clothes) and one-third of all robberies.[90] From 1960 to 1968 the number of property crimes steadily rose, and most were committed by youth. In April 1969 *Verde Olivo* reported that for two prior months, 96 of the 148 persons apprehended for violent robberies were minors.[91] Moreover, in 1968 rates of sabotage and vandalism among youth dramatically increased. Some students openly displayed their insubordination: police caught many students listening to "bourgeois music and even tearing down posters of Che and Fidel."[92]

The leaders also lamented the "hippie" problem, to which Castro devoted nearly an entire speech on September 28, 1968. The leadership made clear that revolutionary society could not be a haven for bourgeois hippies. Complaining that these young people were wasting time, sitting idle at their hangouts in Havana, Castro warned that hippies would be rounded up and sent to jails, labor camps, and rehabilitation centers.[93] Vagrancy posed similar concerns. In 1969 nearly half of Cuba's fifteen-year-olds and sixteen-year-olds were not engaged in productive labor.[94] In lamenting this unfortunate state of affairs, Castro blamed school administrators as well as the students themselves.[95]

Plainly, most Cuban students failed to adopt Castro's notion of the "new man." In June 1968 *Cuba* magazine interviewed thirty-five students, whose average age was 20.2 years, working as volunteers with the Centennial Youth Column. According to the magazine, the government selected these students to be interviewed because their participation in the Column

---

90. Salas, *Social Control*, pp. 15–16; see also *Bohemia*, April 14, 1967, pp. 78–79.

91. Salas, *Social Control*, pp. 15–16.

92. *Con la Guardia en Alto*, May 1979, pp. 10–17.

93. Salas, *Social Control*, p. 15; see also *Miami Radio Monitoring Service*, September 28, 1968, p. 16.

94. Salas, *Social Control*, p. 20; see also *Verde Olivo* 14 (April 1972): 25.

95. See *Bohemia*, January 10, 1969, for complete text of speech.

illustrated their new revolutionary conscience. The interviewer asked students why they were participating in the Column. Only seventeen of the students—less than half—gave an appropriately "revolutionary" response. Seven male students said they joined to avoid military service. Seven other students claimed to have joined for economic reasons, and thirteen wanted to get away from home. Several students cited being with a lover, being in the countryside, and being pressured by their peers. This was hardly a resounding example of appropriate revolutionary attitudes.[96] *Bohemia* ran numerous articles that discussed the Column's difficulties, including laziness, desertions, shoddy performance, and innumerable and unnecessary absences.

Finally, in the late 1960s both Cubans and foreign visitors commented on the spectrum of problems that had developed on the Isle of Youth. The leadership had hoped the island project would exemplify a new revolutionary youth consciousness. Instead, the "utopia" appeared to the leaders to be plagued by excessive materialism, lack of discipline, and sexual permissiveness. The Isle's objective, to create an idyllic communist society for youth, had never been approached.

Policy Initiatives

To try to remedy these various problems, in 1967 Castro made primary school obligatory for every Cuban child. A year later he abolished the state-operated lottery, a popular prerevolutionary institution that had been allowed to continue to function. The leadership viewed the lottery as promoting laziness, speculation, and greed. Authorities believed that such gambling undermined the creation of a new *conciencia*. According to Castro, young people in particular were fooling away their time, energy, and money.[97]

At the same time Castro initiated a campaign to instruct parents on how to raise their children properly in a socialist society. The government aired instructive television and radio programs, and the leadership encouraged parents to attend CDR-organized block meetings. Once again, authorities penalized the uncooperative with formal and informal sanctions. Those who toed the official, revolutionary line, however, were rewarded.

In April 1968 Castro went still further. Cuba's revolutionary leader called on the CDRs to oversee the activities and attitudes of parents and youth. The government instructed the Committees to report unusual, or

96. Domínguez, pp. 485–487.
97. Salas, *Social Control,* p. 65; see also Thomas, p. 873; Nicholson, p. 48.

unacceptable, behavior.[98] The CDRs then introduced an "exemplary parenthood" program, which promoted proper parenting by rewarding those who carried out the official requirements satisfactorily. Exemplary parents were those whose child followed school regulations, studied and passed all courses, kept a 95 percent school attendance record, and participated in voluntary labor, extracurricular, and rural education programs. These parents then had to demonstrate their continuing interest by serving on special committees, periodically visiting the school, and attending school-related meetings.[99] The government noted the performance of "exemplary" parents and publicly praised them. It sanctioned those who failed to meet its requirements.

In the same year the leadership introduced a Plan for Technological Instruction, designed to convert all agricultural and cattle-raising technological institutes to military centers. Castro placed these institutes under the direction of the Office of Military Centers for Intermediate Education, an office within the Ministry of the Armed Forces. The Ministry of Education was to supervise the technical and teaching portions of the programs. Major Belarmino Castilla Mas, Deputy Minister for Technological Military Training, explained the military's responsibility: "It is our job to determine where and how this army of technicians is to be trained, where we are to employ these human resources and in which direction the efforts must be aimed."[100] In these boarding institutions, one observer wrote, "students live under strict military discipline . . . and complete their military draft obligations while they study."[101] By 1970, twenty-three institutions participated in this new program.[102]

The Cuban government also established more rehabilitation vocational schools and work armies to reeducate "maladjusted" youngsters. These programs, regulated by either the Ministry of Education, the Armed Forces, or the Ministry of the Interior, affected thousands of youth. One government official explained their objectives as follows: "[W]e educate these young people in the sense of collectivity. We want to change the basic pattern of their conduct, which has been one of individualism."[103]

Considered as a whole, the second phase of the Cuban government's policies toward youth elevated the objective of ideological instruction over that of basic education. In addition, the Cuban leadership attempted to exercise its authority in other realms of life, in part by steadily increasing

98. Salas, "Juvenile Delinquency," p. 264.
99. Domínguez, p. 261; see also *Con la Guardia en Alto*, January–February 1972, p. 63.
100. Read, p. 216.
101. Ibid., p. 215.
102. Ibid.
103. Wald, p. 282.

the military's role. Finally, the leaders demonstrated their willingness to coerce citizens directly in order to force changes in stubbornly independent attitudes and behavior.

Nevertheless, despite the government's inclination to employ substantial coercive measures to mold the ideology of young men and women, the leaders continued to confront resistant, uncooperative youth. Truancy and theft abounded, as did idleness, homosexuality, and the hippie lifestyle. All this nonconformity proved quite discouraging to the Marxist-Leninist leaders. Leave it to the children, Fidel Castro had said. "They will carry the Communist virus into their homes. They will infect entire villages with it."[104] But by 1970, after a decade of revolutionary education, Cuban youth still showed few signs of developing into Che Guevara's "new socialist men." Castro and his associates had grown tired of trying to woo, praise, bribe, and coddle the children. They would no longer brook the dissent of individualists. The time had come for harsh measures.

PHASE THREE

The new decade dawned with extreme economic, social, and political burdens resting on Fidel Castro's shoulders. The Cuban leader struck back, in part, by adopting a less tolerant approach to youth problems. The leadership began to worry less about correct attitudes and began to focus more on proper behavior. Castro announced that he would soon implement stern measures to remedy Cuba's youth problems. The new policies came in two waves.

Coercion Intensifies

In the first wave Castro declared that religion, especially the Afro-Cuban variety, caused antirevolutionary attitudes among children. The government, he insisted, would work harder to eradicate this evil and to punish those who encouraged it among youth. Next, with the help of the FMC, the Ministry of Education began distributing to parents packets of "guidance cards" that set forth approved child-rearing practices for parents to follow. Parents were to study the cards and to discuss their content at required parent-teacher meetings.[105] Moreover, although by 1972 more

104. K. S. Karol, *Guerrillas in Power: The Course of the Cuban Revolution* (New York: Hill and Wang, 1970), p. 353.
105. Leiner, pp. 153–155.

than fifty-five work-study schools were operating in Cuba, the leaders decided the island needed much more of this brand of education. Castro announced that within the following few years all schools would be converted to a work-study basis.[106] He conceded that through these schools, "we [the Cuban leadership] run the risk of replacing the father by the state," but insisted that the very survival of the Revolution was at stake.[107]

Further Education Reforms

In February 1970 Castro introduced a plan to improve the performance of teachers. The "Plan de Titulación Maestros" sought to review, evaluate, and retrain revolutionary teachers.[108] A year earlier the report of the Seventh National Assembly of the People's Organizations in Education stated that "we need teachers whose motivation is to form new men. . . . True revolutionary teachers."[109] Then, in 1971 the government expanded the teacher-training program to include *círculo* staff members. One official explained that the *círculo* teachers had to be included because "the principle pursued in the child-care centers is to form the child completely— the child for the new society, children who will replace today's workers."[110] An official explained that these teachers must "create" children with "a sense of solidarity and collectivity." He continued:

> They shouldn't be selfish; they should be able to identify with the group. . . . They should know that we all work together to produce what we have, and that we then all share the things we have created. . . . Work should be seen as something fulfilling and rewarding; not just something you have to do to stay alive. They should respect all kinds of work, if that work serves the Revolution.[111]

Perhaps most important, the leadership dictated that the *círculos* were no longer to be reserved only for children of working mothers. Instead, all young Cuban children were encouraged to attend. The government set out to have every Cuban child in a *círculo* by his first birthday.[112] Once

106. Nicholson, p. 27.
107. Matthews, p. 45; Fidel Castro speech at the University of Chile on November 15, 1971.
108. Karol, p. 313; see also Paulston, p. 388.
109. Read, p. 215.
110. Wald, p. 120.
111. Ibid., p. 119.
112. Ibid., p. 128.

children left the child-care centers at the age of five or six, they went directly to boarding schools (*internados*), semiboarding schools (*semiinternados*), or day schools. In the *internado* programs, expanded during the early 1970s, instructors emphasized political consciousness. The children read articles and stories on imperialism, guerrilla warfare, and revolutions in Cuba and other parts of the world.[113]

In 1971 Castro expanded the rural work-study program to include primary schools as well as secondary schools. He also announced that forty work-study primary schools would be constructed within the following year.[114] In the rural program children grew vegetables, made handicrafts, cared for fruit orchards, packaged and assembled toys, and prepared herbal teas. The students, who lived in dormitories, worked four hours in the classroom every morning and four hours in the field every afternoon. Much of their time was devoted to cultivating coffee, pineapple, citrus fruits, and sugar cane. An average day lasted from 6:30 A.M. to 11:00 P.M. The products, of course, went to the state for sale or distribution.[115] One official explained:

> [T]he children's work in the field was not amateurishness and not play, but a serious contribution to agriculture. Being so young . . . they are quicker and more supple and do not mind bending over so much. They do not, of course, have the strength or stamina of adults, but their contribution is real, especially considering the shortage of farm labor.[116]

Through these work-study programs the leadership sought to inculcate in the children revolutionary duty, communist civic-mindedness, military discipline, and obedience as well as technical competence. Above all, the government stressed conformity. As a Cuban teacher explained:

> We work in collective groups, and it's important for the students to be the same. . . . If we permit one student to be different in dress, hair, or behavior, what can we expect from the rest? . . . We have to create similarity among the students and form them with a collective philosophy. That is a basic tenet of communism.[117]

While participating in these programs, students were to concentrate on three goals: attaining military skills, performing useful, productive work,

113. Ibid., pp. 38, 136.
114. Matthews, p. 346.
115. Wald, p. 180; Matthews, pp. 346–347.
116. Matthews, p. 347.
117. Nicholson, p. 29.

and gaining basic knowledge and a firm footing in Marxist-Leninist ideology. Indeed, as one scholar explained, schools sought to instill a tripartite commitment to *estudio, trabajo y fusil* (study, work, and the rifle).[118]

These work-study programs offered the Cuban government yet another opportunity to influence directly, and on a daily basis, the upbringing of the island's children. Not only did work-study programs reduce the rate of truancy but the government no longer had to face continual parental influences and objections. Teachers, selected and trained by the government, taught children the role and importance of manual labor in a socialist society. And, isolated from their parents for extended periods, the children provided the government with a large, free labor force that was in no position to object to its treatment.

Cuban schools thus became powerful instruments for state revolutionary socialization of children. The government's growing control over children disrupted the traditional Cuban family and subordinated parental influences.[119] Promoting cooperation, loyalty, and conformity among students became a cardinal objective of the education system.

As for young men and women, Fidel Castro saw a university education as essentially a political endeavor and an "opportunity to produce." The university was not a place for detached political, philosophical, or scientific inquiry. On December 8, 1972, Fidel Castro announced, in a speech at Havana University, that the Revolution would "take a decisive step in university education by combining study and work."[120] Students would be able to gain a university education only if they simultaneously worked for the state. Castro continued: "In our country, the need to combine study and work was more than obvious! . . . [T]he application of the principles of universal study is possible only to the extent that work is also made universal. . . . [T]he gap between intellectual workers and manual workers must gradually disappear."[121] The government made it quite clear that "new and old students who lack the necessary and moral conditions" would be expelled forthwith.[122]

By the end of 1972 the University of Havana had enrolled sixteen thousand students in work-study programs. José M. Millar Barrueco, then the rector, envisioned that by 1980 the university would be "a vast complex of schools, factories, farms, mines, hospitals . . . where students are workers and workers are students. [I]n Cuba, a factory is . . . a branch of the

118. Juan M. del Aguila, *Cuba: Dilemmas of a Revolution* (Boulder: Westview Press, 1984), p. 76.

119. Nelson, pp. 152–155.

120. *GWR*, December 17, 1972, p. 9.

121. Ibid., pp. 9–10; see also Matthews, pp. 342–343.

122. Matthews, p. 350; see also *GWR*, July 11, 1971.

university, a part of the educational system. . . . Today, Havana University is an integral part of the revolutionary economy and social system." This process, Millar explained, "encompasses the whole of society, since even the primary-school pupil is being taught the importance of work. The process carries through to the adult, forming a new man."[123]

Youth Problems Worsen

Despite the state's comprehensive control of resources and its willingness to coerce, youth problems continued to dog the Cuban government. In truth, the leadership's repressive measures had little positive effect. Youth at all levels continued to display signs of insubordination and noncompliance. Perhaps most seriously, many students rejected Castro's work-study programs. The leaders lamented that the majority of young people avoided entering fields that required labor. This state of affairs touched off another reprimand from Fidel Castro, who declared: "What is discouraging is that in 1971 and 1972 fewer and fewer students want to study in agricultural and industrial subjects. I ask myself why. And I ask you . . . who is going to produce the material goods in the future and now?"[124]

Other symptoms of educational malaise soon appeared. The vocational and technological schools, which the government created in the mid-1960s and crowned a success at that time, no longer attracted many students. By 1972 the number of registered students had dropped dramatically; in fact, some schools actually stood empty. Students displayed little interest in agriculture and industry; they enrolled instead in such "nonproductive" fields as languages and the social sciences. Twelve years of revolutionary rhetoric and coercion apparently had done little to persuade Cuban students to pursue "productive" occupations in agriculture and industry. Castro asked: "Who wants to go to work in the countryside? [It] is rough, it is poor . . . it doesn't change from one year to the next [and it will stay as it is] for years to come."[125]

Students also quite plainly lacked respect for government officials, state

123. Matthews, pp. 343–344. Gerald Read describes the effects of these work-study programs in Cuba in the early 1970s: "The island at the present time can be characterized as a vast reformatory, or, more charitably, a comprehensive school, with the Party showing no sign of discouragement in its mission to inculcate revolutionary enthusiasm, commitment, and morale" (p. 218).

124. Fidel Castro quoted in Matthews, pp. 343–346.

125. See Carmelo Mesa-Lago, *Cuba in the 1970s: Pragmatism and Institutionalization* (Albuquerque: University of New Mexico Press, 1974), p. 94; see also *GWR*, April 16, 1972, pp. 2–4.

property, and socialist values. According to the Minister of Education, students lost or destroyed more than half of their school books every year. Castro complained: "There's something wrong when we have to educate our young people in the need to care for socialist property."[126] The leadership also railed against "extravagant foreign fashions" and the obsession with American music and "decadent" literature. The government claimed that "residual manifestations" of prostitution and homosexuality prevailed among the island's youth.[127]

Rates of truancy and vagrancy among youth also climbed steadily. Since 1968 the school drop-out rate had steadily risen. The government estimated that by April 1971 more than 300,000 youngsters between the ages of four and sixteen were neither attending school nor working.[128] On December 31, 1970, Raúl Castro complained that in one year "300,000 to 400,000 children between 6 and 16 . . . drop out of school for one reason or another."[129] Although the antiloafing law cut that figure to 215,513 by 1972, that still left 44.3 percent of Cuba's fifteen-year-olds and 60.2 percent of Cuba's sixteen-year-olds neither working nor attending school. In the leadership's view these young loafers were contributing nothing productive to Cuban society.[130]

Moreover, in 1971 juvenile delinquency soared to an all-time high. Children committed more than 50 percent of all crimes, a significant jump from the 41 percent figure in 1968.[131] And for the first time ever suicide rose in 1971 to the tenth leading cause of death among Cuban youth. By 1972 it had climbed to eighth, and by 1973 it reached seventh.[132] The illegal use of prescription drugs spread in popularity among university students, especially those in medicine. A 1969 survey concluded that more than one-third of the University of Havana's medical students regularly used mild drugs.[133] These problems suggest that Cuban youth, many angry and disenchanted, had lost faith in the early promise of the Castro government. In defiance of the government youth committed petty crimes, refused to work, dropped out of school, and demonstrated nonconformity by openly listening to American music and dressing and acting in unacceptable ways. Indeed, some youngsters illustrated their dissatisfaction with life in Cuba by committing suicide.

As the years passed, Cuban leaders and the press repeated their bitter

126. GWR, May 9, 1971, pp. 4–5.
127. Mesa-Lago, p. 94; see also GWR, May 9, 1971, pp. 4–5.
128. Mesa-Lago, p. 93.
129. Speech in GWR, January 10, 1971.
130. Mesa-Lago, p. 93.
131. Salas, Social Control, pp. 14, 17.
132. Ibid., p. 178.
133. Salas, Social Control, pp. 53–54.

disappointment with youth on the island. In 1972 the Secretary General of the UJC, Jaime Crombet, denounced the organization, pointing out that ten years after its founding its "poor" and "erratic" membership had slipped badly. Indeed, Crombet complained that the group's lack of discipline and dedication had seriously hindered any attempt to raise the consciousness of Cuban youth.[134] In an April 1972 speech Castro complained that Cuban youth "are willing to do anything except to study hard."[135] He also chastised students for unacceptably high levels of cheating, truancy, and laziness. What explanations could Cuban leaders offer for these disappointing statistics? Castro blamed the schools and their rigidity and lack of discipline. He reproached Cuban parents and grandparents for fostering unacceptable attitudes. He rebuked teachers, the CDRs, and youth organizations. But Castro saved his choicest criticism for the youngsters themselves.[136] Cuban youth were letting down the Revolution.

To analyze and solve these problems, the government called for a special congress. In April 1971 nearly eighteen hundred delegates from across the country gathered in Havana for the first National Congress of Education and Culture. Delegates discussed teaching methods, educational objectives, methods for "popular" education, formation of the children's conscience, and effects of outside environmental factors.[137] In making recommendations, participants reaffirmed that the Revolution had entered an especially intense phase in which Cuban leaders would have to exercise even more authority over education and youth. The Congress closed with an official declaration: "Education must reflect and stimulate the changes flowing from the revolutionary transformations. It must above all tend to create a new man ... a new people who, at the same time that they untie the strings of the past, are capable of creating conditions for higher individual and social existence."[138] Given the record of Cuban youth rebelling against prior government efforts, cultural transformation must have seemed to many a distant goal.

The Government Responds to Youth Resistance

Faced with rising disobedience and the repeated failure of government policies, Castro opted for further repression. The high rates of drop-outs

134. *GWR,* April 19, 1972, pp. 2–3.
135. *GWR,* April 16, 1972, pp. 2–4.
136. Fidel Castro, speech at the final session of the Second Congress of the Young Communist Union; full text in *GWR,* April 16, 1972, pp. 2–4. See also Mesa-Lago, p. 94.
137. Leiner, pp. 181–183; Mesa-Lago, pp. 97–101.
138. Quoted in Matthews, p. 350.

and drug use, truancy and vagrancy, and crime prompted a second wave of policies, demonstratively harsher than those of 1970. First, Castro declared truancy to be a crime.[139] Then, in 1973 he announced that the Centennial Youth Column and other labor groups would be disbanded. The young members would begin working in labor groups led by the UJC and directed by the Armed Forces.[140] The government placed most students in the Army of Working Youth (EJT), founded on August 3, 1973. The EJT, a paramilitary body devoted to labor and other "shock tasks," included both delinquents being "reeducated" and young adults fulfilling their military responsibilities. Others simply volunteered their services either as a display of genuine support for the government or as a means to gain access to opportunities and goods. The EJT eventually took in approximately one-third of Cuba's young people.[141] To encourage students to remain in school, the government created rehabilitation work armies for truants.[142]

In addition, the Castro government reopened Party schools, where students prepared to be future leaders by studying ideology and Marxism-Leninism. These schools, closed since the late 1960s, underscored the continuing, and perhaps even intensified, emphasis on indoctrination.[143] To influence further the development of youth consciousness, the government also began to distribute a weekly magazine, the *Pionero*, to members of the Young Pioneers. One official explained the magazine's purpose:

> [O]ne of the fundamental objectives ... is to aid in the integral formation of the child. . . . [T]his is political. . . . Within this context we try to give them a sense of history, of internationalism, a hatred of imperialism—remember, Che talked about how hatred for the enemy is as important as love. . . . We also want to reinforce the individuality of the child, which is something quite separate from individualism. . . . [The] individual is always seen as part of the collective. . . . We see the magazine as . . . a vehicle to help create all these ideas and attitudes in the children.[144]

In June 1973, to combat juvenile delinquency, Castro reduced the age of criminal responsibility. Sixteen-year-olds now became wholly respon-

139. Salas, *Social Control*, p. 15; see also *Gaceta Oficial de la República de Cuba*, June 1, 1971, law no. 3664.

140. *GWR*, July 26, 1971; August 12, 1973, p. 2; see also Domínguez, p. 321; Mesa-Lago, p. 96.

141. *GWR*, August 12, 1973, pp. 2–3; see also Mesa-Lago, p. 96; *Juventud Rebelde*, September 2, 1971.

142. Domínguez, pp. 359–360; Matthews, p. 301; *GWR*, August 2, 1973.

143. Domínguez, p. 339.

144. Wald, pp. 211–214.

sible for their crimes and liable for punishment as adults.[145] Next, the government enacted a series of strict laws to deter youth from using illegal narcotics. These laws, especially harsh for foreign nationals, called for three to eight years in prison for drug sales. Possession of narcotics, in most countries considered a less serious offense than drug distribution, was to be punished in Cuba even more harshly with from seven to fifteen years imprisonment.[146] During this period the leadership also passed laws to eradicate "extravagant foreign fashions, customs, and behavior." Any "maladjusted minors" who displayed the "antisocial behavior" outlawed under such laws would henceforth be interned in rehabilitation centers. The leaders also introduced severe sanctions, up to life imprisonment, to punish abnormal sexual behavior and crimes against the national economy.[147]

In late 1973 the Cuban leadership introduced an experimental program that required regular military training in high school and university curricula. In 1975 the leadership inaugurated this program, similar to the U.S. college-level Reserve Officer Training Corps (ROTC) programs, across the country. The Cuban program, however, began at the high-school level with FAR officers teaching many eleventh- and twelfth-grade courses. The government also built several additional military-operated polytechnical institutes.[148] One observer wrote that these schools resembled "the military training camp of a modern Sparta."[149] The military thus redoubled its efforts to instill in Cuba "the Communist personality"—"modesty, confidence, honesty, camaraderie, courage, affection, and respect . . . patriotism and conscientious discipline."[150]

A notable part of this second wave of repressive policies directed at Cuban youth concerned detailed record keeping. In January 1974 the Castro government began to compile cumulative profiles on every student. These profiles included academic data, biological facts, socioeconomic information, personality traits, political evaluations, and any additional observations. The leadership referred to these files throughout the student's life, and the accumulation of facts had a substantial impact on many careers.[151]

---

145. *Gaceta Oficial de la República de Cuba,* June 23, 1973, law no. 1240; see also Read, p. 218.

146. Salas, *Social Control,* p. 54.

147. Mesa-Lago, pp. 96–97; see also Fidel Castro speech at the tenth anniversary of the creation of the Ministry of the Interior, *GWR,* June 13, 1971, pp. 4, 6; text of speech also in *Granma,* May 26, 1973.

148. Domínguez, p. 348.

149. Dolgoff, pp. 88, 157.

150. Domínguez, pp. 361–362; see also Dolgoff, pp. 171–172.

151. Salas, *Social Control,* p. 28. Also, in 1978 the National Assembly adopted the Child and Youth Code, which identified the functions that various groups within society, including

Did these latest, more repressive measures manage to accomplish what less coercive measures could not? The available evidence suggests that they did not. By the late 1970s problems among youth had not substantially improved. A 1977 *Bohemia* article stated that truancy amounted to a principal government concern. That same year Castro complained to university and secondary students about cheating, wasting time, pretending ignorance, and shunning responsibilities.[152] In several 1978 speeches Castro attacked once again the "materialist attitudes" of Cuba's youngsters.[153]

In the late 1970s crime rates in Cuba also remained quite high.[154] The incidence of theft, robbery, and vandalism, property crime and traffic offenses, particularly among young people, skyrocketed.[155] Both gambling, which had long since been outlawed, and prostitution, which had been virtually eliminated during the early 1960s, appeared again on Havana streets.[156] And, as the black market became more active, Castro complained publicly that most black-market offenders were minors.[157]

PHASE FOUR

Upon launching the "Rectification Campaign" in February 1986 at the Third Party Congress, Fidel Castro declared that a primary target was Cuba's pervasive "youth problems." Alienated and in many cases hostile, Cuban youth did not exemplify the Party leadership's revolutionary values. Castro claimed that the errors and disappointments evident in preceding years—from corruption and negligence to apathy, selfishness, and laziness—undermined the progress that had been made toward creating a new citizen with an appropriate *conciencia*. Nowhere was this more evident than among Cuba's younger generation: largely apathetic, noncompliant, alienated, and uncooperative.

In the eyes of Cuban leaders, youth on the island openly flouted the attitudes and values that the government had so vigorously attempted to

government bodies, mass organizations, the family, educators, and the press, had in the process of raising and socializing youth. See José Ramón Machado Ventura, "Boundlessly Confident in Our Youth," in *World Marxist Review* (September 1985), p. 41.

152. Salas, "Juvenile Delinquency," p. 263.

153. See, for example, *Granma*, January 2, 1978.

154. Salas, *Social Control*, pp. 42–46; see also *Granma*, July 1, 1978.

155. *Granma*, September 28, 1977; July 1, 1978; see also *Bohemia*, January 6, 1978, pp. 8–9.

156. Salas, *Social Control*, pp. 52–54, 66–67, 103; see also *Granma*, July 1, 1972.

157. Salas, *Social Control*, pp. 66–67; see also José Yglesias, *In the Fist of the Revolution: Life in a Cuban Country Town* (New York: Pantheon Books, 1968), pp. 196–199.

instill in them. Various trends among the younger generation particularly concerned the leaders: nonconformity, pervasive materialism, disregard for manual labor, and disrespect for the military. The leadership viewed these attitudes as closely linked to acts common among youth such as cheating, vagrancy, absenteeism, juvenile delinquency, and crimes against the state. The Rectification thus targeted each trend for extensive official attention.

For the Castro government the 1980 Mariel boatlift provided a disappointing measure of the discontent among Cuba's younger generation. To satisfy international demands and to expunge the uncooperative and recalcitrant, Castro allowed more than 125,000 Cubans to emigrate to the United States. Embarrassingly for the government, the Mariel group consisted overwhelmingly of young Cubans, born after the revolutionary triumph. Such emigrés could not be passed off as disgruntled capitalists. Plainly, many members of a new generation had failed to find contentment in revolutionary Cuba. By eagerly grasping the opportunity to leave, these young Cubans rejected and abandoned the island's abstemious and sacrificial revolutionary society. For them, as for many others, the early promise of Cuban socialism had been irretrievably lost.

In the early 1980s the leadership also grew concerned with unacceptable labor attitudes among Cuba's youth. Officials observed that in the workplace young workers, more than older laborers, lacked discipline, performed poorly, scorned work quotas, and often skipped work altogether. In a speech in the mid-1980s Castro chastised youth:

> I wonder if this textile mill were in Brazil, what would happen? . . . There is no appeal to the obligation of the workers? Do we believe that socialism can be built this way? Is there no appeal to the duty of young people, telling them that this is an underdeveloped country that needs to develop, that it can't be on the basis of pie in the sky and all in order for the factory to function? We have to know how to call the young people . . . to their duty and tell them "Produce!"[158]

The government criticized youth for producing less than their elders and for not leading the Revolution's labor "battles." Since the Marxist leadership had so painstakingly modelled and socialized the island's youth, Cuba's young laborers, Castro insisted, should display greater revolutionary awareness in the workplace than did their older peers.

158. Fidel Castro speech, quoted in Rhoda Rabkin, "Cuba: The Aging of a Revolution," in *Socialist Cuba: Past Interpretations and Future Challenges,* ed. Sergio G. Roca (Boulder: Westview Press, 1988), p. 48; *GWR,* April 27, 1986, p. 11.

From the leadership's perspective young Cubans had always enjoyed the benefits of the Revolution. They had never suffered under the misery of capitalism. In a 1990 interview Castro explained that youth "should be among the vanguard and they should be a frontline force of the Revolution during these very important and extraordinary times."[159] A year later he told a group of students that they owed the government much work because "we have done everything for the welfare of our youths." He tried to shame the students by telling them, "[You have had] the privilege of living the time in which you are living . . . of having the honors you have [had]."[160]

Throughout the educational system, from the lower grades through the university level, students plagued the leadership with undesirable attitudes and behavior.[161] In December 1984 Castro chastised students for the widespread abuse of illegitimate medical exemptions, used in order to avoid agricultural labor duties.[162] Similarly, by the mid-1980s the rising number of cheating incidents in schools and at the universities prompted repeated official denunciations.[163] In one especially embarrassing affair the leadership dismissed a UCJ deputy from the National Assembly for participating in a cheating scandal.[164]

Beginning in 1985 another worrisome sign of youth disaffection appeared: unimpressive academic performances. In the mid-1980s the government repeatedly chided students for poor study habits. In a September 1987 speech, for example, Castro complained that students were slacking off, studying little, feigning ignorance, and paying "more attention to television programs than to academic subjects."[165] In the summer of 1986 the Cuban media reported an alarming rate of failure among secondary-school students. Although the government scheduled summer makeup exams, the Ministry of Education sternly warned that no more second opportunities would be forthcoming. In fact, however, only 23 percent of the middle-secondary students in Havana passed their makeup exams. Consequently, school officials felt compelled to offer these exams once more the following year, and the government even dropped the passing grade from 70 to 60 percent to accommodate poor performance.[166]

159. U.S. *Foreign Broadcast Information Service (FBIS)*, October 29, 1990, p. 4.
160. Ibid., March 27, 1991, p. 2.
161. *GWR*, September 18, 1988, p. 3.
162. Rabkin, p. 49; see also *GWR*, December 23, 1984, p. 2.
163. Rabkin, p. 49.
164. Ibid.
165. *FBIS*, September 2, 1987, p. 1.
166. Enrique A. Baloyra, "Political Control and Cuban Youth," in *Cuban Communism,* ed. Irving Louis Horowitz, 7th ed. (New Brunswick, N.J.: Transaction, 1989), p. 434.

The low esteem in which Cuban youth held military service also disturbed government officials. By the mid-1980s young men and women on the island tended to view military service with disfavor, as a dreadful requirement rather than as an honor or a patriotic duty. A December 1984 Politburo document criticized the tendency of youth to regard military service as punishment.[167] And a 1987 *Juventud Rebelde* article explained that many youths took military service to be "a reform school of sorts."[168] Despite the power and privileges accorded military leaders, young Cubans often taunted the Armed Forces and tried to avoid military service.[169]

In the early 1980s the government also confronted a rising number of worrisome incidents among youth. Leaders criticized the rise in automobile accidents involving "careless" and "selfish" young Cubans. In 1986 deaths from automobile accidents jumped 10.5 percent from the year before.[170] Given the island's shortage of automobiles, Castro demanded that Cuban youth be more responsible, particularly since many automobiles were state-owned property. The leadership also criticized high school students for their destructive hooliganism. In 1983, for example, a group of about one hundred high school students started a "rock-throwing" spree against police.[171] Furthermore, the government closely monitored university students, especially those returning from the Soviet Union, for "*perestroika*" contamination, "pockets of subversion," and other "signs of defiance."[172]

Moreover, for nearly thirty years the Cuban leadership had persecuted religious followers and attempted to create through the educational system new citizens who would believe only in Marxism-Leninism and the dictates of the revolutionary government. Until October 1991 the state did not even allow religious followers into the Party. However, a professor at the University of Havana reported that, despite the government's attempt to stigmatize Christians, young people were among the most religious in Cuba. He estimated that youngsters comprised fully 70 percent of those attending Christmas services in Havana.[173]

By the mid-1980s the government found that an astounding number of citizens were practicing a religion. Young Cubans who did not keep their religious activities secret remained excluded from Party membership. This growing and increasingly alienated group of religious believers created a

---

167. *Granma,* February 4, 1985, p. 2; cited in Rabkin, p. 50.
168. Baloyra, p. 432; see also *Juventud Rebelde,* May 12, 1987, p. 2.
169. Rabkin, p. 49.
170. *GWR,* February 15, 1987, pp. 3, 9.
171. *U.S. News & World Report,* July 11, 1983, p. 26.
172. *FBIS,* February 8, 1990, p. 2.
173. *Excelsior* (Mexico City), February 19, 1991, pp. 4A, 39A.

potentially powerful source of opposition. The government feared that the Party, which comprised only 5 percent of the population, was failing to provide a solid foundation of supporters. Thus, at the October 1991 Party Congress the leaders opened the Party to religious believers. In July 1992 the government formally amended the 1976 Constitution by declaring Cuba a secular, rather than an atheist, state.[174] In response to the persistence of religious beliefs on the island, the leadership moved to accommodate a set of traditional values that it had originally sought to eradicate.[175]

Perhaps just as significant, during this period students began to criticize Fidel Castro and his government quite openly. In 1986 Cuba's National Directorate of Police conducted a study of youth attitudes on the island that concluded that 48 percent of citizens under the age of twenty-five expressed apathy, disillusionment, and even open hostility toward the Cuban government. Defiant graffiti frequently appeared on university walls, and some youngsters went so far as to mock Fidel Castro himself.[176] In fact, in early 1990 the government arrested a group of students at the University of Havana, all members of the UJC, for conducting activities aimed at promoting political and economic reform.[177] The government sentenced at least one of these students to a three-year term of "limited liberty," a form of house arrest.[178] A few weeks later police arrested several additional students at the José Antonio Echeverría Higher Polytechnical Institute (ISPJAE). Authorities detained yet another student who had read for nearly two hours underneath an anti-Castro sign he had hung at the university library. In a December 1990 speech Fidel Castro warned the university's history, philosophy, and arts and letters departments to eradicate grave attitude and behavior problems among their students.

The marked increase in crime throughout the 1980s provided yet an-

174. See *Washington Post,* July 12, 1992, pp. A20, A29; *Daily Yomiuri* (Tokyo, Japan), July 14, 1992, p. 1.

175. *Miami Herald,* International Edition, October 13, 1991, pp. 1A, 3A.

176. The survey was carried out by the Directorate Nacional de Policia, para el Comite Central del Partido Comunista de Cuba in 1986. It is cited in Georgie Anne Geyer, *Guerrilla Prince: The Untold Story of Fidel Castro* (Boston: Little, Brown, 1991), p. 13.

177. *FBIS,* January 12, 1990, p. 5.

178. Under Article 34 of the criminal code "limited liberty" (*limitación de libertad*) can be substituted for a prison sentence. It entitles one to live at home and to continue working but without being eligible for promotion or salary raises. In addition, one cannot change one's residence without the permission of the court, must appear before the court whenever called to do so, and must obey the law and respect the "norms of socialist coexistence." The official mass organizations, in coordination with the police, supervise the limited-liberty sentence. If one violates the terms of limited liberty, one serves the remainder of the sentence in prison. See "Tightening the Grip: Human Rights Abuses in Cuba," *Americas Watch* 4, no. 1 (February 24, 1992): 8–9; "Cuba: Behind a Sporting Facade, Stepped-Up Repression,"

other telling indication of the extent of Cuba's youth difficulties. In 1986 the government reported that the crime level during the first half of the 1980s significantly worsened.[179] In 1987 the crime rate jumped another 19 percent, and between 1987 and 1991 the island's crime rate continued to rise.[180] In March 1991 the Academy of Sciences of Cuba issued a report, written by Fernando Barral, which stated that "crime and corruption are endangering Cuban socialism." The document reported that because of the severe economic crisis plaguing Cuban society, the large illegal "second economy" had rapidly gained "ground at all levels of Cuban society . . . including among people who hold positions in the system." The report stated that because many consumer goods had become difficult or impossible to obtain, underground capitalism was "compromising the future of our country." Petty crime and black-market activities, particularly among young people, had taken on wholly "new dimensions." Although noting that police operations undertaken in the fall led to hundreds of arrests, the report concluded that the situation continued to deteriorate rapidly.[181]

In 1986 Fidel Castro rebuked young and old alike for their unabashed disrespect for the government's laws.[182] Five years later, in February 1991, Attorney General Ramón de la Cruz Ochoa complained bitterly: "Criminal corruption in the economic sphere is the principal enemy of our society today. It has grown because we let our guard down." But now, he assured, the "rotten apples are being exposed." He concluded that alongside corruption there existed disrespect for the rule of the law, particularly among young people.[183]

Casting the Blame

The flourishing of materialism and selfishness, greed and individualism, and religious attitudes, the leadership lamented, directly brought about "negative consequences" such as apathy, noncompliance, criminal activities, open defiance, and various other youth problems.[184] We must be "more demanding and intolerant of aberrant behavior," Castro thundered

Americas Watch 3, no. 9 (August 11, 1991): 2. See also *Miami Herald,* International Edition, March 2, 1992, p. 3A.

179. *Granma,* September 29, 1986, p. 6.
180. *GWR,* October 11, 1987, p. 3.
181. *FBIS,* March 27, 1991, p. 7.
182. *GWR,* July 13, 1986, p. 9.
183. *Bohemia,* February 8, 1991, pp. 26–30.
184. For example, see ibid., January 31, 1988, p. 3.

in July 1987.[185] And a 1987 *Granma Weekly Review* stated that the government's first priority was to "eliminate the causes and conditions" that had developed over the past decade and had led to juvenile delinquency and other social problems.[186]

Castro and his associates spread the blame for these various youth problems quite liberally. The leadership scolded the Party for its failure to involve Cuban youth in activities and decision making. As one member of the Politburo explained, the Party has "lacked combativeness" in fighting juvenile delinquency and other unacceptable behavior.[187] The government also denounced teachers for poor performance and for failing to encourage students to study properly.[188] Artists were rebuked as well for producing works that sympathized with selfish bourgeois culture and negatively influenced impressionable youth.[189] In pointing to the prerevolutionary "capitalist" trends that had developed since the mid-1970s, Castro attributed the government's problems to social conditions established during the market experiments of the late 1970s and early 1980s.

Castro also chastised university professors for laziness and called on them to reinvigorate their efforts to mold the values and attitudes of youth. One of your "basic tasks," Fidel told professors, "is to shape . . . values." This, he explained, "needs to be . . . an essential part of education."[190] Carlos Aldana Escalante, a member of the Communist Party Politburo, chided the university for not incorporating José Martí's thought into the curriculum. Institutions of higher education, he complained, ignored Martí's work, which remained virtually absent from programs to train party cadres. He criticized these curricula defects as careless, inconsistent, and intolerable omissions.[191]

The leadership pointed to counterproductive family values and "indifference" at home as another cause of Cuba's intractable youth problems. "Juvenile delinquency," Castro declared, is caused by the "influence of the home, the influences of the family, the influence even of certain traditions in the family."[192] Indeed, in the early 1980s official government publications periodically argued that, while public programs to transform Cuban

185. Ibid., July 5, 1987, p. 4.

186. Ibid., p. 3.

187. *FBIS,* December 18, 1990, p. 12.

188. See, for example, *GWR,* Special Section, December 7, 1986, p. 3.

189. *GWR,* June 15, 1986, p. 3.

190. *FBIS,* December 28, 1990, p. 17.

191. Ibid., February 8, 1990, p. 2.

192. Fidel Castro speech on September 17, 1987, *GWR,* September 25, 1988, p. 11. See also *Bohemia,* March 22, 1991, pp. 26–29.

society had partially succeeded, the family had plainly failed to contribute its share.[193]

Cuban leaders also reprimanded unions, mass organizations, and even certain Party officials for becoming lazy and careless in their responsibility to guide the nation's youth. "As soon as a young man or woman takes a job, the party organization, the UJC and the trade union" must "begin his or her political education, striving to promote the young workers' commitment to discipline," one party member explained.[194] In 1980 Raúl Castro deplored his fellow leaders' dogmatism and unwillingness to communicate with youth: "Today young people are, indeed, more demanding because they are competent, educated . . . and above all display a critical attitude to things. That is not a bad quality—quite the reverse. It would be a mistake to try . . . [to] attain anything with the help of rigid . . . banal . . . or weak arguments."[195]

In closely scrutinizing the official programs to transform youth culture, the revolutionary leaders discovered that little progress had been made. Young Cubans remained intransigent and rebellious. The leadership decided to redouble its efforts.

Revitalizing the Union of Young Communists

At the 1986 CDR Congress a young leader of the Union of Young Communists cautioned his elders: "[I]t is not possible to educate youth with the simple comparison to the capitalist past, because their eyes were opened for the first time in a different world, neither exploitation and misery, nor discrimination, injustice and unemployment, nor illiteracy nor lack of liberty will be their motivations to be revolutionaries."[196] Whether an accurate assessment or not, times had certainly changed. The leadership had to couch its appeals to youngsters in a different manner.

In this spirit the government initiated various policies during the Rectification Campaign aimed at curing Cuban youth of their alienation and estrangement. Since coercion had not brought positive results, and since

---

193. Lois M. Smith and Alfred Padula, "The Cuban Family in the 1980s," in *Transformation and Struggle: Cuba Faces the 1990s*, ed. Sandor Halebsky and John M. Kirk (New York: Praeger, 1990), p. 176.

194. Machado Ventura, p. 41.

195. Cited in ibid., p. 44; original text of speech in *GWR*, February 10, 1980, p. 2.

196. *Granma*, September 29, 1986, p. 3; also cited in Rabkin, p. 50.

the government could no longer afford to motivate students with material incentives, Castro returned once again to the moral suasion strategy of the 1960s. Fifteen years of coercion and material incentives had apparently failed to create in youngsters the proper *conciencia*; hence, Castro said, the time had come to return to the ideas and tactics of Che Guevara. In introducing the new motto "We will be like Che!" Castro told his listeners, "I think that many of Che's ideas have great relevance today." He called on youth to work "as Che worked" and to follow Che's examples in their quest to become perfect communists.[197]

After initiating the Rectification Campaign, the government turned again to moral incentives to infuse Cuba's youth with proper revolutionary attitudes. Young people, Castro claimed, must become "the center of the Revolution."[198] Thus, in the early 1980s the government revived emulation programs and contests. Once again youngsters could win "shaper of the future" badges in recognition of exemplary efforts. The government also instituted special awards for teenage inventors and high-technology buffs.[199] In August 1986 Castro sought to renew the role of the Party in the ideological education of youth. He did this by targeting the Union of Young Communists, the "youth wing" of the Party. To enliven the enervated and increasingly insignificant youth organization, Castro appointed a vivacious, energetic, and popular young leader, Roberto Robaina, as its First Secretary.[200]

Robaina immediately set out to galvanize the UJC and bring disaffected youth back into the Revolution. First, he sought to reestablish the UJC's foremost purpose: to create among young Cubans a complete identity with the Revolution's objectives.[201] This organization, Robaina told his listeners in April 1987 at the Fifth Congress of UJC, must "salvage communication" with the government that "we were on the verge of losing." He later invited Cuban youngsters to "break down" barriers between the government and youth, and he encouraged free and honest dialogue between the two.[202] Moreover, Robaina called on the UJC to lead the effort to socialize the nation's young men and women.

That same month Fidel Castro called on the UJC to resurrect the con-

197. *GWR,* October 18, 1987, pp. 4–6.

198. Ibid., November 4, 1990, p. 1.

199. Machado Ventura, p. 41.

200. *GWR,* January 17, 1988, p. 9; see also May 6, 1990, p. 12. In 1993 Robaina was appointed Cuba's Foreign Minister.

201. Ibid., December 23, 1990, p. 3.

202. Roberto Robaina speech, ibid., January 17, 1988, p. 9; see also Robaina speech, *Granma,* March 7, 1991, p. 3.

cept of "military discipline" among Cuba's youth.[203] Later, Raúl Castro spoke at a UJC meeting and told his listeners that the UJC's "top" priority must be "ideological work."[204] During the same month a *Granma Weekly Review* article called on the UJC to battle against the "dogmatism that emerged over the past 20 years." The article explained that during the 1970s ill-intentioned youth had adopted a "mechanical and well-known" yet wholly unacceptable phrase: "Our Youth is Lost." In the leadership's view the Rectification Campaign would draw on youth participation and suppress this thinking.[205] Several months later Castro told UJC leaders that they must study the disaffection among Cuban youth and "resolve these problems." Moreover, he implored the UJC—perhaps wishfully— to influence youth in political discussions by "clarifying, arguing, enlightening, and convincing" them.[206]

To provide useful activities during free time, to encourage youth to remain in school, and to motivate and energize young people, the UJC initiated various educational and recreational events, including dances, art projects, camping trips, and beach and roller-skating parties. The UJC also created in Havana a recreational center for youngsters. It organized voluntary agricultural work brigades among students to contribute to the labor force and to help to improve youth attitudes toward manual labor.[207] In addition, the UJC encouraged students to volunteer their school vacation time to labor in the vegetable, coffee, sugar, and tobacco fields.[208] In September 1987 Robaina also announced that "Youth Computer Clubs" would be established throughout the country. By March 1991 the government opened 106 computer centers, each with about eight computers. Cuban leaders viewed these clubs as recreational and educational, providing a fun youth activity and preparing youngsters for the "production process."[209]

Under Robaina's charismatic leadership the UJC became involved in a broad spectrum of projects. In community service activities the UJC sponsored street festivals and youth parades to involve youngsters in civic

203. *GWR*, April 19, 1987, p. 11.

204. Ibid., May 13, 1990, p. 5.

205. Ibid., May 6, 1990, p. 12; see also September 23, 1990, p. 12.

206. Ibid., November 4, 1990, p. 1; see also *FBIS*, February 21, 1991, p. 3.

207. *GWR*, Special Report, February 16, 1986, p. 14; see also *FBIS*, February 21, 1991, pp. 1–2; February 22, 1991, p. 3; see also Machado Ventura, p. 40. For a discussion of the UJC's concern regarding the steadily rising number of dropouts, see *FBIS*, April 3, 1987, p. Q8.

208. *Granma*, October 5, 1990, p. 2; see also *FBIS*, February 21, 1991, p. 3.

209. *GWR*, August 19, 1990, p. 2; also see *FBIS*, March 8, 1991, p. 4; March 14, 1991, p. 3.

activities.[210] It also encouraged membership in student organizations, including the Pioneers, the FEU, and the Federation of Secondary School Students (FEEM). At the same time the UJC participated in political affairs. In late 1986 it assisted the government in a sweeping effort to prepare the entire population to defend itself against imperialist aggression. In mobilizing more than seven million citizens, the leaders attempted to inculcate the masses with fears of an impending American attack and subsequent war. This rallied the nation and placed it on a permanent state of alert.[211]

Other Policy Initiatives

The official return to emphasizing youth *conciencia* prompted the Party to reopen additional schools for political and ideological training. Within five years these schools had graduated and prepared for Party leadership positions more than four hundred thousand young Cubans. The essential objective of this education, an official explained, was "to instill in our people a political awareness characterized, above all, by unflinching loyalty to the principles of socialism."[212] To further youth education and *conciencia*, the leadership also created a commission designed to study and improve radio, television, and film production in Cuba. The aim was to enhance the "historical memory of the revolutionary process," to find methods to better educate, inform, and "consciously mobilize" the masses. Cuban leaders believed that the media should contribute to the revived emphasis on transforming the national culture.[213]

The leadership also replaced certain powerful older Party officials with younger leaders. Ramón Suárez Vega, a Party official in the Department of Ideology, explained that the Central Committee must be "renewed" with capable men and women between the ages of twenty-eight and forty. This second generation of leaders would be comprised of those who had witnessed the triumph of the Revolution as children or who had not yet been born when the Revolution began.[214] To further this new policy, in

210. *GWR*, February 3, 1991, p. 1; *Granma International (GI)*, April 14, 1991, p. 4.

211. See *FBIS*, December 15, 1986, p. Q11; December 17, 1986, p. Q1.

212. *GWR*, Special Section, February 16, 1986.

213. *GI*, May 26, 1991, p. 2. The government also assigned to the commission the task of better rationalizing the media's use of resources.

214. *Excelsior* (Mexico City), February 18, 1991, pp. 1, 26; February 19, 1991, pp. 1, 30; February 20, 1991, pp. 1, 33; see also *FBIS*, March 15, 1991, p. 1. See also Jorge I. Domínguez, "Blaming Itself, Not Himself: Cuba's Political Regime after the Third Party Congress," in *Socialist Cuba: Past Interpretations and Future Challenges*, ed. Sergio Roca (Boulder: Westview Press, 1988), p. 8.

July 1985 Castro dismissed Humberto Pérez, the Minister-President of the Central Planning Board (JUCEPLAN), and replaced him with José López Moreno, a considerably younger man. Similarly, in October 1990 the government named forty-eight-year-old Carlos Aldana Escalante as head of the Department of Revolutionary Orientation, an extremely influential position during the Rectification. In 1992 Aldana himself was sacked.

At its October 1991 Congress the Cuban Communist Party dropped from the Politburo a number of older, more conservative members, such as Vilma Espín, President of the FMC, and Armando Hart, Minister of Culture. In an attempt to garner support from Cuba's younger generation, the Party elected to the Politburo a number of younger, popular leaders, including Roberto Robaina and Carlos Lage Dávila. At the October 1991 Congress the Party also elected a new 225-member Central Committee. Here, too, the Party replaced many of the older, more conservative members, such as Vilma Espín, Jorge Risquet, and José Ramón Fernández, a hero from the 1961 Bay of Pigs victory, with younger Party members.[215] In fact, the average age of the 1991 Central Committee dropped to forty-five.[216] Amidst this youth movement, however, Fidel Castro showed no signs of voluntarily relinquishing, or even relaxing, his own grip on power.

Improving Popular Attitudes Toward the Military

During the Rectification Campaign, the government also set out to eradicate pervasive negative attitudes among youth toward the military. To improve the relationship between the FAR and Cuba's younger generations, Cuban leaders tried repeatedly to involve the military in a positive way in youth activities. For example, in the early 1980s the leadership introduced a program called the Society for Patriotic Military Education (SEPMI). In functioning as a "military outreach program" for young Cubans, this association visited historic battle sites, met with people who took part in famous revolutionary events, participated in seminars to study the legacy of José Martí, and promoted military sports such as parachuting and target shooting. At the same time, SEPMI encouraged Cuban patriotism and imparted useful military skills. Within a few years more than one hundred thousand youngsters participated in the organization's activities.[217]

215. *Miami Herald,* International Edition, October 16, 1991, pp. 1A, 4A.
216. Ibid., October 15, 1991, p. 3A.
217. *GWR,* February 16, 1986, p. 14; see also Rabkin, p. 49; Machado Ventura, p. 43.

Another effort to integrate youth into the military occurred when Fidel Castro created the Territorial Troop Militia (TTM), which provided military training to citizens outside the regular army. Raúl Castro explained that the organization aimed to reach the "reservists who do not belong to the units of FAR or Civil Defense, the young workers, peasants, and above all, students who have not been called up for active military service."[218] By 1991 more than a million citizens belonged to the TTM.[219] In 1991 Cuban leaders also opened the Armed Forces National Defense College to give "each Cuban revolutionary the necessary knowledge and means to defend the Fatherland."[220] This college, the government claimed, would provide students with more opportunities for a military education.

While the government tried to portray the Armed Forces in more positive terms, it also warned youth to take military service more seriously. Castro stated in early 1986 that to be a Party cadre and thus to have access to society's resources, one must either manually labor for the Revolution or serve in the Army. No one could doubt Castro's militaristic outlook on life. No better Party official exists, the Cuban leader declared, "than one who at some time or in some way was a soldier."[221]

Coercion and Militarization

Just as the Castro government reintroduced policies of moral suasion directed at Cuban youth, it also stepped up coercive measures. The leaders aimed to change the behavior, if not the attitudes, of young Cubans. To control soaring crime rates and other acts of recalcitrance and defiance among Cuban youth, the government urged the country's many mass organizations to be more vigilant.[222] Castro pressed the Cuban Confederation of Labor (CTC), in particular, to guard relentlessly against absenteeism, youth vagrancy, and criminal economic activity. Pedro Ross Leal, Secretary General of the CTC, instructed union leaders to "fight all manifestations of . . . profit, petty theft, and robbery."[223] The union's role must be to "lead and guide" young workers.[224] The Party also informed organi-

218. Cited in Rabkin, p. 49; Raúl Castro speech, *GWR*, February 8, 1981, p. 12.
219. Geyer, p. 4.
220. See *GWR*, January 27, 1991, p. 4; see also *FBIS*, January 19, 1991, p. 3; February 6, 1991, p. 3.
221. Fidel Castro speech, *GWR*, February 16, 1986, p. 14.
222. Fidel Castro called on the FMC, the Cuban Confederation of Labor (CTC), the CDRs, the People's Councils (PCs), and the National Revolutionary Police (PNR) to increase their role as vigilantes. *FBIS*, December 11, 1990, p. 1.
223. Ibid., September 4, 1990, p. 3.
224. Ibid., February 15, 1991, p. 11.

zations, such as the FMC, that their "work must converge around vigilance and ideological struggle." The leaders implored the FMC to strengthen its "collective ties" with youth, workers, and students.[225] The government also formed People's Councils (PCs) to minimize economic crime and eliminate waste in the workplace. The Cuban leaders soon called on the PCs to watch closely and guard against "antisocial" behavior.[226] The task of the PCs, a *Granma Weekly Review* article noted, is to "undertake [a] tenacious battle against wrongdoing."[227]

Most important, the government moved to restructure the Committees for the Defense of the Revolution in order to increase their effectiveness in watching over Cuban communities. The restructuring effort centralized the organizations and reduced their role to vigilance against crime and other unacceptable behavior. For the first time since the Revolution, Cuban leaders placed the CDRs in the hands of a top-ranked military officer, General Sixto Batista Santana. He moved rapidly to reshape the CDRs into militarized organizations, which, like the Territorial Troop Militia, were incorporated into the Armed Forces. This restructuring, a CDR National Secretariat official explained, would renew the organizations' most critical functions: undertaking careful vigilance of neighborhoods, fighting crime and other "antisocial actions," and generally defending the Revolution.[228] Indeed, the government implored the leaders of the newly restructured CDRs to step up their "aggressive role" in "vigilance and ideological combat" against crime.[229] In March 1990 Castro called on the CDRs to eliminate the "fifth column," a "dangerous enemy of the Cuban nation and socialism."[230] And in November 1990 Central Committee member María Luisa Suárez Campos instructed the CDRs to take on the role of police in order to overcome those defying the state.[231]

During the Rectification Cuban society was becoming ever more militarized. Indeed, in early 1990 the government appointed various leading Army commanders to powerful civilian posts. In February, for instance, the leadership named Brigadier General Juan Escalona Reguera to chair the politically prestigious National Assembly of the People's Government (ANPP). Lieutenant General Abelardo Colomé Ibarra, a combat hero in

225. *GWR*, February 25, 1990, p. 9.

226. Program on Radio Rebelde, March 22, 1991.

227. *GWR*, October 21, 1990, p. 9.

228. Announced on Radio Rebelde, April 5, 1991; see also *FBIS*, September 26, 1990, p. 6; April 9, 1991, p. 6; May 13, 1991, p. 3; June 24, 1991, p. 1; see also *GWR*, February 25, 1990, p. 9.

229. *Granma*, February 17, 1990; also see *FBIS*, February 20, 1990, p. 6; January 25, 1991, p. 2.

230. Tad Szulc, "Can Castro Last?" *New York Times Magazine*, May 31, 1990, p. 13.

231. *FBIS*, November 30, 1990, p. 7.

Angola and Ethiopia, became the new Interior Minister. Since 1959 those three jobs—leader of the CDRs, Interior Minister, and chairman of the National Assembly—had never been held simultaneously by military officers.[232]

To combat further the recalcitrance and noncompliance of the island's youth, the government created in 1986 another organization aimed at promoting internal order: the National Social Prevention and Attention Commission (NSPAC), headed by Vilma Espín. The leaders charged the Commission with strengthening, supervising, and orchestrating the vigilance activities of the CDRs, the National Revolutionary Police (PNR), and the Department of State Security. The NSPAC sought to strengthen the relationship between citizens and police on the local level. It also launched a campaign against alcoholism and harmful, degrading, and antisocial vices, such as prostitution and gambling.

According to Vilma Espín, the government primarily created NSPAC to "battle against crime," especially economic crimes. At a meeting of the Commission in March 1991, members discussed problem youngsters "roaming the streets," the creation of reeducation centers and behavioral schools for minors, and the need for new recreational opportunities for youth.[233] Much like the CDRs, the NSPAC called on citizens to watch their neighbors and report unusual, antirevolutionary activity, particularly among young Cubans. Espín explained: "Wherever someone is seen to have a standard of living . . . surpassing their normal income, that person must be reported, no matter who is involved because such individuals do more harm than a CIA agent."[234] Indeed, the leadership encouraged all citizens, whether associated with NSPAC or not, to watch their neighbors carefully and report any questionable activities.[235]

In early 1991, to guard against ever-increasing juvenile delinquency, the government created 254 "vigilance brigades" in Santiago. Throughout the rest of the country the leadership established similar groups called *destacamentos campesinos de vigilancia* or "peasant vigilance detachments." As part of this project the Cuban state distributed arms to selected detachments of workers brought together to fight crime and other aberrant activities. In ten livestock-agricultural cooperatives Cuban leaders also created National Revolutionary Police Auxiliary Forces to protect against vandalism, livestock theft, and other crimes. These policy initiatives followed a call from Castro for strengthened security at fruit and vegetable farms

232. Szulc, p. 13.
233. *FBIS*, March 19, 1991, p. 7.
234. Ibid., October 18, 1990, p. 4; see also March 14, 1990, p. 9.
235. See, for example, *Bohemia*, March 22, 1991, pp. 26–29.

to stop widespread thieving.[236] This "posse" mentality prompted Cuban leaders in late 1991 to strengthen and combine these armed surveillance detachments to form the "Unified Vigilance and Protection System." The leadership extended the responsibilities of these vigilance brigades to include protecting warehouses, factories, and cargo trains. Bandits had repeatedly attacked and robbed freight trains carrying food and supplies.[237]

At the eleventh Pan American Games held in Cuba in August 1991, Cuban authorities also formed "rapid action detachments" to control public demonstrations or "embarrassing public displays of discontent."[238] These detachments, made up of volunteers from work centers and the CDRs, took on the task of dealing with potential troublemakers. One CDR coordinator explained: "What we cannot allow is for people to go around shouting slogans against the revolution or socialism. We have to confront these manifestations and these people."[239]

Revamping the Educational System

In an effort to curb juvenile delinquency on the island, the Rectification aimed to reform Cuban education. The "main weapon against crime," Fidel Castro asserted, "is education!"[240] And education, he insisted, consists of "the socialization of conduct and habits."[241] According to the leaders, schools and universities would bring about far-reaching changes in youth attitudes and behavior. In a 1987 speech Castro summarized: "The national education system [plays] a key role not just in the process of rectification but also in the construction of socialism and in the essential goal of achieving a communist society."[242]

To reinvigorate the educational system from the bottom up, the Cuban government built hundreds of additional *círculos* (day-care centers). In early 1988 Castro reported that during the Rectification fifty-four day-

236. See *Latin America Weekly Report* (Great Britain), August 29, 1991; see also *FBIS*, December 17, 1990, p. 6; February 11, 1991, p. 3; Susan Kaufman Purcell, "Collapsing Cuba," *Foreign Affairs* 71 (1992): 139.

237. See *Granma*, January 18, 1992, p. 1; see also *Miami Herald*, International Edition, January 20, 1992, p. 3A; March 2, 1992, p. 3A; Purcell, p. 139. See also "Tightening the Grip: Human Rights Abuses in Cuba," p. 2.

238. The Cuban leaders also referred to these brigades as "rapid response brigades." See "Cuba: Behind a Sporting Facade, Stepped-Up Repression," p. 2.

239. *Washington Post*, July 29, 1991, p. 14A; see also *Latin America Weekly Report* (Great Britain), August 29, 1991 (taken from Reuters News Service, July 11, 1991).

240. Fidel Castro speech, *GWR*, September 25, 1988, supplement.

241. Ibid., January 7, 1990, p. 2.

242. Ibid., December 6, 1987, p. 12.

care centers had been built to accommodate 11,340 children.[243] These new day-care centers, he claimed, would not only improve youth *conciencia*, they would also "be worth billions of pesos" of female labor.[244] In addition, in 1987 the government initiated a laudable plan to construct "special schools" to educate youth with problems ranging from mental retardation to speech defects, from hearing and visual difficulties to various "behavior problems." By January 1990, twenty-four of these special schools had been opened.[245] The government also opened various youth orientation centers designed to provide counsel to the increasing numbers of rebellious young Cubans. Jorge Cedeño, a psychologist at a youth orientation center in Cienfuegos, explained that youth had become more problematic in the 1980s: "This is a new phenomenon . . . . they [youth] feel rejected, so they react with more rebellion."[246]

Aside from these special youth projects, Cuban leaders also set out to reform primary and secondary schools. In particular, the leadership strengthened the emphasis on revolutionary consciousness.[247] In late 1991, for example, the popular youth organization the Young Pioneers proposed creating "rapid response brigades" in the schools to deal with children "affected" by foreign ideas.[248] As part of this education initiative, Cuban leaders publicly chastised the island's youth for avoiding labor-intensive tasks and urged faculty members to instill in students a more acceptable attitude toward manual labor. The leadership insisted that education must be inextricably linked with manual labor.[249]

Alongside the difficult effort to change youth attitudes, the Cuban government during the Rectification also tried to bring about behavioral changes among students. By 1987 the economic crisis had severely curbed job opportunities for young graduates. Hence, in an attempt to dissuade students from seeking professional careers and encourage them to pursue technical and "labor careers," the government granted entry to the university to less than one-half of the applicants. Those not admitted had to enter polytechnic schools or join the labor force directly as blue-collar workers.[250]

Although economic considerations principally motivated this new policy, Castro publicly argued that the government simply sought to destroy

243. Ibid., January 10, 1988, p. 3.
244. Ibid.
245. Ibid., December 13, 1987, p. 9; January 7, 1990, p. 5.
246. *Miami Herald*, International Edition, December 27, 1991, pp. 1A, 4A.
247. *Granma*, March 7, 1991, p. 3.
248. "Tightening the Grip: Human Rights Abuses in Cuba," p. 3.
249. *GWR*, February 16, 1986, p. 13; see also January 7, 1990, p. 2.
250. See Baloyra, p. 431.

long-standing barriers between manual and intellectual labor. In insisting that Cuban education not be defined "so narrowly as . . . before," Castro called on young people to be more self-sufficient and labor-oriented, more willing to contribute to the government's new "Food Program." In preferring productive workers to less useful intellectuals, the Cuban leader acknowledged: "There is a need to graduate trained specialists capable of solving daily problems . . . not from behind a comfortable desk, but amid the noise of machines and the experience of workers."[251]

At the thirtieth anniversary of the CDRs in 1990, Castro once again instructed university students to enroll in useful classes and to pursue labor-oriented professions:

> Over 300,000 students are enrolled in the university's regular courses. . . . a historian—a fine interesting profession—can be trained in a directed reading course, but that kind of course couldn't train a single agricultural worker or produce a single bunch of bananas or grow one pound of sweet potatoes. The university has 300,000 students taking all sorts of courses, while the Guira de Melena enterprise, with 4000 hectares of land, has 128 agricultural workers![252]

Everyone has to serve his time, Castro pronounced, "out there in the banana fields." In mid-1991, as the economy continued to falter, the leadership further reduced the number of students admitted to the university. Applicants not admitted were encouraged to take mid-level technician positions.[253]

In 1987 Castro extended his attack against intellectuals to the high schools as well. He announced that additional senior high schools would be built in the countryside as part of the Food Program. For example, in Havana Province students would be expected to pair daily studies with root and garden vegetable production. Castro recounted, "I asked comrades in education and agriculture to figure out how many schools . . . could be built bearing in mind the growing production plans we have for vegetables."[254] For Castro this plan fulfilled two cardinal needs: new schools and higher levels of agricultural production.

To further encourage students to attain a useful education, Cuban leaders vigorously praised polytechnic institutes and the accomplishments of their graduates. A polytechnic institute, a *Granma Weekly Review* article

251. *GWR,* September 18, 1988, p. 3.
252. Ibid., October 4, 1990, p. 4.
253. *Granma,* May 31, 1991, p. 3.
254. Fidel Castro speech, *GWR,* December 13, 1987, p. 10.

explained, resembles "a large industry where teenagers are simultaneously learning and producing." At the institutes youngsters between the ages of fourteen and seventeen are taught by skilled workers rather than by university-educated professors. The "backbone of the Revolution" was to be preferred to its superfluous intellectuals. Experienced laborers taught the youngsters valuable skills such as manufacturing wire fences, wire-winding motors, and assembling switchboards.[255] Education, one Party official explained, must "wed theory to practice, studies to life, training to production, and promote the conscientious attitude to work typical of the new man."[256]

Two years later Fidel Castro reported that university students were still not entering fields most useful to the country. Consequently, he threatened to have the state place graduates, regardless of the nature of their degree, where they would be most "efficient and provide greater production." Government officials would decide where young Cubans would work by "looking at where they will really be most useful."[257] The following year Castro called on the educational system to produce still "fewer university graduates and more workers skilled in agriculture."[258] The Cuban leader also implored students of all ages to volunteer their labor during vacations.[259] He railed at his country's youth, declaring that what the Revolution needed from young Cubans was "more enthusiasm, more energy, more willingness, more decision to struggle."[260] He repeatedly reminded students that only those who volunteered their labor would be admitted to the Party.[261]

As part of this effort to revamp the educational system and improve the revolutionary conscience of youth, Cuban leaders reiterated their absolute unwillingness to tolerate anything but complete ideological conformity within the universities. In March 1990 Felipe Pérez Roque, President of the Federation of University Students, explained the university's strict Rectification policy: "The university is for revolutionaries. . . . The university does not want those who do not live and think like Cuban revolutionaries. . . . He who is not faithful to the revolution cannot be in university. . . . The dialogue [at the university] is with the revolution and for the

255. Ibid., May 20, 1990, p. 6.
256. Machado Ventura, p. 41.
257. *FBIS*, March 5, 1990, p. 2.
258. Ibid., February 7, 1991, p. 11.
259. *Granma*, October 5, 1990, p. 2.
260. *FBIS*, March 7, 1990, p. 5.
261. See, for example, Fidel Castro's speech, *GWR*, Special Report, February 16, 1986, p. 14.

revolution. He who goes beyond those limits is not talking to us."[262] And Fidel Castro emphasized that, in this difficult period of struggle, the university and polytechnic institutes simply would not waste time educating critics. Consequently, in January 1992 the leadership dismissed nine professors from Havana's Superior Polytechnic Institute. Seven of the nine had reportedly signed a petition calling for respect for human rights, democratic reforms, and the release of political prisoners. The Castro government fired the other two because of their association with the petition, even though they had not signed it. In addition, the leadership fired a secretary and a researcher at the institute for their counterrevolutionary activities. The government dismissed two other professors from the Superior Pedagogical Institute in connection with the same petition.[263]

Restructuring the Penal Code

The renewed attack on juvenile delinquency prompted Cuban officials to change the 1979 Criminal Code regarding penalties for "capitalist" crimes. In 1984 the Ministry of Justice, headed by Juan Escalona Reguera, created a commission to analyze the 1979 code and to propose reforms.[264] Eventually the commission's findings led to numerous changes in Cuban law, including two of particular note. The first amendment to the Code, which took effect in January 1991, declared that any act of unlawful gain that had formerly been classified merely as a socially scorned act was now to be regarded as a crime, punishable by up to eight years in prison. The commission argued that unlawful gain, including the crimes of embezzlement, illicit enrichment, and speculation, posed "great social danger and . . . damage to the national economy."

Raúl Amaro Salup, the president of the Supreme People's Tribunal, explained the motive for such penal code revisions by noting that "the problems with so-called missing property, embezzlement, and the theft of social and state property have taken on great importance." In arguing that "the penal policy must be stricter," he cited the increasing prevalence of crimes such as shoplifting, stealing containers, and diverting goods from the official market to the black market.[265] These malicious offenses, a

262. *FBIS,* March 6, 1990, p. 2.

263. "Tightening the Grip: Human Rights Abuses in Cuba," p. 14. See also *Christian Science Monitor,* August 19, 1992, p. 18.

264. *GWR,* February 7, 1988, p. 2.

265. *Granma,* October 30, 1990, p. 3; see also *FBIS,* October 31, 1990, p. 4; December 26, 1990, p. 2; January 15, 1991, p. 2.

Granma Weekly Review article explained, can be detected or manifested in "the transgressor's property or his life-style—spending more than what he legally makes."[266]

The second critical revision of the code regarded sentencing. The 1979 Code had resulted in far more prisoners than the penal system could accommodate. By the mid-1980s Cuba's prisons housed more than fifty thousand people, a per capita rate that was fully double that of the extremely high per capita rate in the United States.[267] Introducing new crimes that required imprisonment could only worsen this embarrassing situation. Consequently, the commission modified the sentences for many crimes from serving time in jail to undertaking "correctional work." Under the revised penal code Cuban courts sentenced the vast majority of criminals to agricultural labor. Not only did that alleviate the burden of overcrowded prisons, it nicely augmented the labor force as well. In late 1988 Castro noted that the government had put to work more than twenty thousand common criminals.[268] By August 1990 more than 70 percent of the sentences imposed in Cuban courts required service in work centers, not prison terms.[269] This freed prison space for those convicted of "capitalist" crimes. The Cuban courts immediately began to convict and sentence hundreds of "economic criminals."

In July 1990, to ease the judicial burden of burgeoning economic-crime cases, the leadership introduced Law 70, which created smaller tribunals consisting of a professional judge and two lay judges, with jurisdiction almost exclusively confined to economic crimes. Then in October 1990, to take advantage of the expanded judicial capacity, the Minister of the Interior launched a major initiative against those involved in capitalist crimes. A Central Committee member, José Ramón Machado Ventura, called for his Party to be "merciless" in prosecuting such cases: "This is a negative phenomenon that we must get rid of immediately."[270] Since the leaders viewed "illicit enrichment" as one evil that required immediate attention, in October 1990 the Attorney General insisted: "[It is] necessary, now more than ever, to respond with an energetic and systematic fight against acts that harm the nation's economy."[271]

266. *GWR*, May 22, 1988, p. 2.

267. Debra Evenson, "The Changing Role of the Law," in *Transformation and Struggle: Cuba Faces the 1990s*, ed. Sandor Halebsky and John M. Kirk (New York: Praeger, 1990), p. 61. See also *La Prensa* (Panama City, Panama), February 1, 1988, p. 5A.

268. *GWR*, September 25, 1988, p. 11; May 7, 1989, p. 4.

269. Ibid., August 26, 1990, p. 9; see also Evenson, p. 60; *GWR*, October 16, 1988, p. 2.

270. *FBIS*, March 11, 1991, p. 3.

271. Ibid., November 26, 1990, p. 6.

Enforcing the Revised Penal Code

Shortly after these changes in the criminal justice system occurred, the Cuban police arrested more than three hundred citizens scattered throughout the country. The government charged some with standard economic crimes like blackmail, fraud, and negligence. Others were cited for engaging in cronyism, squandering money, selling false gasoline coupons, enjoying an ostentatious standard of living, or buying homes, cars, appliances, jewels, or art objects beyond their means.[272] The government first assured citizens that these criminals would be strictly punished; then, in early November, officials announced that more than five hundred persons had been arrested in less than two months.[273]

In fact, the Cuban judicial system did severely punish citizens convicted of committing economic crimes, often at hasty, public trials.[274] The courts sentenced one man to three years in prison for selling beer illicitly. Several individuals were sentenced to ten years for the illegal sale of gasoline coupons.[275] In December 1990 a citizen received nine years for illegal economic activity. In February 1991 the government arrested seven men for illegal gambling; they received three to eight years in jail.[276] During that same month a judge sentenced four Cuban youngsters convicted of auto theft to ten years in prison.[277] A month later a Cuban court sent a Matanza citizen to jail for ten years for stealing an "undetermined amount of money."[278] A week later authorities arrested twenty-eight citizens for embezzlement and illicit profit; they were sentenced to between two and three-and-a-half years imprisonment.[279] The government even arrested nine citizens for illegally selling favorable places in lines at stores in Havana's commercial district. Upon conviction the courts either sent such offenders to correctional labor centers or sentenced them to a year in prison.[280]

272. Between October 23 and November 10, 1990, the government checked 893 gasoline coupons and found 108 violations of regulations through unauthorized sales or unstamped coupons. *GWR*, December 9, 1990, p. 5.

273. *FBIS*, December 26, 1990, p. 2; see also *Granma*, November 26, 1990, p. 1; *FBIS*, October 25, 1990, p. 1.

274. Purcell, p. 139.

275. *FBIS*, April 4, 1991, p. 3; also reported on Radio Rebelde, April 3, 1991.

276. *GWR*, February 24, 1991, p. 4.

277. Ibid., February 5, 1991, p. 2.

278. Ibid., March 13, 1991, p. 1.

279. Ibid., March 21, 1991, p. 9.

280. Ibid., December 14, 1990, p. 3; see also *La Prensa* (Panama City, Panama), December 14, 1990, p. 5A.

Lowly citizens, of course, did not exclusively commit economic crimes. By 1990 theft at state enterprises confounded high government officials. At one point Defense Minister Raúl Castro declared in exasperation: "One million police could not solve the problem!"[281] To counter this social and economic crisis, the state began to prosecute government officials.[282] In late 1990 a Cuban court penalized the former chief of customs at Varadero International Airport with ten years in jail for illegal trafficking in foreign exchange. It also convicted and sentenced the former chief of the economic department of Varadero's customs delegation.[283] The courts handed a former market administrator a fifteen-year jail term for misappropriating funds.[284] In June 1987 the government arrested the president of Cuba's Aeronautic Institute for corruption and improper conduct and sentenced him to twenty years in prison.[285]

Fighting Internal Opposition

The Castro government also set out to eliminate opposition organizations. According to a January 1992 *Granma* article, the government "will not allow internal opposition" in this time of severe economic and political crisis. "We will fight them without quarter, with the force of the masses and the law, in the political field and in the ideological field, with every means and in every arena," *Granma* reported.[286] The government then tightened internal security by directing the "rapid response brigades," composed of civilian groups, to disperse opposition protests, suppress all signs of public discontent, and harass opposition organizations and human rights groups.[287] Cuban leaders also called on loyal citizens to engage in "acts of repudiation" against individual critics and members of organizations that opposed certain official policies. During such an act an organized group of government supporters staged a protest at the home or

281. Quote taken from *Topeka Capital-Journal*, December 25, 1988, p. 8F.
282. *FBIS*, November 6, 1990, p. 5.
283. Ibid., December 17, 1990, p. 6.
284. Ibid., November 15, 1990, p. 3.
285. *GWR*, June 28, 1987, p. 9; see also *FBIS*, September 8, 1987, p. 1.
286. Cited in the *Miami Herald*, International Edition, January 22, 1992, p. 8A.
287. Ibid., January 3, 1992, p. 3A; March 2, 1992, p. 3A. Purcell has described these brigades as similar to Manuel Noriega's "Dignity Battalions" and the Sandinista's "turbas." See Purcell, p. 139. See also Arthur Schlesinger, Jr., "Four Days with Fidel: A Havana Diary," *The New York Review of Books*, March 26, 1992, p. 22; John Newhouse, "A Reporter at Large: Socialism or Death," *The New Yorker*, April 27, 1992, p. 56; "Cuba: Behind a Sporting Facade, Stepped-Up Repression," p. 2.

office of the dissenter it sought to humiliate.[288] In order to prevent the internal seizure of Cuba by "enemies from within," the leaders even went so far as to encourage citizens to intimidate those "with political and ideological problems."[289]

In December 1991 and the following January, Carlos Aldana, then the Party's chief ideologue, delivered a series of speeches in which he harshly criticized Cuba's dissident human rights organizations, comprised mostly of young defiant citizens. Cuba, he stated, was "under siege." The leaders of these organizations, Aldana claimed, maintain "stable, close ties with the C.I.A." He described Cuba's most visible human rights organization, the Cuban Commission for Human Rights and National Reconciliation, as "squalid, counterrevolutionary garbage." Aldana assured his listeners that the government would deal harshly with the leaders of these organizations, declaring that these crimes would be "summarily punish[ed] . . . with the penalty established for traitors to the nation."[290] In February 1992 the government introduced in the province of Camaguey a "system of unified vigilance and protection," a plan in which the military began to train civilians at Armed Forces facilities for improved vigilance against counterrevolutionary activities. As part of the Camaguey campaign, Communist Party union leaders, as well as members of the CDRs and the Cuban military, arrested numerous citizens. A week later Castro initiated the same program in Havana, where four hundred thousand residents were mobilized in surveillance exercises called "Giron 92."[291]

The government also arrested various young dissident leaders for holding illegal meetings, displaying contempt for Fidel Castro, printing without official permission, and conducting other clandestine activities.[292] According to a February 1992 *Americas Watch* report, Cuban authorities had arrested more than two hundred human rights monitors and activists since 1989. At least forty of the two hundred were serving jail sentences of up to five years. The government sentenced two activists affiliated with the Harmony Movement, a human rights organization, to ten and seven years respectively for their political activities. In addition, between September

288. See, for example, *Washington Post,* August 2, 1992, pp. A29, A31.

289. *Miami Herald,* International Edition, October 27, 1991, p. 3A; March 2, 1992, p. 3A. See also "Cuba: Behind a Sporting Facade, Stepped-Up Repression," p. 3.

290. *Miami Herald,* International Edition, January 14, 1992, p. 1. See also Schlesinger, p. 22; Newhouse, pp. 56, 74–75; "Tightening the Grip: Human Rights Abuses in Cuba," p. 2.

291. *Miami Herald,* International Edition, February 14, 1992, pp. 1A, 3A; March 2, 1992, p. 3A.

292. Schlesinger, p. 22.

1991 and March 1992, authorities arrested twenty-six dissidents and detained briefly dozens of others.[293]

In most cases the government simply punished its critics by dismissing them from their jobs. These activists, depicted as lazy vagrants who shirked work, were often unable to find new employment. They thus became dependent on others.[294] In December 1991 Cuban legislators collectively vowed to fight "all activities deemed capable of undermining the system."[295] A month later Castro himself hinted that he would not hesitate to bring back the death penalty to control internal dissent.[296] A *Granma* editorial described the "counterrevolutionary" activities of Cuban intellectuals, writers, and artists as "simply treason."[297]

Youth Problems Prove Intractable

Despite the various initiatives undertaken during the Rectification Campaign, criminals did not prove to be easily deterred. Rates of crime and juvenile delinquency continued to rise.[298] In response, the leadership considered an even stricter law against corruption and economic crimes.[299] In March the President of the Supreme People's Tribunal, Raúl Amaro Salup, announced that penalties for drug trafficking and embezzlement had been raised to twelve to twenty years.[300] Several months later Castro railed at Cubans for their blatant willingness to resort to crime, corruption, and the black market.[301] In October 1991 Antonio Peña, delegate to the Party

293. *Washington Post,* August 2, 1992, p. A31; also *Miami Herald,* International Edition, March 2, 1992, p. 3A. See also *Miami Herald,* International Edition, October 17, 1991, p. 4A; October 27, 1991, p. 3A; December 6, 1991, p. 3A; January 22, 1992, p. 8A; February 14, 1992, p. 3A; February 27, 1992, p. 19A; March 2, 1992, p. 3A. See also *La Nación* (San José, Costa Rica), February 7, 1991. Those arrested and imprisoned include Pedro Armenteros, Adrian González Marichal, Jorge Quintana Silva, filmmaker Marco Antonio Abad, Bienvenida Cucalo Santana, and poet and journalist Yndamiro Restano. In November 1991 the Cuban government sentenced María Elena Cruz Varela, a Cuban poet and the leader of a small dissident group, to two years in prison for defaming state institutions and holding illegal meetings. See also Schlesinger, p. 22; Newhouse, pp. 56, 74–75. See "Tightening the Grip: Human Rights Abuses in Cuba," p. 3.

294. "Cuba: Behind a Sporting Facade, Stepped-Up Repression," p. 7.

295. *Miami Herald,* International Edition, December 30, 1991, p. 7A.

296. Ibid., January 14, 1992, p. 1.

297. Cited in "Cuba: Behind a Sporting Facade, Stepped-Up Repression," p. 8. See also *Cuba International,* June 23, 1991.

298. See, for example, *Miami Herald,* International Edition, October 14, 1991, p. 1A.

299. *Granma Weekly Review* explained that the current law would be strengthened to sanction transgressors more severely. See *GWR,* February 3, 1991, p. 3.

300. *Bohemia,* March 22, 1991, pp. 26–29.

301. *Miami Herald,* International Edition, October 14, 1991, p. 1A.

Congress, scolded citizens for their "indolence and negligence" and called on the Party to regain "control." Other party delegates deplored the growing problems with fraud and robbery from state construction sites and farms.[302]

To secure desperately needed dollars, rising numbers of young women turned to prostitution, often at Cuba's tourist facilities.[303] Other Cuban youth were pressed to even more desperate lengths. In February 1991 the Castro government announced that, for the first time since Cuban independence, suicide had become the sixth leading cause of death on the island. For Cubans between the ages of forty-five and forty-nine—those who had been teenagers during the early years of a revolution that had promised so much and delivered so little—suicide stood as the leading cause of death.[304]

Government officials themselves conceded that students were not performing adequately in school and had failed to exhibit respectful attitudes toward the Party and the military. A Cuban exnaval officer who fled the island in February 1992 explained: "Young soldiers, new conscripts, [and] old timers are fed up with Cuba's crumbling system."[305] In response, students increasingly participated in protests and other antisocial incidents; they long failed to exhibit what the leadership considered to be proper work attitudes and habits.[306] In early 1991, for example, the poor performance of young laborers prompted the Cuban Confederation of Labor to launch another investigation of juvenile delinquency.[307] The government also complained that most youths refused to participate in the Rectification's various UJC activities.[308]

Moreover, Cuba's young citizens responded with resentment and disillusionment to official policies barring Cubans from luxurious tourist facilities. The Castro government forbade its citizens from legally holding dollars, taking "tourist" taxis, renting "tourist" cars, buying gasoline at "tourist" gas stations, and even entering the country's posh "tourist" hotels, restaurants, and stores. The government allowed only dollar-paying foreigners access to exclusive places, full of fashionable beach clothes,

302. Ibid., p. 4A.

303. *Washington Post*, August 9, 1992, p. A31.

304. *GWR*, February 17, 1991, p. 4. See also Geyer, p. 14.

305. Cuban exnaval officer Danilo Paneca at press conference in Miami. See *Miami Herald*, International Edition, February 23, 1992, p. 3A.

306. A January 1991 uprising among Cuban and African students on the Isle of Youth resulted in several injuries and considerable damage to a number of buildings. *FBIS*, February 7, 1991, p. 4.

307. Leal assured workers that delinquents would suffer from strict measures. Ibid., April 2, 1991, p. 3.

308. See the following articles, *GWR*, May 6, 1990, p. 12; September 23, 1990, p. 12.

high-quality foods and sweets, and local cigars and rum. Meanwhile the basic food ration of the average Cuban shrunk.[309] One young professional commented: "It fills me with rage. . . . It makes me feel like something inferior in my own country."[310] In August 1992 Cuba's deputy minister for economic collaboration, Raúl Taladrid, admitted that the island's younger generation had reacted most negatively to the government's tourism policy. The disparity between that available to Cubans and that to tourists, Taladrid conceded, is "a bitter pill for some to swallow, especially the young."[311]

As a consequence of this profound disenchantment with the course of the Cuban Revolution, in the early 1990s the number of Cubans, mostly youth, who escaped the island by raft and attempted to risk the often deadly voyage to the United States, increased dramatically. In 1991 more than 2,400 Cubans, the vast majority of whom were in their twenties, arrived safely on Florida's shore. These figures more than quadrupled the 1990 total of 467. And American officials estimated that between 25 and 50 percent of the Cuban boat people perished en route.[312] Moreover, throughout 1990 and 1991 many of Cuba's young intellectual elite took advantage of their travel privileges to defect. These young people had been among the small, pampered upper-crust of socialist society, receiving choice benefits from the Revolution. Yet, despite official promises of a bright future, they too opted to flee the revolutionary society. In recent years substantial numbers of military officers, athletes, musicians, artists, pilots, engineers, and doctors, most of whom are young enough to have been raised and socialized under revolutionary guidance, wholly abandoned Castro's revolution.

Military officers, many decorated and a few even labeled as heroes by the revolutionary government, comprised a surprisingly large sector of the

---

309. See *Washington Post*, August 9, 1992, p. A31. In July 1992 the Cuban citizens were given a monthly ration of ten ounces of beans, six pounds of rice, four pounds of potatoes, and twelve ounces of chicken—including bones. Citizens also received one piece of bread a day. Meat, eggs, and vegetables were unavailable to most citizens. See *Washington Post*, July 27, 1992, p. A10. According to an August 1992 article in Tokyo's *Daily Yomiuri*, citizens in Havana, although forbidden from raising pork for health purposes, had found a way to raise their own pigs and evade detection by neighboring members of the CDRs. Havana residents resorted to removing their pigs' vocal cords in an effort to keep them from squealing and being discovered. See *Daily Yomiuri*, August 12, 1992, p. 5.

310. Ibid., p. 11.

311. *Washington Post*, August 9, 1992, p. A31.

312. Gillian Gunn, "Death in the Florida Straits," in ibid., July 14, 1991, p. C5. See also *Washington Post*, August 11, 1991, pp. 1A, A32; December 15, 1991, p. A44; *La Hora* (Guatemala City), May 11, 1991; Purcell, p. 137; Newhouse, p. 83.

defectors. In May 1987 a former deputy commander of the Cuban Air Force defected. In March 1991 a twenty-eight-year-old Air Force pilot flew his unarmed MiG-23 to Key West. In early January 1992 another young colonel decorated in the Cuban Air Force for service in Angola escaped with thirty-four others by stealing a helicopter and flying to the United States.[313] The following month two Navy officers fled Cuba with their families on a motorized raft.[314] At much the same time a Cuban Air Force officer swam across Guantanamo Bay and requested asylum at the U.S. naval base at Guantanamo.[315]

While travelling abroad, various Cuban athletes, musicians, artists, and writers requested and received political asylum. In July 1991 a young, widely popular Cuban baseball player defected during a sports-related trip to the United States.[316] In August 1990 two dancers with the Cuban National Ballet, both in their mid-thirties, defected in Spain.[317] The same year a popular Cuban jazz trumpeter also defected. In January 1991 a renowned Cuban ballerina requested political asylum in Rome. A Cuban violinist and the musical director of the Cuban National Ballet also fled the country. In June 1991 a singer from the Cuban Show Tropicana defected in Costa Rica.[318] Also, in February 1992 a well-known Cuban painter and head of a department at Cuba's Film Arts Institute requested political asylum in France.[319] In July 1992 the executive secretary of Cuba's Union of Artists and Writers defected in Madrid.[320]

During this mass exodus of elites Cuba also witnessed the departure of pilots, engineers, architects, doctors, and other professionals. A Cuban commercial pilot defected after landing his commercial aircraft in Canada in the spring of 1991.[321] A few months later a well-known civil engineer defected in Costa Rica.[322] In January 1992 a Cuban physician asked for asylum in Costa Rica.[323] A month later two young Cuban doctors working in Nicaragua requested asylum in Costa Rica.[324] Even Raúl Castro's

313. *Miami Herald*, International Edition, January 13, 1992, p. 5A.

314. Ibid., February 23, 1992, p. 3A.

315. Ibid., February 27, 1992, p. 3A.

316. *FBIS*, July 15, 1991, p. 2; see also *Miami Herald*, International Edition, October 27, 1991, p. 3A.

317. *La Prensa* (Panama City, Panama), August 6, 1990, p. 5A.

318. *La Nación* (San José, Costa Rica), June 13, 1991, p. 8A.

319. *Miami Herald*, International Edition, February 13, 1992, p. 3A.

320. *Christian Science Monitor*, August 19, 1992, p. 18.

321. *Washington Post*, December 15, 1991, pp. A33, A44.

322. *La Nación* (San José, Costa Rica), June 13, 1991, p. 8A.

323. *Miami Herald*, International Edition, January 17, 1992, p. 2A.

324. Ibid., February 27, 1992, p. 3A.

brother-in-law defected to Costa Rica with his wife and their three children.[325]

According to the Cuban American National Foundation, more than 455 members of the Cuban elite defected between April 1990 and October 30, 1991. At least a quarter of these defectors were members of the UCJ, supposedly a bastion of young, pro-Castro stalwarts.[326] By the early 1990s an extremely high number of Cubans, mostly of a generation raised in the Revolution and supposed to exemplify the "new man," had fled the island. The many defections from the revolutionary society provide yet another example of the widespread disillusionment evident among Cuba's young "revolutionary" generation.

CONCLUSION

A review of the Castro government's policies toward youth during the first three decades of the Revolution leads to several conclusions. First, throughout the first fifteen years the government steadily expanded and centralized its authority over society's educational institutions and youth organizations. By the mid-1970s the Cuban government oversaw virtually every aspect of education: day-care centers and children's organizations, schools and universities, polytechnic institutes and teacher-training programs, scholarships and rehabilitation centers. Using its unchallenged control over society's educational resources, the leadership established a system of reward and deprivation. The government provided its faithful supporters and followers with substantial benefits: goods and career opportunities, leadership promotions and bonuses, and admission to schools and universities for their children. These same benefits were denied to passive or resistant citizens.

Cuban leaders repeatedly used voluntary membership in children's organizations to expose the attitudes and values of the parents. Authorities amply rewarded cooperative parents who encouraged, or required, their children to participate in revolutionary events and organizations. Officials denied benefits to those who failed to encourage their children to join and participate in revolutionary youth activities.

Through the years the role of the Cuban military in youth affairs increased considerably. By 1973 the military exercised substantial influence

---

325. *La Nación* (San José, Costa Rica), June 13, 1991, p. 8A. See also Purcell, p. 137.
326. *Washington Post*, December 15, 1991, p. A44.

in the polytechnical schools, the universities, the children's organizations, the rehabilitation centers, the CDRs, the high schools, and the youth labor brigades. Throughout the latter part of the 1980s and early 1990s, the Rectification Campaign further expanded the military's role through the Society for Patriotic Military Education, the Territorial Troop Militia, and the Committees for the Defense of the Revolution. The government even took the unprecedented and revealing step of appointing certain military officials to critical political positions.

Moreover, the leadership replaced its early policies of encouraging volunteers by imposing mandatory labor. By 1974 the entire educational system, from first grade to the university, operated on a work-study basis. Cuban students labored every day. Although the government labelled compulsory work as "participatory education" and a "revolutionary experience," in truth it amounted to little more than unpaid institutionalized labor for the state.

At the same time official policies became more directly coercive. While the government markedly retrenched from the authoritarianism of the late 1970s and allowed some freedom of action among its citizens, by the early 1990s no one could doubt the leadership's willingness to repress antirevolutionary behavior. Cuban officials began to enact ever more strict laws, imposing harsh penalties on those out of step with the government's objectives. The coercive measures included humiliation tactics, mandatory military service and labor, the attempt to "educate" parents by enacting a formal system of sanctions and rewards, repression in the universities and religious groups, student profiles, and threats of incarceration, labor camps, job dismissals, and deprivation. In the late 1980s this willingness to coerce surfaced again as the government modified the criminal code to punish severely juvenile delinquents who committed relatively minor offenses.

Cuba's revolutionary leaders discovered, however, that, despite the government's indisputable control of the island's resources and despite the leadership's inclination to coerce citizens to behave appropriately, they simply could not force Cuban youngsters to think and act according to the dictates of Marxist-Leninist ideology. More than three decades after the Revolution, youth remained largely resistant and hostile to Cuba's leaders.[327] Rates of juvenile delinquency, particularly economic crimes, failed to improve.[328] The black market and prostitution flourished. Drug

327. See, for example, ibid., August 16, 1991, pp. B1-B2.
328. Throughout the first six months of 1991 the Cuban leaders incessantly discussed the problems of crime and juvenile delinquency. Moreover, *Granma* and other publications ran

trafficking emerged as a vexing problem.[329] Judging by the series of official newspaper articles on alcoholism in Cuba, that social ill also seriously afflicted young men and women.[330]

The island's youth, who had always lived in Cuba's revolutionary society, had gained little from the sacrifices the leadership required them to make. Volunteering their labor, serving in the military, participating in revolutionary activities, and contributing their time and energy to various mass organizations resulted in few tangible benefits for Cuba's younger generation. Young Cubans saw the Revolution as a failure: it certainly had not brought the economic growth or social and political progress that had long been touted. In short, the "new Cuban man" had not emerged. The island's youth, apathetic and disloyal, did not reflect the appropriate revolutionary *conciencia*. Defying the threat of punishment, some even overtly demonstrated their hatred for the Castro government.

In some cases authorities surrendered to the recalcitrance of youth and accommodated their demands. The government's official recognition of Christianity and its move to lift the religious ban for Communist Party membership demonstrated such accommodation. At other times the government dangled positive incentives to lure youngsters into changing their attitudes and behavior. Nevertheless, Cuban leaders most frequently employed repression to counter the actions of insubordinate youth.

As the battle continued, with no clear winners, many young Cubans concluded that the Castro government had lost its legitimacy. In the late 1980s and early 1990s, after communist systems throughout Europe and Africa and in Nicaragua had collapsed, Fidel Castro and his revolution appeared to be an anachronism, out of sync with the progression of history. Living in a society in which the state tightly rationed nearly all goods, and having little or no opportunity to travel, to express their views, and to enjoy their youth, many young Cubans rejected the revolutionary government and its goals. The views and actions of the island's disappointed and alienated youth had created considerable, indeed, confounding and impenetrable obstacles for the revolutionary leadership and for its ambitious plans to transform Cuban culture.

---

a series of articles and interviews with leaders discussing the causes of crime and the measures to eradicate it. For example, see *Bohemia,* March 1, 1991, pp. 28–31.

329. In March 1991 a Cuban citizen was arrested by police for possession and use of drugs and sentenced to one year, four months. *FBIS,* March 15, 1991, pp. 2–3. In February 1991 nine Cubans were arrested and charged with drug trafficking. Ibid., February 5, 1991, p. 2. Also, in May 1991 the National Revolutionary Police arrested twenty-seven Cubans for their involvement in a drug trafficking organization. Ibid., May 29, 1991, p. 2.

330. *GWR,* January 20, 1991, p. 5.

3
Castro and the Goal of Sexual Equality

> [T]he Cuban Revolution is the business of
> machos. . . . Machos drive jeeps, have big pistols, and
> make revolutions. . . . The Revolution, like certain
> brandies, is only for men. All that rhetoric of
> "assault brigades against the tomato" . . . and other
> belligerent formulas to get people to work, reflect
> the epic-machismo background of the revolution. . . .
> [E]ach leader, each time he zips up his olive green fly
> and checks the lock in his pistol, reinforces his male
> ego and congratulates himself for being such a
> macho.
>
> —Carlos Alberto Montaner

To create an egalitarian society for women and men has long stood as a widely acclaimed goal of the Cuban Revolution. Upon seizing power Fidel Castro and his colleagues in the Cuban government emphasized equality between the sexes and women's rights: the liberation of women from the "chains" of prerevolutionary capitalist society. Castro continually encouraged women to leave the home, join the labor force, liberate themselves from their traditional roles, and view themselves differently in Cuba's revolutionary society. He also insisted that men, too, transform their prerevolutionary views toward women and women's role in Cuban society. In 1966 Castro declared that the women's movement represented a "revolution within the Revolution." He stated forcefully: "The most revolutionary thing that the Revolution is doing . . . is the revolution that is occurring among the women."[1]

Throughout much of the twentieth century, Cuban women, like women from the United States and Latin America, fought for political rights, par-

---

1. Fidel Castro speech on December 9, 1966, *Granma Weekly Review (GWR)*, December 18, 1966, Special Section, p. 2.

ticularly the right to vote.[2] During the 1960s, after the triumph of the Revolution, women's issues took on new prominence in Cuban society. At a time when women's movements throughout the rest of Latin America remained weak and insignificant, women in Cuba made some dramatic strides. They did so contemporaneously with the United States civil rights movement and before many of the advances of the more recent American women's rights movement.

Women's liberation in Cuba, however, took on quite different meanings and assumed quite different objectives from the campaign in its northern neighbor. Unlike the movement in the United States, which finally became a strong political force nearly a decade after the Cuban Revolution, women's liberation in Cuba originated from official objectives rather than from the aspirations of women outside of government. As Susan Kaufman Purcell has written, "the impetus for the modernization of Cuban women comes from above. . . . Cuban women are to be made equal by governmental direction and means."[3]

In the United States, Mexico, Argentina, and other countries, by contrast, women's liberation movements are not government-based. In the United States, for example, private groups and individuals provide the impetus, funding and support, ideas and direction. Although federal and state government bodies in the United States have implemented equal opportunity laws, the movement to bring equality to women is organized and led by the citizens themselves. Indeed, on regular occasions women's rights in the United States have collided with the objectives and ideals of the administration in office.

In Cuba, however, the women's movement operated at the direction of, and hence with the full support of, the revolutionary leadership. Since the Cuban movement functioned completely under government auspices, the women's organization took an approach that appears more traditionally "feminine" than "feminist."[4] Women's liberation in Cuba never denoted individual achievement, personal development, and independence, as it has in the United States and other countries. The Cuban movement subordinated the independence of women to service and loyalty to state and soci-

2. For an interesting discussion of these female activities, see Lynn Stoner, *From the Houses to the Streets: The Cuban Women's Movement for Legal Reform, 1898–1940* (Durham: Duke University Press, 1991).

3. Susan Kaufman Purcell, "Modernizing Women for a Modern Society: The Cuban Case," in *Female and Male in Latin America,* ed. Ann Pescatello (Pittsburgh: University of Pittsburgh Press, 1973), p. 258.

4. Alfred Padula and Lois P. Smith, "Women in Socialist Cuba," in *Cuba: Twenty-Five Years of Revolution, 1959-1984,* ed. Sandor Halebsky and John M. Kirk (New York: Praeger, 1985), p. 83.

ety. Although the leadership referred to liberation as women's freedom from responsibility in the home and for the children, the objective was not simply, or even primarily, personal fulfillment for Cuban women. Instead, the goal was to free women to serve the Revolution more completely. "An individual alone can do nothing," Castro stated, "an individual alone is very little, but an individual integrated into the strength of society is everything."[5] The Cuban leader continued: "The liberation of women is dependent upon the Revolution's success in attaining its primary objectives: to establish a wholly socialist economy and society. Women can be free only to the extent that they commit themselves first and foremost to the Revolution."[6]

WOMEN IN PREREVOLUTIONARY CUBA

Women in prerevolutionary Cuba had achieved a more respectable status vis-à-vis men than women in any other Latin American country, with the possible exceptions of Argentina and Uruguay.[7] With regard to political rights, Cuban women received the vote in 1934. Among the Latin American states only women in Uruguay, Brazil, and Ecuador obtained voting rights earlier.[8] Rates of abortion and divorce in prerevolutionary Cuba were among the highest in Latin America. In education the percentage of female students from ages five to fifteen approximately equaled that of male students.[9] According to Cuba's 1953 census, the percentage of illiterate males (26 percent) exceeded that of illiterate females (21 percent).[10] Within Latin America only Argentina and Chile had higher female literacy rates (85 percent and 79 percent respectively).[11] With regard to work positions and social status, the percentages of Cuban women working out-

5. Oscar Lewis, Ruth M. Lewis, and Susan M. Rigdon, *Four Women Living the Revolution: An Oral History of Contemporary Cuba* (Urbana: University of Illinois Press, 1977), p. x. See also Bertram Silverman, ed., *Man and Socialism in Cuba: The Great Debate* (New York: Atheneum, 1971), p. 374.

6. Lewis, Lewis, and Rigdon, p. xvii.

7. José Moreno, "From Traditional to Modern Values," in *Revolutionary Change in Cuba,* ed. Carmelo Mesa-Lago (Pittsburgh: University of Pittsburgh Press, 1971), p. 478.

8. Olivia Harris, "An Overview," in *Latin American Women,* ed. Olivia Harris (London: Minority Rights Group, 1983), p. 7.

9. Moreno, p. 479. Also see Purcell, p. 260; and Richard Jolly, "Education: The Prerevolutionary Background," in *Cuba: The Economic and Social Revolution,* ed. Dudley Seers (Chapel Hill: University of North Carolina Press, 1964), pp. 166–167.

10. Moreno, p. 479.

11. *Statistical Abstract of Latin America* (Los Angeles: Center for Latin American Studies, University of California at Los Angeles, 1961), p. 61.

side the home, attending school, and practicing birth control surpassed the corresponding percentages in nearly every other Latin American country.

Before the Revolution women had been elected to Cuba's House of Representatives and Senate. They had served as mayors, judges, cabinet members, municipal counselors, and members of the Cuban foreign service.[12] The Constitution of 1940, one of the most progressive in the Western Hemisphere with regard to women's status, prohibited discrimination on the basis of sex and called for equal pay for equal work.

Susan Kaufman Purcell has attributed the relatively higher status of prerevolutionary Cuban women, when compared to women in most other Latin American countries, to three factors. First, the Catholic Church played a lesser role in the colonization of Cuba and remained less powerful and influential on the island than throughout the rest of Spanish America. The patriarchal traditions of the Church, particularly in the nineteenth century and before, tended to subordinate women and confine them to childbearing and child rearing in the home. Such an influence proved to be somewhat less important in Cuba than in neighboring Latin American countries.

Second, unlike most other Latin American countries, Cuba never developed a dominant *hacienda* system emphasizing traditional patriarchal authority. Rather, Cuban plantations employed a wage-earning labor force. This agricultural structure engendered a stronger, more independent role for women in society. Finally, the island's proximity and economic ties to the United States substantially influenced Cuban culture. North American social mores, which have been considerably more sexually egalitarian than those of much of Latin America, affected significantly Cuban social mores, especially in the urban areas.[13]

To be sure, prerevolutionary society retained certain extreme inequalities between the sexes. Despite the early date in obtaining relatively advanced legal rights, prerevolutionary women were far from equal partners in governing the state. Women "seldom [ran] for office nor [did] they appear often as members of boards, commissions, or other appointive positions at the policy-making level." Nearly all women in politics or public office found themselves relegated chiefly to subordinate roles.[14]

Moreover, although Cuba was less influenced by the Catholic Church and somewhat more socially egalitarian than other Latin American states, an authoritarian and patriarchal family structure, part of the island's Hispanic legacy, did indeed influence society to a considerable degree. This

12. Purcell, p. 260.
13. Ibid., pp. 259–260.
14. Lowry Nelson, *Rural Cuba* (Minneapolis: University of Minnesota Press, 1950), pp. 144–145; see also Purcell, p. 261.

was particularly the case in the isolated, rural areas, which encompassed more than 43 percent of the population.[15] Within the Cuban family a double standard prevailed that required "good" women to demonstrate unquestioned fidelity, while allowing, indeed encouraging, infidelity among men. Cuban society taught young boys to demonstrate their *machismo:* a Latin notion of male superiority and aggressiveness demonstrated by virility, strength, confidence, courage, and power. Young girls, however, were expected to be gracious, attractive, retiring, virtuous, and virgin.[16]

Prior to the Revolution most Cubans believed that the woman's place should center on the home. Although in practice only upper-class women had the security necessary to focus all their attention on the family, middle-class women tended to emulate this ideal whenever possible. By the late 1940s, however, Cuban society had accepted the idea that upper-class and upper-middle-class women might choose to work in the absence of financial need, provided the labor occurred in a "respectable" professional or bureaucratic setting. At the same time lower-class women, who often had to perform low-status menial labor outside the home, could rarely afford what was seen as the luxury of unemployment.[17] Organized child care in prerevolutionary Cuba remained extremely limited. Often, lower-class working women took their older daughters out of school to supervise younger children and, in essence, to serve as surrogate mothers. This contributed to a high drop-out rate among girls.[18]

Unquestionably, women in prerevolutionary Cuba held an inferior position in the labor force. In 1943, for example, women comprised only 10 percent of this force. Ten years later the figure had increased to 13.7 percent. Thereafter it grew steadily, though slowly: by 1956 to 14 percent and by 1959 to 17 percent.[19] Although dramatically underrepresented in

15. Purcell, p. 260. See also Carmelo Mesa-Lago, "Economic Policies and Growth," in *Revolutionary Change in Cuba,* ed. Carmelo Mesa-Lago (Pittsburgh: University of Pittsburgh Press, 1971), p. 280.

16. Marvin Leiner, *Children Are the Revolution: Day Care in Cuba* (New York: Viking Press, 1974), p. 10; see also Purcell.

17. Purcell, pp. 260–261; see also Nelson, *Rural Cuba,* p. 183.

18. Leiner, p. 10.

19. These statistics were taken from the *Yearbook of Labor Statistics,* International Labor Office, Geneva, and the United Nations *Demographic Yearbook,* New York. See also Moreno, p. 479. A 1986 *Granma Weekly Review* article stated that in 1953 women comprised 17.3 percent of the Cuban work force. That number is significantly higher than either Moreno's or that of Lewis, Lewis, and Rigdon. See *GWR,* April 6, 1986, p. 2. Carmelo Mesa-Lago presents numbers considerably lower. See Mesa-Lago, *The Economy of Socialist Cuba: A Two-Decade Appraisal* (Albuquerque: University of New Mexico Press, 1981), p. 118. At the same time the percentages of women in the work force presented by Domínguez are

white-collar and blue-collar jobs, women did account for approximately 46 percent of Cuba's professionals and semiprofessionals. Of course, 60 percent of these women worked in the traditional occupations of nurse and teacher. In 1957 women filled more than 48 percent of jobs in the service sector. About one quarter of working women were employed as domestic servants. Indeed, more than 90 percent of all domestic workers were female. Fewer than 3 percent of Cuban women, however, worked in agricultural, fishing, construction, and transport industries.

As was true throughout the region, most Cubans tended to view higher-paying positions as male jobs. Nevertheless, in 1956/1957 Cuban women did enjoy more job security and stability than men and were less affected by unemployment.[20] On the eve of the Revolution the number of women in the work force was increasing steadily. And the legal status of women had improved substantially beyond that of women in many other Latin American countries.

PHASE ONE

In August 1960 the Cuban leadership founded the Federation of Cuban Women (FMC) to organize and develop the movement. Fidel Castro selected his brother Raúl's wife, Vilma Espín Guilloys, to lead the organization. In the three decades under Espín's leadership the Federation regularly and faithfully turned to the government for guidance and instruction. Its ultimate responsibility to the Cuban Communist Party was never seriously challenged. Indeed, Castro and his colleagues determined the direction of the movement. They dictated the women's goals and the extent of change in women's social roles. Although Raúl Castro assured observers that Fidel "clearly understands . . . the problems of women in society and their decisive role in the Revolution," the FMC's unflinching commitment to promoting the Castro government's objectives raises serious questions concerning the extent to which women's voices were heard within their own women's rights movement.[21]

Certainly, the Cuban movement enjoyed significant benefits. Aside

significantly higher. See Jorge I. Domínguez, *Cuba: Order and Revolution* (Cambridge: Harvard University Press, 1978), p. 499.

20. Moreno, p. 479; Purcell, p. 261; Jolly, pp. 166–167; see also Clifford R. Barnett, *Cuba: Its People, Its Society, Its Culture* (New Haven: Human Relations Area Files Press, 1962), pp. 343–344.

21. *GWR*, December 7, 1975, p. 4.

from minimal membership dues, the state provided funding. Since the government always covered its expenses, the Federation operated without serious concerns about financial security. Nor did the movement have to fight antiquated laws or constitutional provisions. In creating laws compatible with its ideological rhetoric and objectives, the Cuban Revolution eliminated legal obstacles to equality. The government also undeniably served as a public relations instrument to promote and endorse its women's movement. This governmental support provided the FMC with a degree of legitimacy, and authority, over Cuban women.

These advantages must, of course, be balanced against substantial drawbacks. Most important, the government determined the rate and scope of initiatives to bring about social change. The Castro leadership, not Cuba's women, decided what was and was not necessary and appropriate concerning women's rights and needs. Throughout the first thirty years of the Revolution, women exercised little control over which aspects of the movement the government chose to emphasize. Women traditionally carried out FMC activities under government direction, supervision, and leadership.[22] Perhaps as a consequence of the movement's domination by revolutionary leaders, the vast majority of whom were men, the Federation consistently emphasized economic goals. Other conceivable objectives for a liberation movement, such as women's independence and personal development, were all too often ignored.[23]

Participation in the Revolution

With the establishment of the FMC, Cuban leaders made a concerted effort to involve women in the Revolution. According to the Federation's President, Vilma Espín, the organization's purpose was to prepare women "educationally, politically and socially to participate in the Revolution." The FMC mainly sought "the incorporation of women in work."[24] As one article in *Mujeres,* the FMC's official magazine, read, "We cannot cease being underdeveloped while all women able to work are not doing so."[25] The Federation sought not only to bring women into the labor force by teaching basic skills and disseminating employment information but also to politicize and resocialize them. The 1965 FMC Constituent Congress stated: "Women can enjoy *all* their rights, so that they can participate in

22. Purcell, p. 259.
23. Lewis, Lewis, and Rigdon, pp. xi–xii.
24. Speech by Vilma Espín, quoted in Purcell, p. 263.
25. *Mujeres,* January 1971, p. 7.

all forms of work, free themselves from domestic slavery and the heavy burden of prejudice."[26]

Cuban women, however, proved to be noticeably reluctant to join an organization created by the government, somewhat artificially perhaps, to look after their needs. Initially, relatively few women became members: by the end of 1960 the FMC numbered fewer than 100,000 women.[27] Over time, however, increasing efforts by the Federation and the government, particularly during the Revolutionary Offensive, succeeded in markedly raising membership figures. By the end of 1968, 981,105 Cuban women had joined the Federation. By 1977 FMC membership peaked at 2,182,953. At that time more than 80 percent of Cuban women over thirteen years of age belonged to the organization.[28]

What were the Federation women doing during these years of increasing membership? In 1961 the FMC sponsored campaigns to encourage women to enter the labor force and to combat male prejudice against females by taking jobs traditionally set aside for men. The Federation hung posters throughout the cities calling for women to liberate themselves from oppression.[29] In assisting the Ministry of Education in assembling school textbooks, the FMC kept a close watch to avoid using stereotypic photos of women. The FMC sought to depict a different view of Cuban women in school texts by portraying women as factory workers and agricultural laborers on state farms. Moreover, the textbooks showed children as independent and revolutionary. In one text a young girl encourages her mother not to hurry home at dusk but to remain at the factory to work a few hours more.[30]

Women and Education

The FMC also played an important role in organizing and directing the literacy campaign of 1961 in which more than fifty thousand women ulti-

---

26. "The Federation of Cuban Women Is Five Years Old," in *Women of the Whole World* 12 (1965): 18; see also Purcell, p. 263.

27. José Yglesias, *In the Fist of the Revolution: Life in a Cuban Country Town* (New York: Pantheon Books, 1968), p. 259; see also Purcell, p. 262.

28. These numbers are cited in Domínguez, pp. 267–268. Susan Kaufman Purcell, however, provides considerably smaller numbers. For example, she argues that in 1979 only 1,343,098 women belonged to the FMC. This indicates that a mere 54 percent of Cuba's women (fourteen years of age or older) were members of the FMC in 1979. Purcell, p. 263.

29. *Granma*, March 14, 1971, p. 1.

30. Mohammed A. Rauf, Jr., *Cuban Journal: Castro's Cuba As It Really Is* (New York: Crowell, 1964), p. 45.

mately participated.[31] For the first time the Cuban government sent adolescent girls out on their own, far from home and the protection of their parents. Such a policy would have been astonishing, unthinkable perhaps, only a few years before.

This wholly new experience for Cuban girls caused a great deal of anxiety for parents.[32] To assuage their fears, Fidel Castro insisted that the girls working in the countryside with the literacy campaign would remain "virtuous." They would not be living with the peasants. The girls would be more closely supervised than their male counterparts and would be housed in huts with females only. The sexual revolution had not reached Cuba, and the leadership tacitly assured parents that the familiar sexual double standard still prevailed. Nevertheless, such female participation in the literacy campaign was quite extraordinary for Latin America in the 1960s. The literacy campaign workers canvassed from house to house persuading illiterate people of both sexes to sign up for instruction.[33] During these visits the FMC also encouraged women to send their children to school.

After the literacy campaign the FMC organized schools to educate domestic servants. Young teachers, who had been trained for the literacy campaign, taught sewing, reading, writing, and other basic skills. Academic subjects included history, geography, current events, physical education, and the laws of revolutionary Cuba. By the end of 1961 the government had established sixty schools for domestic servants with a total of twenty thousand pupils.[34]

The Cuban leadership also charged the FMC with the responsibility of raising the educational level and the standard of living of peasant women. In 1961 about fourteen thousand rural women came to Havana for six months to study dressmaking, cooking, and hygiene, and "to develop their cultural knowledge and study at first hand the achievements of the Revolution."[35] The government rewarded the graduates of these courses with equipment and material, such as sewing machines and fabrics. Upon returning to the countryside, the graduates could teach other women the same skills. By 1968 more than fifty-five thousand peasant women had graduated from these courses. For illiterate women not yet incorporated

31. Padula and Smith, "Women in Socialist Cuba," p. 82. Moreno states that the number was closer to ninety thousand (p. 480). Purcell quotes twenty-five thousand women (p. 264).

32. Padula and Smith, "Women in Socialist Cuba," p. 82.

33. Richard Fagen, *The Transformation of Political Culture in Cuba* (Stanford: Stanford University Press, 1969), p. 48.

34. Purcell, p. 264; see also "Women's Access to Education," in *Women of the Whole World* 1 (1968): 27; Jolly, pp. 209–210; Domínguez, p. 267.

35. See "Women's Access to Education," p. 27; see also Purcell, p. 264.

into the labor force, the FMC sponsored courses on subjects ranging from health care and personal hygiene to typing and handicrafts, from gardening and physical education to traffic directing. Equally significant, perhaps, the courses were designed to teach a rather traditional set of social mores: instructing women on how to be "ladies" and to carry out "women's responsibilities."[36]

Curbing Prostitution

In 1961, with the assistance of the FMC, the Cuban government vigorously set out to curb prostitution, which it labelled a repugnant "social illness." The leaders considered prostitution not a crime but a product of prerevolutionary society's selfish capitalist culture. Government troops raided the prostitution sections of Havana, rounded up hundreds of women, photographed and fingerprinted them, and required each woman to have a complete physical examination.

Curiously, while the government outlawed pimping in December 1961, it never actually prohibited prostitution. Wary of taking such a radical step, Castro even announced publicly that the traditional *posadas,* government-run hotels, would remain open to allow men and women to rent a room by the hour. *Posadas,* he insisted, "satisfy a social need."[37] While *posadas* did afford married and unmarried couples privacy that might be lacking at home, their managers could not be expected to screen out prostitutes and their customers. Thus, in reality, the government sought only to control prostitution, not to prohibit it.[38]

Cuban leaders did, however, make an effort to educate women who wished to quit prostitution by sending them to schools to learn hairdressing, typing, and sewing. The women were taught to "dress and fix their hair in ways that were not ornate. They were briefed on table manners and helped to break other bad habits."[39] The government then issued the reformed prostitutes uniforms and assigned them to factories and other places to work. Although the government scorned prostitutes who refused these new jobs and barred them from working for specified periods, it rewarded cooperative women with diplomas at special graduation ceremonies.

36. Purcell, p. 264.
37. Herbert L. Matthews, *Revolution in Cuba* (New York: Charles Scribner's Sons, 1975), p. 378.
38. Luis P. Salas, *Social Control and Deviance in Cuba* (New York: Praeger, 1979), p. 100; see also Lewis, Lewis, and Rigdon, p. 276; *Gaceta Oficial de la República de Cuba,* December 19, 1961, Law 993.
39. Salas, p. 101.

Despite some successful results, the government's attempt in the early 1960s to diminish prostitution and restore the dignity and self-esteem of prostitutes revealed that the leaders themselves harbored certain discriminatory attitudes. Taking women from the countryside and the slums and sending them to schools to learn hairdressing, typing, sewing, and cooking, how to dress and how to fix their hair, hardly amounts to a revolutionary break from traditional *machismo* attitudes. Moreover, rewarding women with sewing machines reveals something of the leadership's inability to eradicate its own prerevolutionary gender attitudes.

Day-Care Centers

Aside from promoting literacy and curbing prostitution, the Cuban government, assisted by the FMC, also created day-care centers. Many women, regardless of educational and occupational opportunities, simply could not join the labor force because they had children that required care. Thus, in 1961 the FMC opened the first *círculos infantiles,* state-operated day-care centers that took over certain traditionally female duties and responsibilities. The FMC also established schools at which teachers and directors of the *círculos* were taught psychology and human relations, hygiene and first aid, history, politics, and ideology, teaching techniques, and child care.

The purpose of the day-care centers, FMC leader Clementina Serra declared, was to allow women to enter the work force liberated from their traditional roles. The *círculos,* Serra maintained, sought "to take care of the children of working mothers, free them from responsibility while working, and offer them the guarantee that their children will be well cared for and provided with all that is necessary for improved development."[40] To bring the day-care message to most Cuban families, the government sponsored radio and television programs and personal interviews with mothers. It published a monthly magazine *Simientes,* which explained and discussed the day-care program.[41] The *círculos* thus became a costly centerpiece of the Castro government's social initiatives.[42]

That the day-care centers could serve ideological purposes other than

40. Leiner, p. 12; see also "Report on the *Círculos Infantiles*" by Clementina Serra, distributed on July 13, 1969, in Cuba.

41. Leiner, p. 151.

42. As Marvin Leiner explained: "[T]he cost of organizing, equipping, staffing, and training for the *círculos* is considerably greater than that of day-care efforts in most other countries. In terms of its effect on the Cuban economy, however, [the government believes] it is a price worth paying" (ibid., p. 13).

liberating women most likely helped to justify to the Cuban leaders their high costs. Consequently, the day-care program was never designed solely to liberate women. In the *círculos* children could be separated from values at home that were incompatible with those of the leadership.[43] In addition, the government opened boarding schools for older children. The day-care centers and boarding schools thus augmented the revolutionary government's direct influence over the education of Cuban children. Since the *círculos* employed only women, they became female bastions that provided numerous job opportunities for women in search of employment. Cuban tradition dictated that no men would seriously be considered for any day-care position. As one young revolutionary explained, "Men can't behave like women, since men can't be mothers like women can."[44] Leaders and citizens alike, wrote an observing scholar, believed that women were "better prepared by nature to care for young children."[45] Another wrote, "No one seemed ready to imagine men staffing the day-care centers."[46] Often the leadership staffed the day-care centers with women who had been prerevolutionary domestic servants because they had experience in caring for children. And, not surprisingly, day-care workers were the lowest paid of all occupational sectors in Cuba; their wages equalled a mere 77 percent of the average national wage.[47]

Once again the Castro government's rhetorical zeal for equality between the sexes masked sharp limits in practice. Not only did the day-care centers employ only women but they taught certain subjects, such as embroidery and sewing, only to girls. In the mid-1970s the Cuban Minister of Education affirmed, "We just can't have little boys sewing and crocheting. . . . [T]he parents would never accept it."[48] The leaders, then, accommodated and protected many attitudes that contrasted markedly with the official goal of the women's movement: complete equality between the sexes.

As part of the campaign to increase the size and productivity of the Cuban labor force, in the early 1960s the government initiated a program to provide three meals a day in the workplace. This measure lightened the burden of housework for women and allowed the state to control food rationing more effectively. On May 1, 1966, Fidel Castro revealed an un-

43. Ibid., p. 151.
44. See generally, Leiner. See also Karen Wald, *Children of Che: Childcare and Education in Cuba* (Palo Alto: Ramparts Press, 1978), p. 58.
45. Ibid., pp. 124, 223.
46. Elizabeth Sutherland, *The Youngest Revolution* (New York: Dial Press, 1969), p. 184.
47. Domínguez, p. 501; see also Leiner, pp. 35–36.
48. Quoted in Wald, p. 180.

derlying economic motive behind FMC programs like the *círculos,* boarding schools, and meal plans in commenting: "[T]he entire nation profits from the incorporation of thousands . . . say of a million women into production; if each one of those million women produces the value of a thousand pesos per year, a million women means a thousand million pesos in created wealth."[49]

During the early 1960s the FMC carried out other duties as well. It sponsored political education and emulation programs; it organized vaccination efforts, voluntary work programs, and Women's and Red Cross Brigades.[50] In addition, the FMC began distributing a magazine, *Mujeres,* which discussed women's contributions to education, production, and culture. A traditional, even paternalistic, view of women marked much of the writing in *Mujeres;* indeed, it nearly always contained a statement by Castro praising "exemplary women." *Mujeres* published articles discussing how to make toys, knit and sew, care for sick children, use and care for a pressure cooker, and make the home more attractive. These articles in the official publication of Cuba's women's movement tended to reinforce prerevolutionary attitudes toward women in society.[51]

Thus, the Castro government, while formally espousing equality between the sexes, did not vigorously refute many prevailing notions regarding the suitability of particular roles for females. Women were still expected to be chiefly responsible for home and child care. The leadership made little effort to change the traditional belief that women are more suited for certain occupations, such as teachers and day-care workers.[52] Even Che Guevara, the Revolution's most outspoken advocate of sexual equality, viewed the daily business of Revolution as largely a man's project. As Che explained:

> Our vanguard revolutionaries must idealize their love for the people. . . . They cannot descend with doses of daily affection to the terrain where ordinary men put their love into practice. The leaders of the revolution have children who do not learn to call their father with their first faltering words; they have wives who must be part of the general sacrifice of their lives to carry the revolution to its destination.[53]

49. Fidel Castro, May 1, 1966, speech.
50. *GWR*, August 31, 1969; see also Moreno, p. 481; Sutherland, p. 173.
51. See Purcell, pp. 267–268.
52. Ibid.
53. Che Guevara, "Notes on Man and Socialism in Cuba," in *Che Guevara Speaks,* ed. George Lavan (New York: Merit, 1967), p. 136; quoted in Domínguez, p. 494.

Gains Made by Women

Despite the fact that revolutionary rhetoric far outdistanced the government's actual practices, Cuban women during the 1960s did make remarkable social gains in many areas. For instance, the government increased the number of women in the Committees for the Defense of the Revolution. By 1963 women comprised nearly 44 percent of CDR members.[54] CDR membership provided women an opportunity to participate actively in the Revolution. The government also began to distribute free contraceptives, thus giving some women an opportunity to avert pregnancy.

Moreover, FMC members, perceiving divorce as a woman's way out of an excessively authoritarian marriage, successfully urged the government to facilitate divorce proceedings. The organization also effectively pressured courts to enforce alimony payments more thoroughly.[55] During these years the government also legalized abortion. Castro, who personally considered abortions "repugnant," had ensured that the state outlaw them in the early years. However, after numerous clandestine abortions continued to occur, the government opted to make abortion services legal, available, and free for all women. Each of these measures could be viewed as a considerable concession to Cuban women.[56] Certainly, each significantly weakened the traditional bonds between women and family life and provided women with greater freedom in making decisions regarding pregnancy.

In 1968, however, almost a decade after the triumph of the Revolution, women still comprised only 15.6 percent of the Cuban work force.[57] This figure was not substantially higher than the 1958 figure of 14.8 percent.[58] In this respect the vast amount of energy and money expended on *círculos,* publications, boarding schools, television and radio programs, and women's educational programs failed to bring about a substantial increase in the number of women in the Cuban work force.

Moreover, surprisingly few parents chose to send their children to daycare centers. In 1968 fewer than one out of ten children attended *círculos* while their mothers worked. Several reasons may help to explain why par-

54. Fagen, p. 83.

55. Domínguez, p. 501.

56. Chris Camarano, "On Cuban Women," in *Science and Society* (Spring 1971): 53; see also Purcell, p. 265; Lois M. Smith and Alfred Padula, "The Cuban Family in the 1980s," in *Transformation and Struggle: Cuba Faces the 1990s,* ed. Sandor Halebsky and John M. Kirk (New York: Praeger, 1990), p. 180; *Granma,* February 16, 1989, p. 4.

57. Domínguez, p. 499.

58. Lewis, Lewis, and Rigdon, p. xix; see also Padula and Smith, "Women in Socialist Cuba," p. 83. These figures vary among sources by a percentage or two. See also Purcell, p. 261.

ents refused to commit their children to government day-care. First, at this early date in the Revolution, many families still had live-in relatives or domestic hired help with whom to leave their children. In addition, in the early stages of the day-care programs, many parents perceived facilities as insufficient and day-care staff as inexperienced and unskilled. Lacking confidence in the programs, parents avoided enrolling their children. Perhaps even more important, women continued to cling to traditional values and standards. As Ruth and Oscar Lewis observed, many lower-class women saw "liberation" not as being incorporated into the labor force but as "*release* from outside work, taking care of their own homes, and having time to spend with their children." Prior to the Revolution, economic necessity had forced these women to work as servants, cooks, and janitors. Joining the revolutionary labor force did not answer their dreams of liberation and freedom.[59]

At the same time middle-class and upper-class women—whether to pacify their husbands or to suit their own values—often resisted taking outside jobs. In truth, these women simply did not march forward, demanding the opportunity to leave the home and enter the work force. Instead, many Cuban women seemed consumed with the burdens of household management, a task decidedly more difficult than before the Revolution. In the 1960s the Castro government began to ration significantly food and consumer goods. The leadership also required husbands to spend extended periods away from the home on voluntary labor assignments. It nationalized, and made more cumbersome, basic services, such as laundries, repair shops, and dry cleaners.

Middle-class Cuban women thus certainly found housework more time-consuming. Some may even have found it more challenging as well. Perhaps even more important, since the government legally guaranteed their husbands a steady wage, many women for the first time in their lives felt economically secure without having to work. Indeed, as consumer goods became scarce, their prices inflated, and the supply of money abundant, many Cuban women saw a secondary income as less desirable.[60]

Cuban men also resisted the leadership's drive to bring women into the workplace. Husbands rejected the idea of "their women" working outside the home and interacting with other men in the workplace.[61] The government leaders, still overwhelmingly male, expected women to volunteer their time to participate in the CDRs, parent-teacher committees, voluntary labor projects, and FMC activities. Thus, neither men nor women in

59. Lewis, Lewis, and Rigdon, p. xv.
60. Ibid., p. xviii; see also Padula and Smith, "Women in Socialist Cuba," p. 85.
61. Lewis, Lewis, and Rigdon, p. xviii.

Cuba wholeheartedly supported official initiatives to bring women into the work force.

For each of these reasons the turnover rate for women in the Cuban work force remained quite high. In 1969, for example, 106,258 women joined the work force. That same year, 80,781 women quit and returned to their home.[62] Women who joined the work force may have become disillusioned to find that few working women held high-level jobs. Moreover, the vast majority of the female labor force was still clearly doing what had always been considered "women's work."[63] Thus, despite much revolutionary rhetoric, and despite new job opportunities, Cuban women on the whole remained extremely reluctant to take on more outside work and responsibilities.

PHASE TWO

In 1968, as attention turned to the future sugar harvests, the Cuban leaders greatly stepped up their efforts to recruit women into the work force, especially the agricultural and industrial sectors. During this period of the Revolutionary Offensive, the FMC assisted this intensive campaign to encourage women to labor for the Revolution. After a year's efforts, including 396,491 recorded home visits to women, the project actually succeeded in meeting, and even surpassing, its overall goal of hiring 100,000 additional women. This figure raised the percentage of women in the labor force from 15.6 percent in 1968 to 17.7 percent in 1969. Although still within sight of the 1959 figures, the numbers of Cuban working women had clearly risen in impressive fashion. In fact, the 2.1 percent jump surpassed the combined gains of the nine previous years of the Revolution.[64]

Nevertheless, the Revolutionary Offensive concerned itself more with numbers than with equality. Although more Cuban women went to work, their occupations remained much the same. During this period the Cuban government decided that society needed more women to sew, to teach, to nurse, and to perform other traditional tasks. Thus, in urging women to work, Fidel Castro had in mind "suitable" jobs: that is, jobs that did not require physical labor.[65] Castro often stated that although women should participate in "farm work," they must not "do heavy agriculture."[66]

62. Padula and Smith, "Women in Socialist Cuba," p. 85.

63. Jean Stubbs, "Cuba: The Sexual Revolution," in *Latin American Women*, ed. Olivia Harris (London: Minority Rights Group, 1983), p. 18.

64. Lewis, Lewis, and Rigdon, p. xix. See also Purcell, p. 261.

65. Nicola Murray, *Feminist Review* 2 (1969): 69.

66. *GWR*, September 4, 1966, p. 1.

Women, he pronounced, are most suited to be teachers and day-care workers.[67]

In any event, by 1970 the FMC claimed to have incorporated 113,000 women into the work force.[68] The Federation persuaded about one out of four women to go to work. What can account for the success of this campaign? Perhaps most important, the patriotic appeal of the harvest campaign and the energetic propaganda of the "Revolutionary Offensive" attracted many previously unemployed women. The increased availability of day-care centers and boarding schools, combined with a decade of vocational and adult night-school training, also provided better opportunities for female employment.

Moreover, the government took steps in 1969 to make housework chores and household management more convenient and less time-consuming for women. The state extended store hours and gave working women priority at laundries, groceries, and department stores.[69] The government permitted women to stay with ailing relatives at hospitals and allowed women time off from work should illness strike a family member. Since the government never afforded men these special shopping and work privileges, Cuban leaders plainly viewed shopping, laundering, and caring for the ill as primarily female responsibilities.[70] Nonetheless, the government did take practical steps to make work outside the home more attractive for Cuban women.

Women Resist

More than 75 percent of Cuban women, however, did not choose to join the work force at this time. According to a survey in a 1969 *Granma* article, the "weight of tradition" prevented women from entering the labor force. Women cited such reasons as "a woman's career is marriage" and "the woman's place is in the home" for not accepting employment. Of the women who opted out of work outside the home, 59 percent, or nearly three hundred thousand, attributed their negative response to family obligations. Apparently, the 40 percent without family obligations simply valued their freedom from work.[71] With the state's implicit permission, these women chose to remain unemployed.

67. See, for example, *Foreign Broadcast Information Service (FBIS)*, March 7, 1990, p. 4.
68. *Granma*, August 8, 1969.
69. Lewis, Lewis, and Rigdon, p. xix.
70. *Granma*, March 7, 1985, p. 1; Smith and Padula also discuss this in "The Cuban Family," p. 179.
71. *Granma*, August 8, 1969, pp. 1, 3; see also *GWR*, August 31, 1969; Douglas Butterworth, *The People of Buena Ventura* (Urbana: University of Illinois Press, 1980), pp. 35–36;

In a 1969 report the Cuban Academy of Sciences argued that women were avoiding the labor force, in part, because of unstable homes and families. The report found the "Cuban family to be in a state of crisis."[72] The lack of shared responsibility between spouses, the tendency of male laborers to be shifted among work sites, the disillusionment of women who still considered their families to be their chief priority, and a general disorganization of family life permeated Cuban society.[73] Such difficulties, the report contended, kept women in the home.

Moreover, some evidence suggests that both men and women in Cuban society continued to view the woman's role in marriage as inferior and subordinate to that of the man's. A 1970 survey, conducted among twenty-six divorced men and forty-three divorced women in metropolitan Havana, asked who should have the authority in a marriage: the man, the woman, or both? Over 60 percent of divorced men and of divorced women selected the man. At the same time, beliefs reflecting the philosophy of women's liberation or the revolutionary government's ideology concerning work appeared among only a sixth of the respondents.[74]

After the 1970 sugar harvest failed to meet its ten-million-ton objective, Castro expressed disappointment at the low number of women in the labor force. He also noted that, despite official efforts, prostitution still flourished on the streets of Havana.[75] Shortly thereafter, the government—viewing prostitution as a growing, social problem—outlawed it. The authorities rounded up prostitutes, now considered criminals, and incarcerated them or assigned them to labor camps.

In speeches during this period Castro regularly lamented the breakdown of the family and lashed out at women and men for their irresponsible attitudes. He blamed women's reluctance to join the work force on unstable and insecure homes as well as on the daily burdens of housework and family worries. In response, in August 1970 Castro introduced the "Brigades of Militant Mothers for Education." The brigades were to assist

Sutherland, pp. 175–176; Lewis, Lewis, and Rigdon, pp. xviii–xix; Gil Green, *Revolution Cuban Style: Impressions of a Recent Visit* (New York: International Publishers, 1970), pp. 102–103.

72. Padula and Smith, "Women in Socialist Cuba," p. 84.

73. Rene Dumont, "The Militarization of Fidelismo," in *Dissent* 17 (September-October 1970): 420.

74. Cited in Domínguez, pp. 497–498. In the same survey women were significantly more likely than men to believe that women should work for pay outside the home, though 26 percent of the sixty-nine respondents believed an increase in divorce was attributable to women's liberation, while 17 percent said that women ought to work for pay "to help the country's development." As Domínguez has pointed out, this survey suggests that basic beliefs about the family and authority in marriage were still quite traditional.

75. Salas, pp. 102–103; see also Yglesias' discussion of Havana's prostitution problem.

Cuban women with their daily chores and encourage them to join the labor force. These roving groups of housewives counselled women, checked on student attendance, assisted in school upkeep, helped children in collective and individual study, and taught classes as substitute teachers.[76]

To encourage women to work outside the home, the leaders redoubled their verbal pedagoguery. In a speech to the Cuban Confederation of Labor, Castro implored workers to change the "traditional" attitudes of the old Cuba "when women lived off their husbands and served as household decorations."[77] A few months later Castro stated that "work ... [is] the most vital necessity" and that women must join the labor force. Castro underscored his words by announcing the construction of more *círculos* and workplace cafeterias. The "maternity law" of 1974 permitted working mothers to take eighteen weeks of paid maternity leave. The law also offered new mothers an optional nine months of unpaid leave. In addition, the law offered six months unpaid leave for women with children under age sixteen to attend to "family matters." Men were not offered these benefits. Again, the leadership, for all its progressive policies, apparently viewed "family matters" as chiefly a woman's responsibility.

Legislating Sexual Inequality

Despite its continuing idealistic rhetoric, the Cuban government still plainly retained traditional attitudes toward women. The introduction to the new Constitution, for example, made no reference to fatherhood, but instead stated that the government "protects the family, motherhood and matrimony."[78] Moreover, the March 1971 antiloafing law, adopted to combat serious absentee and vagrancy problems among workers, did not apply to women. Neither did the Compulsory Military Service Law.[79] Minister of Labor Jorge Risquet explained the rationale for excluding women from the antiloafing law:

> There are men and there are women. The problem isn't the same for both. Women have the job of reproducing as well as producing.

76. *GWR,* August 30, 1970; see also text of Fidel Castro's speech to the FMC on August 23, 1970, in *Our Power Is That of the Working People* (New York: Pathfinder Press, 1970).

77. Fidel Castro speech on November 15, 1973, full text in *GWR,* November 25, 1973.

78. The complete text of the Family Code can be found in ibid., April 3, 1975, pp. 3–5; see also April 20, 1975.

79. Lewis, Lewis, and Rigdon, pp. xxv–xxvi; see also Maurice Halperin, *The Taming of Fidel Castro* (Berkeley and Los Angeles: University of California Press, 1981), p. 148.

That is, they have to take care of the house, raise the children and do other tasks along these lines and this is no cinch. From the political point of view our people wouldn't understand if we were to treat women and men alike. While people are incensed on seeing a lazy man, the problem isn't always viewed the same way when it involves the case of an idle girl who doesn't study, work or take care of a house. . . . The problem isn't viewed the same and really, it isn't the same thing.[80]

In a December 1973 speech Castro characterized women as "nature's workshop where life is formed."[81] The Cuban leader encouraged women to join the labor force, claiming that the workplace needed "female virtues."[82] A year later, in a speech to the FMC, Castro referred to special "inequalities" between men and women. Since nature had made women "physically weaker than men," Castro claimed that women were entitled to "certain small privileges" and to "special considerations" and courtesies. He also called for greater efforts to instill in children proper standards of conduct and "proletarian courtesies," such as "men giving up their seats to women on buses":

If women are physically weaker, if women have to be mothers, if on top of their social obligations, if on top of their work, they carry the weight of reproduction, and are the ones that carry in their innermost beings the child to be born . . . it is just for society to give them all the respect and consideration that they are worthy of. . . . If in human society there should be any privilege, . . . there should be small privileges and inequalities in women's favor. . . . Proletarian chivalry should exist, proletarian courtesy . . . and consideration toward women.

Castro continued:

Men . . . are . . . obliged to give their seat to a pregnant woman in a bus, or to an elderly woman. . . . You must always have special considerations for others. We have them for women because they are physically weaker, and because they have tasks and functions and human burdens which we do not have![83]

80. *Granma*, September 9, 1970, p. 5; see also Salas, p. 346.
81. *GWR*, December 30, 1973.
82. Lewis, Lewis, and Rigdon, p. xxvii.
83. Fidel Castro speech on November 29, 1974, cited in Domínguez, p. 270; see also Carlos Alberto Montaner, *Secret Report on the Cuban Revolution* (London: Transaction Books, 1981), pp. 96–97.

Certainly, most Cuban women, like most Cuban men, preferred to be treated courteously, yet Castro chose to couch his discussion of courtesy in terms of a traditional chivalry toward women, not a progressive attitude of equality with women.[84]

In a 1975 survey, undertaken to discern why so few Cuban women had joined the labor force, most of the 251 women questioned complained about the burdens of their housework. The survey revealed that women worked an average of 24.5 hours a week in the house. Understandably, since their husbands remained unwilling to assist with housework, many Cuban women were strongly disinclined to accept full-time work.[85] Indeed, Castro frankly acknowledged that full equality between the sexes did not yet exist in Cuba. "After more than 15 years of Revolution," Castro conceded in a 1974 speech, women's rights are one area in which "we are still politically and culturally behind."[86]

A critic might well question whether Cuban leaders sincerely believed that women deserve the same rights as men. Certainly, many would support as a laudable objective for any society Castro's stated goal of supporting equal opportunities for women in politics and in the workplace. Yet although Article 41 of Chapter V of the 1976 Constitution states that sexual discrimination is prohibited, Article 43 states: "In order to assure the exercise" of women's right to work, "the state sees to it that they are given jobs in keeping with their physical makeup." In fact, the Cuban government barred women from nearly three hundred occupations that the leadership viewed as inappropriate for women.[87] While officials defended this decision by claiming to be concerned about women's well-being, many of the excluded jobs neither posed any obvious danger to health nor required any particular amount of strength. For instance, the government rejected all women as unfit to serve as assistant railway conductors, deep-sea divers, and cemetery workers. Women were even excluded from painting houses that required work five meters or more above the ground.[88] Once again, Castro's paternalism overwhelmed both his egalitarianism and, perhaps, his common sense.

The government's peculiar notions of sexual equality also infected the so-called affirmative action programs designed to implement Article 43. One affirmative action regulation read in part: "In every new factory built

84. See discussion of this in Lewis, Lewis, and Rigdon, p. xxv.

85. Padula and Smith, "Women in Socialist Cuba," p. 87.

86. *GWR,* December 8, 1974, p. 2.

87. See draft of Constitution in ibid., April 20, 1975, pp. 7–10; also in *Granma,* January 15, 1976; see also Padula and Smith, "Women in Socialist Cuba," p. 85; Lewis, Lewis, and Rigdon, p. xxv.

88. Domínguez, p. 501.

in any Cuban town, it must be indicated *what work is to be given to women* so there will be time enough to proceed with the selection and training of those women" (emphasis added).[89] Thus, instead of allowing women to compete with men for the same jobs, the government simply labelled certain jobs as "appropriate for women." Castro rejected the more radical possibility of a quota system that would reserve a representative proportion of jobs for female applicants, in favor of a program that froze certain job categories for women, while closing off others to them.

The policy of giving women protected access to certain "appropriate" jobs guaranteed women a place in the work force. Some might even argue that it ensured the most efficient use of Cuba's labor pool. However that may be, the policy undeniably categorized the least physically demanding and most unskilled jobs as "women's work." The government would deliver to women tasks it considered suited to female skills, while preserving the rest of the jobs for men. This approach, the leaders believed, would avoid problems inherent in prescribing exactly the same job for men and women. However, if one delves behind the leadership's high-minded principles of sexual equality, one might well conclude from the foregoing that Cuban leaders themselves discriminated on the basis of sex in their labor policies.[90]

The Record of Women in Politics

The same sexist attitudes that marred the leadership's labor policies may be found in the internal politics of the time. By the mid–1970s few Cuban women had attained leadership posts. Although by 1975 women comprised 25 percent of the Cuban work force, the state failed to nominate them for Vanguard Worker status or for membership in the Communist Party or the Union of Young Communists.[91] In 1974, nearly fifteen years after the Revolution, women represented only 12.7 percent of the Party. That same year women held fewer than 15 percent of the leadership positions in production, services, and administration.[92]

Moreover, most work sites in which women held leadership posts consisted only of women. Virtually no Cuban woman led or supervised Cuban men in any political or economic field.[93] The status of women in CDRs illustrates their minimal progress. While the military had always

89. *GWR*, December 8, 1974; see also Lewis, Lewis, and Rigdon, p. xxv.
90. See Lewis, Lewis, and Rigdon, pp. xxv–xxvi.
91. *GWR*, December 8, 1974, pp. 2–4.
92. Ibid., December 8, 1974; see also Lewis, Lewis, and Rigdon, p. xx.
93. Purcell, p. 268; see also Yglesias, p. 205.

been dominated by men, the CDRs were a new revolutionary creation that could have served as an example of an egalitarian, revolutionary institution. Yet while women were relatively well represented among activists on the block level, only a tiny handful rose to more significant high-level positions.[94]

The 1974 "People's Power" elections in Matanzas Province highlight the small percentage of women in politics. Women represented only 7 percent of those running for these relatively low-level positions, and women eventually comprised less than 3 percent of the candidates elected in the province.[95] Discussing these results at the FMC Second Congress, Fidel Castro mourned that he belonged to a "party of men and a state of men and a government of men."[96] He later remarked that the Matanzas election result "demonstrates just how women still suffer from discrimination and inequality and how we are still currently backward, and how in the corners of our consciousness [we] live on old habits out of the past."[97]

Through such rhetorical appeals the Cuban government in the mid-1970s encouraged the masses to elect women to middle-rank political offices, particularly on the provincial level. However, the leadership made few serious efforts to recruit women into positions at the highest levels of government. In 1975 only six women served on the Party's one-hundred-member Central Committee. No woman served on either the Political Bureau or the Secretariat. Nor did many women serve in the hierarchy of the Revolutionary Armed Forces. Although fairly large numbers of women attended the FAR's officer-training schools, very few ever rose above the lower ranks.[98]

Cuban leaders also failed to promote women to leadership positions within the legal profession. The government included only a few women on the Law Study Commissions established between 1969 and 1974 to redraft the civil, penal, and family codes and create a new Constitution. Not a single woman served on the Central Preparatory Commission of the First Party Congress.[99] Women were also extremely underrepresented in leadership posts in the Party and in state institutions.

94. Lewis, Lewis, and Rigdon, p. xxi; see also Moreno, p. 482.

95. Stubbs, p. 18; see also Padula and Smith, "Women in Socialist Cuba," p. 86; Lewis, Lewis, and Rigdon, p. xxi.

96. Fidel Castro speech to FMC on November 25, 1974, full text in *GWR*, December 8, 1974; see also Elizabeth Stone, ed., *Women and the Cuban Revolution* (New York: Pathfinder Press, 1981), p. 71. Also cited in Padula and Smith, "Women in Socialist Cuba," p. 86.

97. Complete text of speech in *GWR*, October 23, 1977.

98. Ibid., August 24, 1975, p. 5; see also Lewis, Lewis, and Rigdon, pp. xx–xxi; Montaner, p. 89.

99. Lewis, Lewis, and Rigdon, p. xxi.

The Need for New Policies

By 1975 the Cuban government confronted a labor shortage that women found little incentive to fill. Yet repairing the deteriorating economy would require more laborers. Moreover, many believed that fifteen years of continual efforts to influence women to join the labor force had destabilized the Cuban family. The rhetoric of equality and the revised divorce laws contributed to widespread dissatisfaction among Cuban women with their marriages and a consequent sharp rise in the divorce rate, which reached a shocking 18.1 percent by the early 1970s.[100] Women, almost always granted custody in divorce settlements, often emerged from the broken home with added burdens, responsibilities, and financial woes.

Cuban leaders realized that women on the island remained strapped by social attitudes and by the housework that they alone performed. Before women would feel secure enough to venture out and join the labor force, Cuban men would have to help to shoulder the burden of family care. Thus, in the mid-1970s several major gender-related problems confronted the Castro government. To remedy the situation, the leadership undertook a different set of policy initiatives.

PHASE THREE

In 1974 the Cuban government launched nationwide discussions of women's rights and the relationships between husband and wife, parents and children, and home and community. The discussions, carried out in work centers throughout the country, led to the drafting of the Family Code. This Code, which called for full equality in the home, stated that husband and wife were to share equally in housekeeping duties and in children's education and upbringing. The Code decreed that parents raise children to become "worthy citizens" with proper values and attitudes toward the Revolution. In this regard the Code obligated both parents to set examples for their children by participating in official organizations and in voluntary productive labor campaigns.[101]

The Family Code, adopted on February 24, 1976, thus had three principal objectives. First, in recognizing and reinforcing the pervasive influence of the Cuban family, the Code sought to preserve and strengthen family

100. Lowry Nelson, *Cuba: The Measure of a Revolution* (Minneapolis: University of Minnesota Press, 1972), p. 154.
101. *GWR*, March 16, 1975, pp. 7–9; see also Lewis, Lewis, and Rigdon, p. xxii.

ties, which had loosened considerably during the previous fifteen years. Thus, the Code illustrated the leadership's inclination to accommodate traditional Cuban culture. As government official Blas Roca, who supervised the writing of the Code, explained: "Reality ... should [not] be adjusted to fit institutions; the institutions are what must be adjusted to fit reality."[102] Roca suggested that the state both preserve the traditional family structure and encourage women to join the labor force. Second, the Code also aimed to transfer some of the burdens of housework and child rearing from mother to father, giving women freedom to leave the home and join the work force. Finally, the new law attempted to increase citizen participation in government policies.

The extensive discussions carried out throughout Cuba regarding the new code succeeded in influencing popular attitudes toward women. A 1975 survey found that, of fifty-seven well-paid workers interviewed, nearly all supported incorporating women into the paid labor force. The change in attitudes, however, occurred within clear boundaries. The majority of those interviewed said that women should work only because the Revolution needed the production, not because women might find fulfillment outside the home.[103] Despite extensive government publicity efforts, such traditional gender attitudes proved to be quite resistant to change.

Traditional Culture Remains Unyielding

In April 1975, as people across the island discussed the Family Code, the government issued a survey to find out why so few women ran in the 1974 People's Power elections and why far fewer had been elected. More than 60 percent of men and women surveyed responded that women had too many responsibilities at home to take on the added burden of political duties. In the same survey citizens were asked why men did not have the same responsibilities at home as women. Ignoring years of official rhetoric on the subject, more than 30 percent labelled work in the home as women's work. Many men claimed that doing household chores embarrassed them: men would lose social standing if neighbors saw them doing women's

102. *GWR*, October 20, 1974, pp. 4–5; see also Lewis, Lewis, and Rigdon, pp. xxii, xxvii.

103. This survey was conducted by Marifeli Pérez-Stable. Only one worker—a woman—gave what Pérez-Stable classified as a purely feminist response. Cited in Domínguez, p. 498; Pérez-Stable presented the results of her survey in a paper, "Cuba's Workers 1975: A Preliminary Analysis," at the meeting of the Latin American Studies Association, Atlanta, Georgia, March 1976.

work. Others responded by declaring that the woman's role was to care for the husband and children.

The survey went on to ask what attributes female candidates should have. More than 50 percent of the respondents said women candidates should be "moral, serious, decent," yet less than 20 percent expected these same virtues of male candidates.[104] The findings of this survey have since been replicated. Three years after the leadership adopted the Code, another Cuban study showed that working women's share of household chores remained eight times that of working men.[105] Such opinion polls, conducted more than fifteen years after the Revolution, revealed that traditional attitudes toward women persisted in Cuba.

Moreover, evidence suggests that the sexual double standard continued to prevail in Cuban society. A 1975 survey conducted in the town of Batabano, Havana Province, asked citizens to name the most important inventions of the century. The most frequent answers were antibiotics, the radio, and the miniskirt. At the same time, the thesis, or central document, on women's equality discussed at the 1975 First Party Congress noted that many Cuban entertainment programs continued to portray women as sex objects or as passive and ornamental creatures suitable only for housework and marriage. Beauty pageants for the carnival, for instance, took place across revolutionary Cuba. Rather than calling for the abolition of such contests, the Party Congress asked only for further "study," noting the widespread popularity of this form of entertainment.[106]

Despite the evident failure of its cultural policies regarding women, the leadership did not give up. Following the First Congress of the Cuban Communist Party in 1975, work centers, mass organizations, and study groups discussed a central Party resolution entitled "On the Full Exercise of Women's Equality." The resolution called on Cubans to eradicate their tendencies to make women objects of exhibition and to evaluate men and women equally on "moral problems": "[W]hat is socially acceptable for men should be equally acceptable for women. . . . Both men and women must be equally free and responsible in determining their sexual relationships." It stated that "women will enjoy equal economic, political, and social rights with men."[107] It also declared, "Manliness is not in contradiction with housework and childcare, and femininity does not run contrary

104. Stubbs, p. 18; see also Cynthia Cockburn, "Women and Family in Cuba," in *Cuba: The Second Decade*, ed. John Griffiths and Peter Griffiths (London: Writers and Readers Publishing Cooperative, 1979), pp. 157–168.

105. Survey cited in Smith and Padula, "The Cuban Family," p. 179; see also *Boletin Demanda* 3, no. 1 (Havana: Cuban Institute for Internal Demand, 1978).

106. Domínguez, p. 497.

107. Cockburn, pp. 154–155.

to any field of work, study or responsibilities in daily life."[108] By introducing and publicizing this resolution, the leaders once again reminded citizens, perhaps disingenuously, that gender roles must change in a revolutionary society.

Women in the Labor Force

Despite the efforts manifested in the Family Code, the government's vigorous propaganda campaign, and the resolution at the First Congress to make social equality an important issue, women joined the ranks of Cuban workers quite slowly. In 1976, 600,000 women worked outside the home. Despite lucrative maternity leave, women continued to drop out of the labor force almost as quickly as they joined.[109] For example, women comprised only a few of 1,400 workers at a rice processing center, 12 of 172 laborers at a cattle insemination center, 15 of 107 workers at a tobacco research center, only 30 of 172 workers at a thermoelectric factory in Camaguey, only 40 of 470 workers at a cement factory, only 200 of 1,000 workers at a fishing center in Pinar del Río, and less than 10 percent of the workers at a refrigerator factory in Ciego de Avila.[110]

While some women joined the work force only to drop out shortly thereafter, others remained unemployed because of shortages in day-care programs. By 1976 the government operated 654 nurseries throughout Cuba serving approximately 48,000 families. While perhaps a laudable effort, these day-care centers were not sufficiently numerous to serve a large percentage of the total population. Indeed, by 1980 the *círculos* could still only care for about 8 percent of Cuba's children the age of six and under.[111] Out of economic necessity, however, the leadership regretfully slowed the construction of *círculos.* Alongside the day-care shortfalls, Cuba also lacked enough laundries and cafeterias to ease household management.[112] These reasons contributed to keeping Cuban women in the home.

Throughout the 1970s the percentage of women in the work force did steadily increase. On occasion Cuban women served as cane cutters and citrus-fruit pickers, automotive mechanics and engineers, dentists and doctors, and traffic police.[113] Some became members of the FAR. A few even took charge of coffee plants and sugar mills.[114] Nonetheless, a tradi-

108. Stubbs, p. 19.
109. Cockburn, p. 156.
110. Joe Nicholson, Jr., *Inside Cuba* (New York: Sheed and Ward, 1974), pp. 96–99.
111. Padula and Smith, "Women in Socialist Cuba," p. 85.
112. Wald, pp. 29–30.
113. Purcell, p. 266.
114. See Sutherland, pp. 174–175.

tional division of labor between men and women continued to characterize the Cuban workplace. The vast majority of Cuban working women remained in the traditional, low-paying service sector. In the late 1970s, for example, women made up 80 percent of the work force in the textile industry and 50 percent of those laboring in the plastics industry. Although women dominated social services and welfare, few worked in construction.[115] Often women's work merely supplemented or substituted for men's labor. Women would typically replace men in such tasks as waiting on tables and providing restaurant kitchen help, thereby permitting men to go on to "more productive" areas.[116] In the mid-1970s many women temporarily took the jobs of their husbands who had been called to serve military time in Angola. While the leadership repeatedly endorsed women's rights, sexual equality did not swiftly become an integral part of the Cuban workplace.

By the late 1970s women had, however, gained substantial educational opportunities. Women made up nearly half of the total university students in Cuba, as well as half of the medical students, 30 percent of the engineering students, and 90 percent of the students in education. The government also stepped up its training of women officers at the Military Technical Institute.[117] Cuban leaders contributed to these gains by launching a plan in the late 1970s to build hundreds of additional boarding schools in the countryside. Designed for junior and senior high school students, these new schools included agricultural work as part of the curriculum. Students would be allowed to return home only on weekends for brief visits.[118] This measure allowed women more available time that they could commit to employment.

In 1980, after more than twenty years of official efforts to incorporate women into the workplace, women accounted for 27.3 percent of the Cuban labor force. One might wonder how this number compares to the percentage of working women in Cuba's neighboring Latin American countries. In 1980 women made up 27.8 percent of Mexico's work force, 27.4 percent of Argentina's, and 21.2 percent of Venezuela's work force. In 1984 women comprised 40.8 percent of Colombia's work force.[119] In short, the percentage of women in Cuba's labor force simply remained on par with the percentage of women in other labor forces in the region.

From this perspective the Castro government's long-standing efforts to

115. Leiner, p. 15; see also Padula and Smith, "Women in Socialist Cuba," p. 85.
116. Leiner, pp. 14–15; see also Purcell, pp. 267–269.
117. Camarano, p. 52; see also Purcell, p. 266.
118. Smith and Padula, "The Cuban Family," pp. 179–180.
119. These statistics were taken from the *Yearbook of Labor Statistics,* International Labor Office, Geneva.

bring women into the labor force, when compared to the negligible efforts of other Latin American governments, were disappointing. Moreover, while educational opportunities for Cuban women had improved substantially throughout the first thirty years of the Revolution, the rest of Latin America had also witnessed those significant advances. Indeed, during the second half of the twentieth century, the level of educational achievements among women in most Latin American societies rose to approximately equal that of men.[120]

Contrary to official rhetoric, no true women's revolution occurred in Cuba either in educational institutions or in the work force. Indeed, women still held a secondary position in many areas of society. In 1979, for example, women represented less than 17 percent of participants in competitive sports.[121] Moreover, the concept of *machismo* dominated many social relations, even among younger people in the schools, the FAR, the universities, and the workplace.[122] In this regard it is perhaps revealing that during the 1970s the number of prostitutes in Havana actually increased.[123]

PHASE FOUR

In 1986 Fidel Castro unveiled to the Cuban people his Rectification Campaign. In radically redefining the government's priorities, Castro emphasized uncompromising economic austerity, labor discipline, mass dedication, and struggle. He also called for a revitalized *conciencia* to bolster political support and to encourage sacrifice for the faltering economy. One might wonder which direction women's policies would take in this new stage of Cuba's revolutionary history.

In fact, the evidence suggests that the Cuban leaders no longer viewed women's issues as imperative in creating proper *conciencia*. Certainly the island's overwhelmingly male leadership subordinated the concerns of many Cuban women. At the March 1990 FMC Congress, Fidel Castro publicly informed the Federation that irrelevant "women's issues," such as job opportunities and equal pay, would "be postponed because of other issues of pressing national concern." Rectification, he explained, required

120. *Washington Post,* March 29, 1992, p. A26.
121. Padula and Smith, "Women in Socialist Cuba," p. 87.
122. Leiner, p. 15.
123. In a 1977 speech Castro lamented this social illness. See *Granma,* September 28, 1977; Salas, pp. 102–103. Also see Domínguez, p. 498; *Verde Olivo* 9, no. 40 (October 6, 1968): 61; *GWR,* May 16, 1971, p. 5; June 13, 1971, p. 4.

some goals to be sacrificed for more compelling ones, such as higher production, stronger defense, and unquestioning loyalty to the Revolution. In insisting that we must not "waste our time" on other matters, Castro hinted that the government, for the moment, would simply ignore less important female concerns.[124]

Women in the Work Force

While Castro offered women little in the Rectification Campaign, he fully expected their uncompromising support and unflinching labor. Indeed, he called on women to contribute their "productive energies" to the effort to rebuild the badly crippled economy. In a 1991 speech Vilma Espín encouraged the women of her organization "to join contingents, to work in the fields, to work in the Pan American Games construction works."[125]

In order to lure women into the Cuban labor force to contribute their "productive labor" to the nation, the government continued to open daycare centers. By 1990 Fidel Castro claimed that more than 400,000 students attended "semiboarding" schools and another 140,000 were registered in the nation's 1,100 círculos.[126] To further simplify the chore of child care for Cuba's women, Castro informed citizens that more day-care centers would remain open twenty-four hours so that mothers could contribute even more service to the Revolution. He commented: "At seven at night the day-care center closes. There are 13 hours, we could add—15 or 16 hours—to a service the country could provide to mothers, to working mothers. . . . Now by having the day-care centers . . . operating 24 hours a day, the task becomes easier."[127] Such a measure, it was hoped, would enhance productivity and improve education.

In 1990 the government also announced that, in an effort to address the complaints of Cuban women, it would soon introduce a plan that would allow men to take unpaid leave from work to care for children when their wives held more useful positions in the workplace.[128] Although the government couched this policy in terms of a concession to women and a triumph for women's rights, it may also be viewed as an economically pragmatic move. If a woman contributed more than her husband to the

---

124. *GWR*, March 18, 1990, p. 12.
125. *FBIS*, March 11, 1991, p. 7.
126. Without these schools, Castro asked, "how many women would work?" Fidel Castro speech, *GWR*, March 18, 1990, pp. 7–8; see also ibid., January 21, 1990, p. 10; Castro speech in *FBIS*, March 8, 1990, p. 2.
127. *FBIS*, March 7, 1990, p. 10.
128. Ibid., January 26, 1990, p. 2.

national economy, the government could better afford to release her husband from work responsibilities. And government officials, not the husband and wife, would decide which position provided a more valuable service to society. Once again, Castro's policy initiatives toward women owed much to his sense of economic pragmatism.

Continuing Attitude Problems

By the late 1980s the leadership began once again to chide Cubans for not significantly changing their attitudes toward women. FMC President Vilma Espín blamed parents and boyfriends for continuing to discourage young women from taking jobs in fields not ordinarily viewed as women's work.[129] A 1987 *Granma Weekly Review* article chastised Cubans for harboring unacceptable attitudes toward women. In Cuban homes, the article stated,

> there are still unjust and archaic concepts that place the burden of housework and child care on women. . . . Cuban women have far less free time than men for they spend about five hours on housework. . . . Cuban women still face subjective problems that often prevent them from holding down important positions on the job or doing work traditionally done by men.[130]

Moreover, between 1970 and 1990 the percentage of women in the work force never showed the startling increases the leaders hoped for. Relatively few women joined the labor brigades. In October 1987, for example, only three thousand women worked in the labor brigades of twenty thousand Cubans.[131] In 1990, according to government figures, women comprised 38 percent of the Cuban labor force.[132] Since 1959, then, the percentage of women in the work force increased about 20 percent. While this certainly amounts to a respectable growth, the trend of increasing numbers of working women had begun at least a decade before the Revolution and had been reflected in societies throughout Latin America.

129. Padula and Smith, "Women in Socialist Cuba," p. 87; *Latin America Weekly Report* (Great Britain), March 11, 1983, p. 3.

130. *GWR,* July 19, 1987, p. 9.

131. Ibid., October 5, 1987, p. 1.

132. Ibid., March 18, 1990, p. 7. The Cuban government has also stated that women comprise less than 25 percent of Cuba's economically active population. I am not sure what this figure means. If that is a more accurate number than the 38 percent, then the percentage of women in the Cuban labor force in the 1990s is only slightly above the 1953 figure. The Cubans used this figure in ibid., April 6, 1986, p. 2.

Cuban women also continued to work considerably fewer days and hours than men and earned substantially smaller incomes.[133] Moreover, women did not play a leading role in intellectual fields. At a 1983 international conference in Havana on health, *Granma* identified twenty-one Cubans who were presenting papers. Only one was a woman.[134] In sports, male athletes gained the most acclaim within Cuban society. In January 1991 the Party newspaper *Granma* hailed the seventeen most popular and outstanding athletes of 1990. Only four were women.[135] After decades of government rhetoric, the degree to which Cuban culture remained unchanged strongly suggests that Cubans were unwilling to adopt the revolutionary attitudes toward women espoused by their leaders.

Of course if the leaders of the Castro government themselves retained many traditional attitudes toward women, Cuban citizens may have been receiving conflicting, and therefore less persuasive, signals. At the Fifth Congress of the Union of Young Communists, Castro told youth that schools would have to cut their budgets and could not waste resources on such unnecessary matters as the activities of "girls."[136] At the same Congress Castro predicted that the present crisis would be overcome because "Cuba has a rich history of men of exceptional ideas." That he neglected to mention women was perhaps a telling oversight.[137] Three years later, as Castro urged society to make sacrifices, he warned Cubans that they would be expected to wear out their old clothes before receiving new ones. Yet he hastened to assure men that despite the shortage of textiles, "our women will be well-dressed."[138]

A 1990 *Granma* article on the growing popularity of aerobics among women noted, "The girls here are a dream come true . . . and radiate beauty through every pore."[139] Indeed, in a 1986 speech Castro congratulated women for the progress they had made in achieving egalitarianism. As examples of women's progress he cited the fact that many housewives had been vaccinated for tetanus and that more than 1.5 million women held membership in the "Mother's Movement for Education."[140] Castro's concepts of progress and liberation for women plainly differed from those of most modern supporters of women's rights.

133. According to a 1986 *GWR* article, "The burden of domestic tasks generally forces women to work fewer days or shorter hours than men." Ibid., March 30, 1986, p. 2. See also January 12, 1986, p. 2; December 18, 1988, p. 12.

134. Padula and Smith, "Women in Socialist Cuba," p. 89.

135. *GWR,* January 13, 1991, p. 4.

136. Ibid., April 19, 1987, p. 11.

137. Ibid., April 12, 1987, p. 3.

138. *FBIS,* October 1, 1990, p. 12.

139. *GWR,* April 29, 1990, p. 1.

140. Fidel Castro speech, ibid., February 16, 1986, pp. 12–14.

In August 1992, in a curious semantic sleight of hand, Castro even went so far as to defend prostitution, provided it satisfied the needs of tourists. Cuban women who sell sex, he assured his listeners, could not be considered prostitutes because prostitution "is not allowed in our country." Rather, Castro maintained, these women are "*jineteras*," not prostitutes, since no one forces them to sell themselves to their customers. "Those [women] who do so do it on their own," Castro observed, "voluntarily, and without any need for it." The Cuban leader went on to boast that his country's "*jineteras*" were "highly educated hookers and quite healthy."[141] The contradictions in Castro's views of prostitution suggest, once again, that the government's policies regarding women may have failed in part because the leaders themselves were incapable of changing their views of Cuban women.

Sexist Policies

The Cuban leaders' underlying traditional attitudes toward women also repeatedly surfaced in their policies. For instance, repeating his theme of the late 1970s, Fidel Castro announced in the early 1980s that, because of the world recession and shortage of hard currency, some nonessential workers would be laid off. He assured Cuban men that female laborers would be the first to go and that the best jobs would be reserved, as always, for men.[142] In August 1986 the government again reiterated that men, particularly those who had concluded active military service, would receive the most attractive positions.[143]

In 1988 the leadership moved to "rationalize" employment in order to increase efficiency and productivity. This meant placing workers in jobs most appropriately fit for them. Women seeking employment, Castro explained, would "work in day-care centers."[144] In encouraging women to take jobs as housekeepers and waitresses, Castro tried to reassure women that people had come to view waitressing in a more favorable light. Women have overcome the shame of working in coffee shops, he insisted, since waiting tables was no longer viewed as denigrating, servile labor.[145]

Thus, at the same time that the leadership reserved the best jobs in

141. *Washington Post,* August 9, 1992, p. A31; see also ibid., January 2, 1993, p. A20.

142. *Latin America Weekly Report,* March 28, 1980; see also Padula and Smith, "Women in Socialist Cuba," p. 88.

143. *GWR,* August 3, 1986, p. 1.

144. Ibid., February 21, 1988, p. 3. For another discussion of "rationalization," see *Granma,* April 18, 1991, p. 2.

145. *GWR,* August 24, 1987, p. 8.

society for men, they encouraged women to take the less desirable positions. Once again, Castro reverted to the tactic of substituting rhetoric and propaganda for real progress in pursuing sexual equality. In late 1990 he complained that the state needed agricultural workers so badly that "work in plantain processing centers is accessible to even women." Castro assured Cuba's supposedly fragile women that "it will not be necessary to carry the somewhat heavy bunches. . . . [O]ne does not have to walk too far, but walking is always necessary."[146]

The Weakness
of the Women's Leadership

Throughout the 1980s Cuba's highest leaders rarely mentioned women's issues or equality between the sexes. These topics had clearly moved away from the mainstream of Cuban propaganda. Even the FMC's President Vilma Espín devoted very little time in her speeches to feminist issues. When addressing the FMC, Castro himself mentioned women's issues infrequently, even in speeches of many hours. By the end of the 1980s the evidence suggests that Fidel Castro viewed the FMC as little more than a female labor organization from which to draw loyal workers and public support, useful in domestic and international circles.[147]

Through the years the FMC remained thoroughly incapable of acting without the permission of Fidel Castro. In September 1990, while celebrating its thirtieth anniversary, the Federation thanked Castro for creating and guiding the organization.[148] That same year, at the FMC's Fifth Congress, one member called on the Congress to announce that its primary objective was to "prevent Fidel from being burdened down with the problems of the moment. . . . [W]ith our work and progress we will make him happy."[149]

In her closing speech at the Congress FMC President Vilma Espín advanced the notion that Cuban women were "radiating with joy" because Fidel, "our dear commander and chief," who has guided us "and our work with skillful hands and unyielding firmness," is with us again. Espín lectured women that their job was to work to promote "savings, efficiency, and quality" and to fulfill their part in the food program and in defense.

146. *FBIS,* October 4, 1990, p. 4.
147. See, for example, Castro's speech to the FMC Congress in *Cuba Internacional* (June 1990): 16–21. He did not speak of women's issues.
148. *GWR,* September 2, 1990, p. 9.
149. Ibid., March 18, 1990, p. 12.

In typically fawning terms she told Castro, "We live proudly . . . being your soldiers" and we "reaffirm our willingness to fully devote ourselves to production and defense . . . as Fidel has asked us."[150] Apparently the FMC leadership considered ensuring Fidel Castro's happiness to be a transcendent objective. This can scarcely be considered a particularly feminist, or revolutionary, goal.

In the second half of the 1980s the Cuban government admitted that it had failed to bring about sweeping changes in attitudes toward women. In the mid-1980s two scholars, Isabel Lauguia, an Argentine, and John DuMoulin, an American, both of whom had lived in Cuba since the early 1960s, observed that raising girls with feminine traits results in a serious handicap for Cuban women.[151] In February 1986 Castro himself lamented that only "slight progress" had been made in promoting women to positions of responsibility in state agencies, administrations, and local bodies of People's Power.

Rather than examining the evident shortcomings of its own policies, however, the leadership simply blamed the family for not sufficiently "battling" to bring about sexual equality. A January 1991 *Granma Weekly Review* article blamed parents for raising their children with a "double standard." The learning process, the article argued, "starts with the family." Parents unwisely continued to bring up their "children with a marked difference between boys and girls." Consequently, the article stated, children became heir to a set of values, personal principles, and myths passed on from one year to the next.[152]

Despite all the revolutionary rhetoric, in early 1991 Cuban women still held an unmistakably inferior position in both the Party and the political structure, the essential sources of power in Castro's society. Women comprised only 21.5 percent of the Party, representing only 13.8 percent of the Party cadres and 19 percent of the UJC cadres. Very few held official positions. In the late 1980s women accounted for only 23 percent of the 499 deputies on the National Assembly.[153] Of the 225 Party members elected to the Central Committee in October 1991, only thirty-seven (16 percent) were women. In addition, at this time women represented only about 10 percent of Cuba's ambassadors.[154]

150. *FBIS,* March 7, 1990, p. 9; March 9, 1990, p. 3; *GWR,* March 18, 1990, p. 12.

151. Smith and Padula discuss their work "The Cuban Family," p. 177; see also Isabel Lauguia and John DuMoulin, *Hacía una concepción científica de la emancipación de la mujer* (Havana: Editorial de Ciencias Socialistas, 1983).

152. *GWR,* January 27, 1991, p. 3.

153. Juan M. del Aguila, *Cuba: Dilemmas of a Revolution* (Boulder: Westview Press, 1984), p. 145.

154. Padula and Smith, "Women in Socialist Cuba," p. 89.

In fact, not a single woman ever served on the Secretariat, which the government eliminated in October 1991. Until the 1991 Party Congress, only one woman, Vilma Espín, the head of the FMC and the wife of Raúl Castro, had served on the Political Bureau, the most powerful institution in society. At the Congress the leadership removed Espín from the Political Bureau and named three other women to the twenty-five-member Bureau.[155] While this modest increase in numbers at the Political Bureau may have encouraged some women, the record of the Castro government in appointing women to high political posts fell far short of its revolutionary rhetoric.

By the most recent phase of the Revolution, women's position in Cuban society had weakened substantially. As economic problems consumed the government, authorities abandoned or overlooked women's issues. Although the government continued to demand from women labor, support, and loyalty, it offered few tangible benefits in return.

CONCLUSION

This examination of the women's movement in revolutionary Cuba illustrates three cardinal points. First, Castro's full commitment to sexual equality must be questioned. He was consistently more concerned with augmenting the size of the Cuban labor force than with achieving equality between the sexes.[156] The chief reason the work force needed more workers was the exodus in the early 1960s of more than six hundred thousand Cubans, many of whom were middle-class professionals. This situation created a void in the labor force and an urgent need for agronomists, engineers, doctors, accountants, dentists, and other trained professionals. Moreover, running a socialist government and a centrally planned economy required a vast number of able bureaucrats and technicians, administrators and managers, as well as a significant increase in the number of lower-status laborers.[157] And the significant expansion of social services, from medical to educational, required additional workers. Modernizing women's role in society presented a way to fulfill some of these pressing labor needs.

Bringing women into the work force, however, meant eradicating pre-

155. See, for example, *Miami Herald,* International Edition, October 17, 1991, p. 4A.
156. Purcell, p. 259.
157. Ibid., p. 262; see also Leiner, pp. 11–12.

revolutionary attitudes that stressed the traditional role of women in the home and the belief that women were to avoid work if possible. Such cultural values and opinions clashed with the leadership's primary objective of increasing the size of the labor force. In addition, the discrimination against women, the low level of female aspirations, and the sexually based stereotyping of many traditionally male occupations hindered the government's revolutionary goals. Hence, Cuban leaders created the FMC to mobilize women and to inculcate both men and women with new attitudes that were more appropriate for the state's objectives.

Although women did gain significant rights and status from many of the government's policies, the degree to which true sexual equality ever formed a serious objective for the government is open to debate. Even though the goals of equality and increasing the labor force often complemented one another, Vilma Espín, President of the FMC, seems to have viewed her organization as primarily a labor brigade and a feminine support group for Fidel Castro's policies. She routinely subordinated the aggressive promotion of sexual equality and the personal growth of women to other official objectives.[158]

Second, while Cuban leaders continually claimed to advocate full equality and enlightened social attitudes toward women, they themselves never fully relinquished their traditional views of women's role in society. Although Castro encouraged sweeping changes in attitudes toward women, his government's treatment of women did not set an example for Cubans to follow. Fidel Castro himself was perhaps too much the *caudillo,* and the quintessential gun-carrying, jeep-driving, cigar-smoking *macho,* to change his basic attitudes toward women. His views toward women were perhaps as inherently part of his character and identity as were his army fatigues. In order to succeed in transforming attitudes, the government would have had to change its strategies in dramatic fashion. Carlos Alberto Montaner perceptively observed: "[The government would have to] concoct a different mythology, adopt other manners, and castrate the revolution. . . . [T]he revolutionary thing would be to eradicate the masculine accent, the machismo style which rules over Cuba's public life. . . . But that would be like asking for a different revolution."[159]

Viewed as a whole, the Cuban government's policies reflected both the leaders' clever rhetorical zeal and their lack of commitment to many goals of women. In fact, the leadership essentially accommodated and accepted prerevolutionary attitudes toward women. The government's acceptance

158. See Padula and Smith, "Women in Socialist Cuba," p. 87. See also Purcell, p. 262.
159. Montaner, p. 91.

of traditional sexist attitudes found a place in the new Constitution as well as in the leadership's speeches and actions. Even after the substantial changes of the 1986 Rectification Campaign, these attitudes continued to mark the rhetoric and policies of Cuba's revolutionary leaders.

Finally, despite the vast amounts of money and energy expended by the government and the FMC, traditional attitudes toward gender persisted. The Revolution put great pressures on Cuban women. It called upon them to excel "at work, to volunteer, to study, to participate in sports and politics, and to raise families—to be super women."[160] Yet prerevolutionary attitudes toward female occupations, sexual behavior, women in politics, and women's responsibilities in the home endured.

At the Fifth Congress of the FMC in March 1990, Fidel Castro assured his listeners that "the struggle for women's equality in all aspects is a priority task of our Party.... [I]t was, is and will be a priority task of our revolution."[161] One wonders if those hundreds of delegates listening truly believed that they would soon witness sexual equality in Cuba. Indeed, one might question whether women's equality was still a leading objective of the Cuban government or had become merely a propaganda ploy to bolster the size of the labor force and to justify control over the education of Cuban children.

In short, the substantial disparity between the leadership's rhetoric and its actual policies toward women calls into question the notion that a chief objective of the Revolution was to ensure full equality between the sexes. The government had many opportunities to assure women, through fair, noncoercive measures, equal access to jobs, political positions, and leadership roles. It could have given women equal rights in the workplace, a voice in telling political decisions, and a leadership role in the Revolutionary process. In fact, however, the government repeatedly failed to take the fundamental steps necessary to transform the rhetoric of equality into reality.

At some psychological level Cuba's male leaders may have supported the ideals behind sexual equality. Certainly they seem to have appreciated the subsidiary benefits that egalitarian gender policies might deliver. Yet the Castro government cannot be considered revolutionary in its policies toward women: its rhetoric was not sufficiently supported by its actions.

160. Padula and Smith, "Women in Socialist Cuba," p. 79.
161. *GWR*, March 18, 1990, p. 8.

4

The Revolutionary Battle to Transform Attitudes Toward Labor

> Work must be engaged in happily, to the accompaniment of revolutionary songs, amidst fraternal camaraderie and human relationships which are mutually invigorating and uplifting. . . . [W]ork will be man's greatest dignity . . . [W]ork will be a social duty as well as a true human pleasure and the maximum act of creation.
>
> Everyone must be interested in his own work and in that of others. . . . Youth maintains . . . the mentality of the capitalist world—that is, the attitude that work is . . . a sad duty, an unfortunate necessity. Why does this happen? Because we have not yet given . . . work its true meaning.
>
> —Ernesto "Che" Guevara

> We must learn how to create an honorable concept of labor. All our honor . . . must be gathered together to increase the value . . . the importance of labor.
>
> —Fidel Castro

To create a new *conciencia* toward manual labor was critical to the bid by Cuba's Marxist-Leninist government to reform the island's culture and replace troublesome and reactionary attitudes with a host of more appropriate revolutionary views. Indeed, almost immediately after overthrowing the regime of Fulgencio Batista, Fidel Castro and his revolutionary government turned for guidance to the writings of Karl Marx to set forth proper Marxist-Leninist labor objectives.

Marx argued that labor, although dehumanizing and estranging the worker in capitalist society, took on a different meaning altogether in socialist society. He believed that once the economic forces that had given labor its exploitative and destructive characteristics had been eliminated, work would become a positive, enriching element in daily life. Marx wrote that once "subjective and objective" conditions had been created for workers, labor would become "attractive work, the individual's self-realization."[1] The laborer in a harmonious socialist society, Marx argued, would remain flexible as to what task he performs: he would willingly undertake any kind of work that would redound to the whole society's benefit. The socialist worker, Marx maintained, "[becomes] a fully developed individual, fit for a variety of labors, ready to face any change of production, and to whom the different social functions he performs are but so many modes of giving free scope to his own natural and acquired powers."[2] Marx even went so far as to argue that all individuals in socialist society required regular doses of manual labor in order to find happiness and fulfillment. He wrote, "The individual . . . needs a normal portion of work" in his quest to find freedom and self-realization.[3]

In accordance with such Marxist teachings Fidel Castro urged Cubans to eliminate prerevolutionary attitudes toward labor and create a new set of values and attitudes toward work. The leadership called on Cuban citizens to change their understanding and view of work, to see manual labor as honorable and necessary in constructing a revolutionary society. Throughout the first three decades of the Revolution, Cuban leaders employed a wide range of strategies in a persistent and rigorous attempt to inculcate Cubans with a new national labor ethic. These various strategies passed through four distinct phases.

PHASE ONE

Experimentation characterized the first phase of the Castro government's attempt to transform Cuban labor attitudes. During the early 1960s the revolutionary leaders themselves sharply disagreed as to the proper route to achieve their labor goals. Indeed, two opposing sides engaged in a lively debate about tactics. Ernesto "Che" Guevara and his disciples represented one side. These leaders, considering themselves pure communists, endorsed an idealistic line of thought that advocated gradually eliminating money and other material incentives and nationalizing, centralizing, and

---

1. Karl Marx, *Grundrisse: Introduction to the Critique of Political Economy,* trans. and ed. Martin Nicolaus (New York: Vintage Books, 1973), p. 611.

2. Karl Marx, quoted in John G. Gurley, *Challengers to Capitalism: Marx, Lenin, Stalin, and Mao* (New York: Norton, 1979), p. 61.

3. Marx, *Grundrisse,* p. 611.

collectivizing production. This approach, which departed considerably from the conventional Soviet line, concentrated on creating revolutionary consciousness before establishing a sound economic base. In fact, the Guevarists believed that communism could not be created simply by using market mechanisms. The government, Che insisted, must first create frugal, loyal, and selfless citizens, who would be sacrificing, collective-minded, state-oriented, hardworking, and egalitarian. Che believed that the material foundation, the proper economic structure for society, would necessarily follow. To create this perfect citizen, the Guevarists called on the leadership to mobilize, regiment, and educate politically the masses. Most important, Guevara advocated offering moral incentives to citizens who demonstrated proper *conciencia.*

On the other side of the debate, a group of practical, economic-minded Marxists challenged the Guevarists. Led by Carlos Rafael Rodríguez, this more pragmatic group recommended a wholly different approach that emphasized orthodox Marxist theory. The Pragmatists stressed the primacy of economic policies and a Soviet-line political and social orientation.

In short, Che focused on the initial development of cultural forces such as revolutionary consciousness and morality. The Guevarists believed that Cuba's new economic development plan should be based on moral rather than material incentives. Rodríguez, however, emphasized the importance of establishing a solid economic foundation based on material incentives. Once structural economic forces had been stabilized, then the government could move to developing revolutionary consciousness.[4]

The debate between the Pragmatists and the Guevarists regarding the correct economic model for Cuba created serious tension within the government. And Fidel Castro held an ambiguous position, refusing to endorse fully either side. He did, however, openly support the Guevarist belief in the significance of creating a new work ethic among Cuban citizens. Castro agreed with Che that Cuba could not progress smoothly toward socialism without first thoroughly imbuing the people with transformed attitudes toward labor. In particular, Castro and Guevara viewed the prerevolutionary labor ethic as the product of three acute historical ills: Spanish colonialism, Cuban slavery, and Western capitalism.

From this perspective the Cuban attitudes toward manual labor that so distressed the new communist leaders had developed from the Spanish

4. For discussions of this debate see Carmelo Mesa-Lago, *Cuba in the 1970s: Pragmatism and Institutionalization* (Albuquerque: University of New Mexico Press, 1978), pp. 6–8; Juan M. del Aguila, *Cuba: Dilemmas of a Revolution* (Boulder: Westview Press, 1984), pp. 85–86; Carmelo Mesa-Lago, *The Economy of Socialist Cuba: A Two-Decade Appraisal* (Albuquerque: University of New Mexico Press, 1981), pp. 18–25.

tradition of colonialism and aristocracy. During the colonial period the Spanish Crown brought to the New World both extreme centralization of political power and a hierarchical and authoritarian Catholic religion. The Spanish also imposed an uncompromising Aristotelian concept of classes and their appropriate social functions. These colonial characteristics engendered among upper-class subjects an unwillingness to perform tasks that they viewed as better suited for those at the bottom of the social scale. Among the elites a pervasive disdain for manual labor prevailed.[5] Spanish colonists believed that menial jobs should be left as the exclusive province of the lower classes. The remnants of this view, Castro believed, posed intolerable impediments for Cuban socialism.

Colonial and postcolonial Cuban attitudes toward manual labor stemmed not only from the history of Spanish rule but also from the tradition of slavery. As in all slave societies, masters and slaves perceived labor as degrading: something to be forced by the strong upon the weak. This was as true in Cuba as in much of the rest of Latin America. After Spain abolished Cuban slavery in the late nineteenth century, many lower-class blacks and mulattoes were no more inclined to perform hard manual labor than were many of the upper-class whites. In essence, Cuba became a postslave society that clung tenaciously to the labor attitudes of preslave and slave societies.[6]

Finally, and most important, Fidel Castro traced inappropriate Cuban labor attitudes to exploitative foreign capitalism. As Castro and Guevara saw it, capitalist businessmen, by overworking, underpaying, and generally abusing their employees, had created poor attitudes toward labor among the Cuban people. Like the masters of the earlier slave age, capitalists themselves did not labor but hired less fortunate members of society to perform the work. In a September 1961 speech Castro explained: "In the old society ... there were various kinds of parasites.... There were national parasites and there were foreign parasites, like the great imperialist 'mister' who owned shares in the electricity company, the telephone company, the sugar refinery, or the huge plantation." And Castro asked, "At whose cost did [these "misters"] eat, dress, wear shoes, and live?"[7] Prerevolutionary work attitudes, the Cuban leader insisted, must be

5. See, for example, Castro's comments in *Granma Weekly Review* (*GWR*), January 12, 1986, p. 6.

6. For a superb discussion of this see Carlos Moore, *Castro, the Blacks, and Africa* (Los Angeles: The Regents of the University of California, 1988).

7. Fidel Castro, speech on the First Anniversary of the Committees for the Defense of the Revolution, September 28, 1961, cited in Richard Fagen, *The Transformation of Political Culture in Cuba* (Stanford: Stanford University Press, 1969), pp. 199–200.

swiftly destroyed and speedily replaced with a labor *conciencia* more appropriate for a nonexploitative revolutionary society.

Official Rhetoric: Promoting Proper Attitudes Toward Labor

Relying on this analysis of the ills of Cuban labor, the Guevarists publicly called upon the people to eradicate capitalist labor attitudes. Throughout the early 1960s they appealed to Cubans to eliminate their disdain for manual labor. In June 1960, even before Castro announced the Marxist-Leninist nature of the Revolution, Che Guevara stated: "The government will have to ask sacrifices . . . of workers. . . . A revolutionary government cannot demand sacrifices from above; they must be the result of everyone's will—of everyone's conviction."[8] The following August Che pronounced:

> In Cuba a new type of man is being created. . . . A profound social change demands equally profound changes in the mental structure of the people. . . . In order to change a way of thinking, it is necessary to undergo profound internal changes . . . especially in the performance of our duties and obligations to society. . . . We must, then, erase our old concepts.[9]

On May 14, 1961, Castro reiterated: "Wealth is created by manual labor. . . . Go from here conscious of the fact that you are going to work."[10] Four months later he again encouraged citizens to think differently about manual labor. For the first time Castro focused attention upon *"gusanos,"* the social parasites who did not work:

> The Revolution is for all those who do useful work for the public. . . . In the old society there were those . . . who did not work but who nevertheless dressed, ate, wore shoes, slept, and lived. They did absolutely nothing useful. . . . Although we have rid ourselves of many of the *gusanos,* we have not yet come near to wiping

---

8. Ernesto (Che) Guevara, speech delivered to Havana assembly of workers, June 18, 1960, in John Gerassi, ed., *Venceremos! The Speeches and Writings of Ernesto Che Guevara* (New York: Macmillan, 1968), p. 95.

9. Che Guevara, speech delivered to militiamen, August 19, 1960, in Gerassi, ed., pp. 113–116.

10. *El Mundo,* May 16, 1961, pp. 6, 8.

them out. . . . And what right has anyone to live as an idler? . . . You must work.[11]

In October 1962 Che reminded a youth assembly that communism required a new labor ethic. "Sacrifice," Che said, "this is the education best suited to a youth preparing for communism: a form of education in which work ceases to be the obsession it is in the capitalist world and becomes a pleasant social duty."[12] Three months later Che told a group of cane cutters that the Revolution seeks "the development of the consciousness of the entire nation concerning the necessity of productive work."[13]

Policy Initiatives: Moral Incentives

The leadership did more than just encourage the development of a new labor culture in stirring speeches. It complemented the rhetoric by instituting rigorous labor policies. In this way the government imposed on the Cuban population the official belief that workers should perform out of a moral obligation to revolutionary goals. In 1961, for example, Castro and his associates created grievance committees (*comisiónes de reclamaciónes*) to discipline poor behavior, to encourage workers to improve their performance, and to manage disagreements in the workplace. These committees, made up exclusively of the workers themselves, primarily handled conflicts between labor and management. Significantly, although the leadership designed these committees to deal with labor conflicts, it did not allow them to make a final decision on any particular conflict. The Ministry of Labor reserved that right for itself.[14]

In 1961 Che Guevara introduced "socialist emulation," another policy based on moral incentives and defined as "fraternal competition to increase the output of the community." Emulation, a measure employed widely throughout socialist societies, was a form of competition meant to rally workers to labor more energetically and produce more goods. In essence, it provided a means by which the government, without any mate-

11. Fidel Castro, speech on the First Anniversary of the Committees for Defense of the Revolution, September 28, 1961, cited in Fagen, pp. 199–209.

12. Che Guevara, speech delivered to an assembly of communist youth, October 20, 1962, cited in Gerrasi, ed., pp. 211–215.

13. Che Guevara, speech delivered to sugar cutters in Camaguey, February 9, 1963, cited in ibid., p. 230.

14. Roberto E. Hernández and Carmelo Mesa-Lago, "Labor Organization and Wages," in *Revolutionary Change in Cuba*, ed. Carmelo Mesa-Lago (Pittsburgh: University of Pittsburgh Press, 1971), p. 220.

rial loss to the state, could reward appropriate attitudes and behavior while simultaneously increasing the labor supply and the level of production.[15] Competition occurred among groups, brigades, sections, regions, and factories.[16] Winners' prizes went to those who fulfilled or exceeded norms, who improved themselves educationally, who succeeded in savings or quality, and who impressed with attendance and punctuality. The government awarded such model citizens medals, "moral" titles, or public recognition of some kind, such as sitting on a podium with Fidel Castro or perhaps even attaining Communist Party membership. As Che Guevara commented, "Emulation is a weapon to increase production and an instrument to evaluate the consciousness of the masses."[17] Che further explained:

> The best workers, the men that demonstrate a revolutionary attitude with their daily labor, [will be] rewarded. . . . Those . . . have the possibility of becoming a member of the party. . . . The Marxist must be the best . . . a tireless worker who gives all . . . a hard worker who gives his hours of rest, his personal tranquility, his family, or his life to the Revolution.[18]

The government first began experimenting with emulation among the cane cutters. Later the leaders enacted national legislation to regulate and expand the emulation program to other industries.

Public Denunciation of Uncooperative Workers

On the one hand, by praising and rewarding workers the government encouraged the development of new labor attitudes. On the other hand, the leadership reprimanded apathetic workers who failed to fulfill labor requirements. In September 1961 Castro complained that industrialization had stalled because the Cuban worker was not "cooperating properly

15. Terry Karl, "Work Incentives in Cuba," *Latin American Perspectives* 7 (Supplement 1975): 27; see also Robert M. Bernardo, *The Theory of Moral Incentives in Cuba* (University: University of Alabama Press, 1971), p. 57.

16. Bernardo, p. 57.

17. Che Guevara quoted in Hernández and Mesa-Lago, p. 235.

18. Che Guevara, "The Role of a Marxist-Leninist Party," in *Che: Selected Works of Ernesto Guevara*, ed. Rolando E. Bonachea and Nelson P. Valdés (Garden City, N.Y.: Anchor Books, 1968), pp. 109–110.

and was not imbued with revolutionary spirit."[19] Castro lamented that many workers were taking advantage of their guaranteed wage. Throughout 1961 and 1962 government officials took up Castro's theme and repeatedly railed against labor apathy and absenteeism.

The government managed to personalize these reprimands through turning to public humiliation, a measure designed to improve worker performance. By publicly admonishing recalcitrant laborers before their peers, the leaders aimed to embarrass shameful offenders into compliance and to deter others from neglecting labor requirements.[20] The government praised work sites in which all laborers joined the program and publicly criticized uncooperative workers. Lázaro Peña, Secretary General of the Cuban Confederation of Labor, congratulated work sites where "posters are placed on the walls denouncing the absentee workers, commissions are organized to visit the sick [to determine if they really are sick], . . . the absentee worker is criticized and . . . is obligated to engage in self-criticism in front of a general assembly of the workers or those of a department."[21]

A New Role for the Unions

In August 1961 the government passed a law that redefined the chief tasks of Cuban trade unions. In the future, labor unions were to improve administration in the work force, organize and carry out political education activities, encourage fulfillment of production and development plans, and promote efficiency and expansion of social and public services. The government frankly expected unions to serve the Revolution without compromise. Cuban leader Blas Roca explained: "Today the fundamental task of the unions is to fight for an increase in production."[22] Raúl Castro reiterated: "Today the great task confronting the . . . unions is to increase production, recruit voluntary workers, tighten labor discipline . . . and improve the quality of what is produced."[23]

Union leaders, accustomed to thinking in terms of improving labor

19. Manuel Urrutia Lleo, *Fidel Castro and Company, Inc.* (New York: Praeger, 1964), pp. 169–170; see also Luis P. Salas, *Social Control and Deviance in Cuba* (New York: Praeger, 1979); *Revolución*, September 25, 1961.

20. Theodore Draper, *Castroism: Theory and Practice* (New York: Praeger, 1965), p. 185; see also Salas, p. 335.

21. *Revolución*, September 2, 1962; cited in Salas, pp. 335–336.

22. Hernández and Mesa-Lago, p. 212.

23. Raúl Castro, *Revolución*, January 23, 1963; also quoted in Hernández and Mesa-Lago, p. 213.

conditions, rebelled at their new role of ensuring labor productivity. Some union members refused to go to work; others merely ignored the official labor requirements. Extreme tension thus developed rapidly between the demands of the government and the desires of the unions.[24] Indeed, by late 1961 the revolutionary government had come to view the negative response by Cuban labor as a political act of resistance against the state.

Fidel Castro, of course, would not readily accept such blatant nonconformity. The government quickly assured all workers that those who did not accept their revolutionary responsibility to work supportively and enthusiastically would be categorized as criminals and punished as enemies of the state. In the future, the authorities declared, absenteeism would not be tolerated. In November 1961 the Minister of Foreign Relations stated emphatically that absenteeism reflected "not only the laziness or negligence [of workers] but was linked to counterrevolution."[25] The same month, in scolding the workers of Cuba's largest textile enterprise for losing twenty-six days of work between January and September 1961, Lázaro Peña attributed this poor labor performance to a "counterrevolutionary attitude on the part of the worker."

Should these incidents of "counterrevolutionary behavior" not be eliminated, Cuban leaders threatened to take more formidable measures. In September 1961, for instance, Che Guevara told a group of workers that if they did not sacrifice, volunteer their labor, and practice work discipline, he would propose "compulsory measures . . . to sustain production." He stressed that "absenteeism has recently assumed alarming proportions. . . . Until now, it has been an evil spoken of in abstract terms without being analyzed critically. This is an evil encountered in all industries."[26] In April 1962, *Revolución,* the official newspaper of the 26th of July Movement, quoted Che: "[I]t has come time to use compulsive measures [against workers] because we have to ensure production."[27]

That same month the government announced that it would deprive "problem" workers of selected goods. At the general assembly of the CTC, Lázaro Peña attacked Cuban labor for increasing displays of resistance, particularly absenteeism. He announced that the names of recalcitrant, noncompliant workers would be placed on "special lists." Their goods and bonuses would be denied and their salaries cut.[28] A few months later President Osvaldo Dórticos defended these measures claiming, "in

24. Hernández and Mesa-Lago, p. 213.
25. Salas, p. 335; see also *Verde Olivo,* November 5, 1961.
26. Che Guevara, *Revolución,* September 25, 1961, quoted in Urrutia Lleo, p. 169.
27. Che Guevara speech, quoted in Salas, p. 335; see also *Revolución,* April 16, 1962.
28. *Hoy,* April 14, 1962.

the face of this evil, it is necessary to use the greatest of revolutionary severity."[29]

Legislating Harsher Penalties

For the first time the Cuban government's efforts to deal with the country's labor problem had moved beyond mere verbal exhortation. To ensure proper work behavior, the leaders concentrated on implementing mildly coercive measures, such as the denial of necessary goods. This became the opening salvo of a much more comprehensive labor campaign. Castro's Minister of Labor, Augusto Martínez Sánchez, later recalled, "We opened an offensive against absenteeism at a time when labor discipline had relaxed extraordinarily ... when absenteeism had reached extraordinary proportions."[30]

On August 29, 1962, the leadership drafted into Cuban law this attempt to control the behavior of laborers. The Labor Ministry issued Resolution 5798, the first measure to penalize passive, unproductive workers. This resolution introduced penalties for tardiness, early departures from work, and unexcused or unjustified absences. The punishment, relatively mild, included wage reductions and cuts in benefits. The government also passed a number of other laws that empowered the state to set wage levels, to transfer and reassign workers without their consent, and to require workers to carry identification cards at all times.[31]

In addition, the leadership established a rehabilitation center at a labor camp in Guanahacabibes. Officials sent disobedient laborers and supervisors to this camp for training and instruction. In 1963, as a form of punishment and worker rehabilitation, Cuban leaders also introduced a military draft that encompassed all males between the ages of sixteen and forty-five.[32] The government divided the drafted army into two groups, one engaged in defense and the other in production. The former included those recruits who were "free of suspicion" of counterrevolutionary tendencies, while the latter took in all who were "not politically integrated" into Cuban society.[33] By 1965 the government had sent the most "deviant"

29. *Revolución*, September 10, 1962.

30. *Hoy*, October 28, 1964; see also Draper, p. 185.

31. Lowry Nelson, *Cuba: The Measure of a Revolution* (Minneapolis: University of Minnesota Press, 1972), p. 120; see also Urrutia Lleo, pp. 168–170; Hernández and Mesa-Lago, pp. 168–170; Salas, p. 335.

32. Salas, p. 336.

33. Carmelo Mesa-Lago, "Unpaid Labor in Cuba," in *Fidel Castro's Personal Revolution in Cuba: 1959-1973*, ed. James Nelson Goodsell (New York: Knopf, 1975), p. 201.

of the recruits into the "production" sector to perform agricultural labor in military brigades called Military Units to Aid Production (UMAP). Within the following three years the state drafted about ninety thousand persons.[34]

Between 1965 and 1967 the UMAP became a catch-all for delinquents who had been denounced by their neighbors or the CDRs. These military units took in any person who failed to conduct himself in accordance with the official definition of proper behavior. The UMAP housed persons rounded up as vagrants, counterrevolutionaries, and so-called deviants: homosexuals, juvenile delinquents, and religious followers, including Catholics, Baptists, and Jehovah's Witnesses. The UMAP also conscripted workers who had displayed what state officials considered inexcusable ignorance, carelessness, or disrespect.[35]

The UMAP quickly gained notoriety for its inhumane treatment of workers. In 1967 the National Union of Writers and Artists in Cuba strongly denounced the arrest of several intellectuals and university faculty members who had been accused of homosexuality and placed in the UMAP. In response to this protest Castro disbanded the UMAP after the 1967 harvest and conceded that such treatment did not contribute to revolutionary objectives. However, the government did not hesitate to establish other, somewhat less repressive, forced-labor camps.[36]

Despite the leadership's rhetorical flourishes and the various mildly coercive methods implemented by the state, Cuban workers during this first period of the Revolution plainly resisted official efforts to change their attitudes and behavior. Many laborers carried out quiet, discreet acts of resistance, such as evading rules, performing poorly, or even skipping work. Others openly rebelled, some to the point of setting fire to their workplace.[37] In late 1962 Maurice Zeitlin, an American scholar, surveyed 202 Cuban workers to determine whether the government had successfully altered work attitudes. He concluded that 53 percent of the workers had not changed their attitude at all and 3 percent had a worse attitude toward labor than before the Revolution.[38]

34. Ibid.

35. Nelson, pp. 120–121; also see Salas, p. 336; Jorge I. Domínguez, *Cuba: Order and Revolution* (Cambridge: Harvard University Press, 1978), p. 357. Also, for a revealing description of the UMAP, see José Yglesias, *In the Fist of the Revolution: Life in a Cuban Country Town* (New York: Pantheon Books, 1969), pp. 275–276.

36. See *Granma*, April 14, 1966, p. 8; see also Domínguez, p. 357; Yglesias, p. 275. For a personal account of the UMAP, see José Conesa Martínez, *Ocho Amigos* (Miami: Noya Printing, 1978).

37. Urrutia Lleo, p. 171.

38. Domínguez, pp. 487–488; see also Maurice Zeitlin, *Revolutionary Politics and the Cuban Working Class* (New York: Harper Torchbooks, 1970), pp. 13–30; 197–199.

Thus, after three years of official efforts, still a relatively short period of time, the available evidence indicates that labor attitudes in Cuba were not proving to be as easily modified as the leaders had hoped. For most workers labor attitudes had apparently not undergone sweeping changes. One year later an American journalist, Mohammed Rauf, visited Cuba. After noting the "excessive use" of "childish and sophomoric" slogans being used to motivate Cubans to change their views toward labor, Rauf remarked on the surprisingly poor attitudes exhibited by the Cuban labor force toward work. A Cuban official with the National Institute of Agrarian Reform in Havana explained to Rauf: "[Y]ou don't understand the Cuban mentality. . . . If we don't keep goading our workers like this, they would go back to sleep. We have to keep needling them. . . . You may not need the slogans, but our workers do."[39]

Throughout 1963 and 1964 Castro complained about the careless, sloppy performance of workers and the resulting low productivity.[40] In October he insisted that Cubans needed greater "pressures" to make them work harder.[41] At the same time Castro chided the union's grievance committees for seeming "to be on the side of absenteeism and vagrancy." Guevara himself criticized the committees for being unacceptably lax, and he labelled them a "barrier" to improving production. Guevara commented: "[T]hey will be able to accomplish a very useful task only provided that they change their attitudes. Production is the fundamental task."[42] Meanwhile, Minister of Labor Martínez Sánchez observed that the new labor laws had not successfully cut down on worker absenteeism.[43]

The Law of Labor Justice

In October 1964, profoundly disappointed with Cuban labor attitudes, the leadership introduced the "Law of Labor Justice." Martínez Sánchez claimed that this new law would strengthen labor discipline and increase productivity. He explained: "There are still undisciplined workers and for them we have to have discipline measures. . . . We still find workers who have not taken a revolutionary step and tend to . . . protest any measure coming from the administration."[44]

39. Mohammed A. Rauf, Jr., *Cuban Journal: Castro's Cuba As It Really Is* (New York: Crowell, 1964), pp. 77–78.

40. Draper, p. 32.

41. Ibid., p. 184.

42. Salas, p. 337; Hernández and Mesa-Lago, p. 220.

43. *Hoy,* October 28, 1964. See also Draper, p. 185.

44. Salas, p. 337; see also *El Mundo,* October 27, 1964, pp. 7–10; *Hoy,* October 28, 1964.

This comprehensive law targeted all "violations of labor discipline" and established severe sanctions to be imposed against laborers who failed to produce as Cuban leaders required. The Law of Labor Justice singled out for punishment not only those workers who committed generally recognized economic crimes like fraud but also those who merely displayed signs of laziness or vagrancy, absenteeism or tardiness, foot-dragging or inefficiency, damage to equipment or lack of respect for superiors.[45] As Carlos Rafael Rodríguez, President of the National Institute for Agrarian Reform, announced, "[S]anctions will be applied to correct anti-social attitudes, negligence, laziness, and to those that ... manage to work less than the eight hours established for all kinds of work."[46]

This new law attempted to force Cuban workers to change their attitudes and behavior by threatening them with discipline. Indeed, the government paired particular violations with three grades of punishment: light, moderate, and serious penalties. The light penalties ranged from a simple warning to a modest wage cut. The moderate called for a major wage cut or for transfer to a different job in the same work center. The serious penalties ranged from transfer to a different work center, often far from family members, to permanent discharge. The law, which imposed a "system of coercion more oppressive than anything the Cuban working class had known," met much popular opposition.[47]

As part of the new law the government also further curtailed the role of Cuba's labor unions. It abolished the grievance committees and created labor councils to deal with worker violations and conflicts between labor and management. The significance of these committees, however, was more apparent than real; in practice, the Ministry of Labor curtailed the ability of these councils to operate freely. For example, the Ministry could dismiss and replace council members as it saw fit. The Ministry could recall a case heard by the council and resolve it without any further right to appeal. Indeed, the Ministry could even annul any decision made by the council. Clearly, the role of formal labor unions had been sharply constricted.

In 1966 the Twelfth National Congress of the Cuban Confederation of Labor issued the Declaration of Principles and Union Statutes. This declaration stated that the main task of the labor movement, which would be "directed and guided by the Party," was to mobilize the masses and strengthen the Marxist-Leninist ideology in Cuban society. The leadership expected unions to cut costs, increase production, promote the

45. Salas, p. 337; also see Draper, p. 185.
46. Nelson, p. 120.
47. Draper, pp. 185–186; see also Adolfo Gilly, *Inside the Cuban Revolution* (New York: Monthly Review Press, 1964), pp. 18–19.

government's labor legislation, and encourage proper revolutionary consciousness. At the 1966 CTC Congress the newly elected Secretary General of that body, Miguel A. Martín, was asked what remained of the unions. The unions, he answered, could still help to organize and discipline workers and to change prerevolutionary attitudes of selfishness.[48] By this relatively early date most impartial observers would conclude that Cuban labor unions existed in name only.

By the final years of the 1960s Maurice Zeitlin, a sympathizer of the Revolution, wrote that Cuban trade unions had simply "withered away." In truth, of course, the unions had not died of neglect; Fidel Castro and his colleagues had purposefully and vigorously uprooted them, as Karl Marx had advised. Zeitlin noted:

> The workers do not have an independent organization which takes the initiative in the plant, industry or country as a whole, to assure—let alone to demand—improved working conditions. . . . No organization exists, as an autonomous force, to protect and advance the immediate interests of the workers as they see them, independent of the prevailing line of the Communist Party or policies of the Revolutionary government.[49]

In 1966 another Castro sympathizer, economist Joan Robinson, wrote: "The trade unions . . . represent the view of the Party and government rather than that of the workers."[50]

As was once observed of Benito Mussolini's Italy, even ruthless discipline could never make the trains arrive on time. Despite the enactment of the law and the government's enhanced control over the labor unions, Cuban production continued to founder. Ignoring the cumbersome nature of the economy, the Castro government continued to blame the country's economic woes wholly on absenteeism and worker resistance. Consequently, the leadership intensified its verbal attacks on the Cuban worker. Government officials continued to preach the virtues of hard work, voluntarism, and sacrifice. In a January 1964 speech Che Guevara stated: "We have to change the workers' consciousness rapidly so that they understand clearly the new nature of their work, the new nature of sacrifice. . . . We must create a new awareness that will permit us to enormously accelerate our transition to communism. We salute you who go

48. Hernández and Mesa-Lago, p. 213.

49. Maurice Zeitlin, "Inside Cuba: Workers and Revolution," *Ramparts* 8 (March 1970): 20; cited in Hernández and Mesa-Lago, p. 213.

50. Joan Robinson, "Cuba–1965," *Monthly Review* 17 (February 1966): 17; cited in Hernández and Mesa-Lago, p. 213.

happily to work, who identify with their labor."[51] In August Che again reiterated: "The man who works with that new attitude is perfecting himself. . . . [V]oluntary work is the factor that develops the conscience of the workers more than any other." And Che concluded, "We must do it so well that every worker loves his factory."[52]

After nearly a half decade of leaders railing against the ills of Cuban labor, the traditional labor culture of the Cuban people continued to confound the Castro government. Simple moral suasion and moderate coercion had failed to transform the attitudes and behavior of the workers. In 1965 a frustrated Cuban official lamented:

> I don't understand these people. . . . [A]t the time of the Bay of Pigs invasion, these peasants took up their guns and enthusiastically hurried to their posts, ready to lay down their lives. . . . A few months later, I saw them dozing in the fields, shirking work. Why, I ask myself, are they ready to die for the Revolution, but not to work for it?[53]

Moral Incentives Further Encouraged

The Cuban leadership, though bedeviled by traditional culture, was not yet ready to succumb to it. Toward the end of the first stage of the Revolution, the Castro government redoubled its efforts to create the new Cuban citizen. To transform labor attitudes even more quickly, Che explained, the state must increase its moral suasion and multiply its efforts. Che cautioned that the creation of *conciencia* "does not come about automatically." It is something the government must create with energy and enthu-

51. Che Guevara speech, given on January 11, 1964, cited in Bonachea and Valdés, eds., p. 308; also published in *El Mundo,* January 12, 1964.

52. Che Guevara, speech delivered to workers, August 15, 1964, in Gerassi, ed., pp. 335–339.

53. Peter Schmid, "Letter from Havana," *Commentary* 40, no. 3 (September 1965): 57. In 1965 Che complained: "It is clear that work still has coercive aspects, even when it is voluntary: Man has still not transformed all the coercion surrounding him into conditioned reflexes. . . . [H]e still produces under the pressure of the environment. . . . He is still to achieve complete spiritual creation in the presence of his own work, without the direct pressure of the social environment but bound to it by new habits. That will be communism." Che Guevara, letter addressed to Carlos Quijano, editor of *Marcha* (Montevideo), March 1965, cited in Bonachea and Valdés, eds., pp. 155–169; also published in *Verde Olivo,* April 11, 1965.

siasm.[54] Plainly, the notion of a model revolutionary worker still fascinated the Cuban leadership.

In March 1965 Che wrote a significant essay heralding the appearance in Cuba of the "new man."[55] The Revolution, he explained, was entering another phase, a phase that would require an even more extraordinary national effort to create revolutionary *conciencia*. This campaign, Che argued, must become the government's chief goal. By 1966 this line of reasoning had apparently convinced Fidel Castro. He officially endorsed the Guevarist approach which advocated creating a revolutionary work ethic by eliminating material incentives.[56]

Cuba's rapidly weakening economy made even more attractive the strategy of diminishing the importance of material rewards. Shortages forced the government to curtail the number of bonuses it could distribute. Thus, the government initiated yet another labor policy, this one aimed at developing a new socialist citizen while conserving national resources through emphasizing moral incentives.[57] Cuban leaders argued that moral incentives would help to create a revolutionary consciousness by appealing to man's sense of obligation instead of his individualism, egoism, and selfish capitalist desires. From this perspective material incentives, Castro reasoned, led men to behave "as a wolf to other men" and thus might actually obstruct the creation of new labor attitudes.[58] Moral incentives, however, were thought to bring out the best in citizens.

On May Day 1966 Castro optimistically declared that "work is no longer . . . a means of enriching a privileged minority. . . . [W]ork is no longer—nor will it ever be again—a means of exploitation."[59] In the same speech the Cuban leader argued that since the Revolution the "consciousness of our people has grown" and that "for the masses of our country the concept of work and of the worker has changed profoundly." A few months later he reiterated: "Workers of our country have advanced considerably in the area of ideology. . . . [W]ork is the fundamental instru-

54. Cited in Bonachea and Valdés, eds., pp. 155–169.

55. Che wrote: "We can see the New Man who begins to emerge in this period of the building of socialism. . . . Work must acquire a new condition. . . . We [must do] everything possible to give work this new category." Che Guevara, cited in Bertram Silverman, ed., *Man and Socialism in Cuba: The Great Debate* (New York: Atheneum, 1971), pp. 337–354.

56. Carmelo Mesa-Lago, "Economic Policies and Growth," in *Revolutionary Change in Cuba*, ed. Carmelo Mesa-Lago (Pittsburgh: University of Pittsburgh Press, 1971), p. 300.

57. Domínguez, p. 485.

58. Fidel Castro, speech in the Chaplin Theater, April 19, 1966, cited in Martin Kenner and James Petras, eds., *Fidel Castro Speaks* (New York: Grove Press, 1969), p. 189. Also in *GWR*, July 28, 1968, p. 3.

59. Fidel Castro, speech delivered at May Day Celebration, May 1, 1966, cited in *Fidel Castro* (Havana: Campamento 5 de Mayo, 1968), p. 32.

ment for the liberation of a people … a fundamental social duty."[60] Shortly thereafter, Che echoed the same view, declaring that "in a relatively short time the development of conscience does more for the development of production than [do] material incentives."[61] A *Granma* article on September 27, 1966, stated explicitly:

> The revolution has advanced in the most extraordinary and diverse ways. All the steps to date … have aided … in the fundamental task: the formation of the new man, a man with a profound consciousness of his role in society and of his duties and social responsibilities.… The construction of Communism demands … the formation of the new man; and it will not terminate until this job has been completed.[62]

Despite all of the leaders' rhetorical efforts to convince themselves and the rest of Cuban society that worker attitudes were improving, attitudes and behavior among laborers actually remained a vexatious, indeed, an intractable, problem. From time to time the leadership's frustration and disappointment broke through their outward optimism. In September 1966, speaking at the Twelfth Workers' Congress of the Cuban Confederation of Labor, Castro stated dejectedly:

> Can we say … every worker in our country changed his whole mentality, his old concept of society … and acquired a collective view with a clear *conciencia*? … A completely socialist consciousness has not yet been formed. Many workers did not see work as a means of creating social wealth, of creating benefits for all.… [T]hey did not see that work was their fundamental duty.[63]

In early 1967 the government issued a report entitled "Industrial Development in Cuba" which stated that workers in most agricultural production centers were not even approaching their capacity for work. The laborers were putting in significantly less than eight-hour days.[64] In a May

60. *GWR*, September 4, 1966, p. 3.

61. Herbert L. Matthews, *Revolution in Cuba* (New York: Charles Scribner's Sons, 1975), p. 295.

62. *Granma*, September 27, 1966; also cited in Fagen, pp. 17–18.

63. *GWR*, September 4, 1966, p. 3.

64. *Industrial Development in Cuba: Report Presented by the Cuban Delegation to the International Symposium on Industrial Development* (1967), pp. 32–33; cited and discussed in Leo Huberman and Paul M. Sweezy, *Socialism in Cuba* (New York: Monthly Review Press, 1969), pp. 141–142.

speech that same year Castro warned Cubans that "all must work productively and work hard and long hours . . . for the good of the whole society and without material reward."[65]

On July 26 Castro complained that the "old ideas" of capitalist society had not yet disappeared: not everyone was behaving in a revolutionary manner. The Cuban leader noted: "There are those whose ideas are completely apart from collective interests. . . . [We] see in many towns the loafers who produce nothing."[66] Castro and Guevara thus sought to motivate Cubans to adopt revolutionary work attitudes out of love, respect, and support for the Revolution and its leaders. Che continued to argue vigorously that only when Cubans had developed the proper *conciencia* would the island successfully build the material base for a communist society. Indeed, by 1967 Che's views had prevailed. The goal of transforming Cuban culture, of building a new citizen, became the transcendent objective of the Castro government. The pragmatic Soviet line that counselled industrializing Cuba and establishing a firm material base had been relegated to a secondary position in the Cuban leadership's hierarchy of goals.

PHASE TWO

By 1967 government policies had taken a radical turn, heralding a period marked by extraordinary pressure to create a new labor *conciencia* among the masses. In late 1967, after the death of Che Guevara, the effort to establish the "new man" reached a crescendo. The Revolution would skip socialism altogether, the leaders proclaimed, and move directly to pure communism. In late 1967 President Osvaldo Dórticos declared: "We are about to build Communism. . . . The aim of our revolution is not to build a socialist state, but to move with minimum delay toward full Communism. . . . We have to prepare for it . . . by partial transformation of our society."[67]

In March 1968 this new phase of ideological fervor peaked as Castro launched the "Revolutionary Offensive" that sought to speed the construction of "real" communism and the molding of the new Cuban citi-

65. Nelson, p. 115.
66. Fidel Castro, speech delivered in Santiago de Cuba, July 26, 1967, in *Fidel Castro*, pp. 67–68; see also Huberman and Sweezy, pp. 150–151.
67. K. S. Karol, *Guerrillas in Power: The Course of the Cuban Revolution* (New York: Hill and Wang, 1970), pp. 357–358.

zen.[68] In July Castro announced that the "great task of the Revolution is . . . forming the new man."[69] To hasten this goal, the government moved quickly to further centralize and nationalize the economy. The government extended its reach by immediately seizing the vast majority of the state's remaining private enterprises.[70]

A New Labor Sanction: Worker Transfers

Since material disincentives had thus far failed to discourage defiant attitudes and behavior, such as absenteeism, inefficiency, vagrancy, and negligence, the Cuban government deemphasized salary cuts to penalize unacceptable labor attitudes. Instead, the leadership began to rely on penalties targeted at "reeducation," such as worker transfers. Leaders claimed that this change in penalties brought about less oppressive forms of punishment. Although at first glance this may seem correct, economic considerations suggest otherwise.[71] At the time excessive amounts of money circulated in Cuba. Yet because of the shortage of consumer goods, the Cuban worker had little real buying power. In reality, the labor sanctions, involving transfers to different work sites instead of economic punishments, penalized workers more harshly. These new coercive measures often forced workers to leave the family, live away from home, and suffer personal insecurity. In the end, since money could purchase little, many workers probably feared work transfers more than salary cuts.

Mobilizing and Militarizing Production

But the government did not aim the Offensive merely at eliminating material incentives and private profiteers. It targeted more specifically the attitudes of Cuban workers. The Castro government sought to inspire productive enthusiasm and to "wage war" on parasitism and individualism as well as selfishness, carelessness, laziness, and indulgence. To thwart such

68. Edward González, "The Limits of Charisma," in *Fidel Castro's Personal Revolution in Cuba: 1959–1973*, ed. James Nelson Goodsell (New York: Knopf, 1975), pp. 301–308; also see Karol, pp. 440–441.

69. *GWR*, July 28, 1968, p. 3.

70. The government seized 16,634 private businesses in Havana alone. This figure included 9,179 craftsmen working on their own. Karol, p. 442; see also del Aguila, p. 91.

71. See Hernández and Mesa-Lago.

problems, the leadership set out to mobilize virtually the entire Cuban nation for agricultural work.

Once the leaders launched the Offensive, a broad range of officials exalted work and used military terms, even war dispatches, to describe their goals. Speeches adopted dramatic militaristic phrases, equating the labor force with a "heroic battalion" and routinely describing labor efforts as "struggles" or "wars." More than twenty thousand workers in Havana alone left their jobs and headed to Camaguey to "do battle" in the cane fields. In many cases the wives of the workers took over their abandoned jobs.[72]

Once Cuban society had mobilized for its labor "war," the government allowed no one in Havana to relax until their forces achieved victory. Nothing was to jeopardize the government's success. The leadership closed every bar, restaurant, and theater in the city. Brooking no dissent, Castro cancelled holidays—Easter, Christmas, and New Year's Day—and prohibited their celebration. The leaders viewed these holidays as distracting the workers, as occasions that promoted laziness, religious fervor, and other nonrevolutionary attitudes. A *Granma* editorial claimed, perhaps optimistically, that laziness had been dealt a severe blow and would soon vanish forever.[73]

Yet, in an April 9, 1968, speech Fidel Castro acknowledged that after a month of "war" production levels still had not increased; indeed, they had actually decreased. To encourage spirited work and total commitment to raise productivity, Castro introduced a new "war" objective: the national crusade to produce ten million tons in the 1970 sugar harvest (*zafra*).[74] He called for "heroism," asked all Cubans to accept necessary deprivations, and presented the crusade as an achievement on which national honor rested. The *zafra* was touted as the true test of the Cuban Revolution.[75]

At this point moral rewards had been proven wholly ineffective. Material benefits had been excluded as both economically unfeasible and antirevolutionary in nature. To ensure proper work habits and high productivity, Cuban officials had chosen to militarize labor with a vengeance. Castro thus moved firmly to bring the Revolutionary Armed Forces into the labor sector. The FAR took command of the two leading sugar-producing provinces, Oriente and Camaguey. The leadership assigned junior officers to manage primary sugar *centrales* (mills), and the Armed Forces organized all work sites along military lines with columns, bri-

72. Karol, p. 446.
73. Ibid., p. 447.
74. Although Fidel had set this goal in 1963, he had not publicly emphasized it until now.
75. González, p. 306; see also Huberman and Sweezy, p. 141.

gades, and battalions.[76] Cuban leaders replaced farm machinery managers with lieutenants and established military-operated schools for tractor drivers and machine operators.[77]

This militarization of labor culminated in the organization of the Che Guevara Trailblazers Brigade. Officers commanded this brigade of workers much like a military battalion. The Trailblazers Brigade, a huge work force composed of thirty-six mechanized squads, each comprising 117 men and twenty heavy tractors and bulldozers, cleared land, dug reservoirs, and built dams and roads. The workers, mobilized and organized in military-style units, performed just as ordinary soldiers might carry out their commander's orders. Of this effort René Dumont wrote:

> The clearing of the land followed a line of march roughly parallel-ing that of the rebel columns ten years before—a sentimental, guerrilla-like work criterion that did not allow for adequate eco-nomic evaluation. . . . Following behind the noble squads of the bulldozers come the modest foot soldiers, a group of unskilled la-borers who, with their little axes, endlessly chop. . . . It was genu-ine war, complete with communiques. . . . The Cuban people were made increasingly subservient to the Party and the Army, and it was becoming more and more difficult to distinguish between the two, inasmuch as both groups wore uniforms and carried re-volvers.[78]

In a 1968 May Day speech Raúl Castro, Minister of the FAR, explained the objective of this "unprecedented mobilization" of labor:

> The goal was to achieve perfect control of all the provinces' re-sources. . . . Ninety-three thousand people were mobilized. . . . [W]orkers were organized into Civil Defense squads, platoons, companies, battalions. . . . When the siren sounded at 6 P.M., on April 11, 93,000 workers were gathered. . . . [W]ith clocklike preci-sion, the workers set off for their work places, as if forming a large army, in perfectly organized truck caravans, with . . . routes, traffic regulators and controllers, [and] time schedules.[79]

To ensure high levels of productivity, Raúl Castro announced that the 1970 sugar harvest would be organized in this same regimented manner.

76. González, pp. 308–309; see also Huberman and Sweezy, p. 145.

77. René Dumont, "The Militarization of Fidelismo," *Dissent* 17 (September-October 1970): 420.

78. Ibid., pp. 408–419.

79. Huberman and Sweezy, pp. 146–148.

Putting Youth to Work

As part of this all-encompassing campaign, the Cuban leadership in 1968 encouraged youth to volunteer their labor. The government established the Youth Centennial Column with an official goal of sending fifty thousand young people into the field to work. The Column called for volunteers who would sign up for three years in lieu of compulsory military service. Since most young Cubans drafted into the military ended up laboring in the agricultural sector, the choice was more apparent than real. A June 23 *Granma* editorial read: "The Youth Centennial Column's aim is to have 100,000 young people for next year to participate in the great ten-million ton sugar harvest in 1970. One hundred thousand representatives of our youth's tradition of heroism will take up this task for the honor of the Revolution."[80]

In another effort to promote proper work attitudes, the Castro government introduced "School Goes to the Country," a program in which children from cities and towns spent six to ten weeks every semester working in agricultural camps, while simultaneously carrying on studies at a reduced pace. Cuban officials saw this not only as economically rewarding through increasing the labor supply but also as an opportunity to place children in a positive work environment. On the farms they would work with their hands, think and act collectively, and live apart from their families. This initiative provided children with a healthful rural experience and the government with more influence over ideological education.[81]

To bolster the sugar harvest effort, the leadership put to work all who had requested permission to leave Cuba. Castro sent these *"gusanos"* to the fields to labor until their time to leave. On September 28, 1968, Castro declared that these "Johnsons" would "earn by the sweat of their brow the Cuban bread they consume before their departure." Historians have estimated that this group numbered about seven hundred thousand citizens.[82]

Thus, by the end of 1968 Cuban society had witnessed a genuine military takeover of the faltering agricultural sector.[83] The government viewed militarization as the only means to confront the general disorder, mismanagement, and resistance of Cuban labor. In November Castro announced that the military would oversee the "super mobilization" for the 1970 harvest. The FAR, Castro claimed, is "the institution with the most experi-

---

80. *Granma*, June 23, 1968.
81. Huberman and Sweezy, p. 151.
82. See Karol, p. 444; see also *Granma*, September 29, 1968.
83. See Dumont, p. 419, for a discussion of this.

ence in organization; they are the ones with the most discipline. They must contribute that spirit of organization and discipline ... as well as their experience."[84]

Moral Suasion

While the government dramatically moved toward militarization, it continued to employ some moral suasion. Throughout 1968 Castro and other leaders preached the importance of creating a communist *conciencia* with new labor attitudes. And the media echoed the revolutionary words of the leaders. In July 1968 Castro explained:

> A Communist society is one in which man will have reached the highest degree of social awareness ever achieved. . . . Communist consciousness must be developed at the same rate as the forces of production. An advance in . . . consciousness . . . must accompany every step forward in the development of the productive forces. . . . We should not use money or wealth to create political awareness. We must create wealth with political awareness.[85]

The state introduced several other programs to promote appropriate labor attitudes, including the Advanced Guard Movement, for which all exemplary workers could be chosen. This program had a dual function of developing *conciencia* and increasing production. To be an Advanced Guard member, a worker, ideally at least, had to demonstrate punctuality, produce high-quality work, overfulfill production quotas, and willingly work overtime. Apart from maintaining a correct ideological attitude, laborers were supposed to use their free time to further their education. In the first year the government chose 10 percent of the Cuban work force to be Advanced Guard members. By early 1969 some 235,000 workers, or 18 percent of the organized work force, had been selected.[86] Perhaps these workers had succeeded in reaching the goals that the leaders had set. Perhaps this small group had adopted the attitudes and ideas, the labor *conciencia,* of the revolutionary elite. But most Cuban workers, perhaps even the vast majority, were still not cooperating.

Across the economy labor problems continued to perplex the leaders. Many workers kept displaying the subtle forms of resistance that so frus-

84. González, p. 309.

85. Complete text of speech in *GWR,* July 28, 1968.

86. Ibid., August 17, 1969; see also Domínguez, p. 275; Karl, p. 32; and Salas, pp. 339–340.

trated the Cuban government. By late August 1968, despite the extraordinary efforts of the Revolutionary Offensive, the leadership showed increasing signs of disillusionment. Some even began to express doubts about the feasibility of creating the "new man." Once again, traditional Cuban culture was proving to be a formidable foe for the revolutionary government.

An August 1968 issue of *Bohemia* quoted Castro: "[I]f it is admitted that man is incapable of learning, of developing *conciencia*, then those brainy economists will be proven right: the Revolution will fail." *Granma* reported a speech, delivered in Camaguey by Minister of Labor Jorge Risquet, in which he declared that every Cuban man would be forced to labor in the upcoming sugar harvest: "All men of working age in the rural areas" must be incorporated into "stable production units." Risquet also stressed the need for "daily checking . . . of attendance at work and fulfillment of the eight-hour day."[87]

By adopting such measures as "eight-hour days, twenty-four days in each month," Risquet claimed, production would double.[88] This suggests that Cuban officials believed that workers in the Camaguey Province were working only about half of their potential. Such an estimate is supported by other studies as well. According to Huberman and Sweezy, in 1968 the average Cuban work day lasted only about four hours, and "it was generally agreed that absenteeism [was] a significant problem." Thus, the Cuban agricultural labor force was "utilized at somewhere around 50 percent of practicable capacity."[89]

During this period a *Granma* article reported that poor handling of equipment and unacceptable work attendance gravely undermined labor performance and productivity. Figures in the article revealed that one unit "worked only 1,421 hours with 114 machines instead of the scheduled 4,220 hours with 211 machines." Thus, the unit only worked one-third of the hours planned.[90] According to Carmelo Mesa-Lago, in 1968 the production lines in the agricultural sector lost from 40 to 75 percent of the workday as a result of shutdowns, breakdowns, and lack of labor discipline.[91] Moreover, a 1968 study revealed that the average Cuban worker wasted from one-fourth to one-half of the workday.[92] Undoubtedly, the

87. *Bohemia,* August 2, 1968, p. 52; *Granma,* August 4, 1968.

88. The article's headline read "Wasting Manpower is a Crime against the Revolution." This article is discussed in Maurice Halperin, *The Taming of Fidel Castro* (Berkeley and Los Angeles: University of California Press, 1981), p. 291. See article in *Granma,* August 4, 1968.

89. Huberman and Sweezy, pp. 142–144.

90. *Granma,* December 1, 1968.

91. Mesa-Lago, *The Economy of Socialist Cuba,* p. 137.

92. *Bohemia,* May 10, 1970, pp. 32–37; see also Carmelo Mesa-Lago, *Cuba in the 1970s,* p. 36.

prevalent labor attitudes and patterns of behavior among Cuban workers were hardly in keeping with the leadership's lofty goals.

In late 1968 the Castro government's frustration with the Cuban worker suddenly erupted. Although some officials continued to coax workers with gentle rhetoric advocating moral incentives and voluntarism, other leaders began to criticize bitterly the disappointing performance of Cuban workers. Ever more frequently officials berated Cuban laborers and threatened further militarism if workers failed to improve their performance. A *Granma* article read: "The heads of all who try to destroy the Revolution will fall.... Military Law will apply to all youngsters over fifteen who are not engaged in studies. In the future, they will be put into uniform. The law will have to be amended but we already have army units composed of technical students."[93]

The leaders also informed the country's laborers that they would be required to carry "labor cards," a kind of worker report card on which all breaches of discipline and insubordinate acts would be noted. The leadership explained that it would periodically review these cards. Cooperative workers would be rewarded. However, should a worker receive unacceptable marks on his labor card, he would be sent to a labor camp and thus deprived of goods and services.

Then, during 1969 the government jailed many citizens charged with "lumpen vagrancy." To take one example, a March 14, 1969, *Bohemia* article reported that three hundred vagrants had been picked up and interned at a rehabilitation camp. Cuban officials locked up undesirables— vagrants, criminals, homosexuals, religious advocates, and others—in prison cells or sent them to rehabilitation camps.[94] In addition, the government eliminated overtime pay. Faithful workers were still expected to work overtime, but they were to do so as volunteers. The leaders hoped, wistfully perhaps, to increase the revolutionary dedication of the country's workers by encouraging unpaid, overtime volunteer work.[95]

In September 1969, to supplement the labor-card regime, the Cuban government introduced Law 1225, a more severe labor measure that required all workers to have labor dossiers. These dossiers contained the workers' history: level of competence and skill, merits and demerits, amount of formal education, and degree of revolutionary awareness. The leaders referred to these dossiers in determining promotions, salaries, retirement benefits, and distribution of housing and other necessities.[96]

93. *Granma*, September 9, 1968.

94. *Bohemia*, November 7, 1969, p. 5; see also March 14, 1969, pp. 66–76.

95. Domínguez, p. 274.

96. Salas, p. 339; see also Karol, pp. 448, 517; del Aguila, p. 89; Rolando E. Bonachea and Nelson P. Valdés, eds., *Cuba in Revolution* (Garden City, N.Y.: Doubleday, 1972), pp. 416–420. The law stated that "anyone guilty of falsification, loss, or total or partial destruc-

The Cuban government found, however, that it could neither legislate cultural change nor enforce satisfactory worker compliance. Despite the new law, poor labor attitudes and behavior abounded. In a September 1969 *Bohemia* article, CTC Secretary-General Miguel Martín described labor attitudes as a "morass of indiscipline, irresponsibility, and superficiality."[97] While other factors, such as weather-related problems, the U.S.-imposed economic blockade, and poorly made Soviet equipment, contributed to the weakening economy, the most critical problem was the negligence of workers and government officials.

Because such overwhelming energy had been directed at the 1970 sugar harvest, other neglected economic sectors rapidly declined. Goods spoiled on the docks or in warehouses. Lack of maintenance caused costly breakdowns. Construction projects stalled. Newly built factories sat idle. Much equipment deteriorated. To make matters worse, workers in other sectors continued to perform carelessly and with little regard for state property. As Mesa-Lago explained, the railroad transportation industry faced a serious crisis because fully "half of the locomotives in existence were wrecked by careless workers." Moreover, poor treatment of fifty thousand imported tractors resulted in a 70 percent drop in their usefulness.[98]

In addition, militarizing the economy proved costly. Incompetent at matching resources to needs, the Armed Forces could not even extract necessary labor discipline. The military, inefficient and wholly lacking essential knowledge and expertise, created a rigid economic system that further undermined Cuban production. In addition, as del Aguila argued, using military personnel in productive tasks probably affected its morale. Cutting cane is rarely viewed in as prestigious terms as "defending the fatherland."[99]

The Economy Falters

By the end of 1969 the Cuban economy could be accurately described as stagnant. Production of virtually all goods had sharply fallen. The 1969 *zafra* yielded about 4.5 million tons, slightly below the 1968 figure of 5.16 tons and substantially less than the production rate throughout the

---

tion of the Labor File and Work Force Control Card shall be charged with a criminal offense."

97. *Bohemia,* September 12, 1969.

98. Mesa-Lago, *The Economy of Socialist Cuba,* pp. 25–26.

99. del Aguila, p. 96.

Table 1. Sugar Production in Cuba, 1958–1975

Year	Raw Output	Year	Raw Output
1958	5.86 tons	1967	6.24 tons
1959	6.03 tons	1968	5.16 tons
1960	5.94 tons	1969	4.46 tons
1961	6.87 tons	1970	8.53 tons
1962	4.88 tons	1971	5.92 tons
1963	3.88 tons	1972	4.32 tons
1964	4.47 tons	1973	5.25 tons
1965	6.16 tons	1974	5.92 tons
1966	4.53 tons	1975	6.31 tons

SOURCE: Mesa-Lago, *The Economy of Socialist Cuba,* p. 58.

1950s.[100] The government's expectations seemed to drop apace. On November 6, 1969, Castro announced that each worker must cut between 1,150 and 1,300 kilograms of cane a day. Since a good worker can cut more than four tons a day (over 4,000 kilograms), and a champion *machetero* can bring in seven tons (7,000 kilograms), this amounts to a substantially scaled-back objective. Clearly, in 1969 workers were producing considerably less than they had produced before the Revolution.

In late 1969 Harvard economist Wassily Leontief visited Cuba and found the economy in shambles. He described the behavior of workers as follows:

> One's first question about the present state of the Cuban economy, after one has seen the innumerable public posters, read the long articles in the daily press, and heard the interminable exhortations on the radio urging every inhabitant of the city . . . to grasp a machete, and go to the country to cut cane, is: Why all the fuss? Why ten years after the glorious revolution does Cuba have great and increasing difficulties in cutting six million tons of sugar now? When before it was able to harvest more than seven million without much trouble and without extracurricular assistance from people living in the cities?[101]

The September 12, 1969, issue of *Bohemia* published an inquiry into labor problems at a Camaguey railway workshop. Workers in Camaguey

100. Ibid., p. 95.
101. *New York Review of Books,* August 21, 1969, p. 16.

were said to be shunning voluntary work and ignoring government calls to increase efficiency. According to the article, in April 1969 only five men out of sixteen hundred had responded to the appeal to cut cane without pay. Those who did volunteer their work labored less than thirty minutes before quitting! Absenteeism accounted for more than 4611 lost days.[102] These certainly did not amount to the worker attitudes that Che Guevara and Fidel Castro had envisioned and sought to create.

During this second period of official efforts to transform attitudes toward labor, the Cuban leadership deemphasized its use of material incentives and stepped up moral suasion. Toward the end of the second phase, however, the leadership moved away from moral suasion and began to implement harsher methods. To increase production and improve attitudes, it reinstated material deprivation. At the same time the government placed the Cuban labor force under military direction. Despite these various and sometimes contradictory policies, the Cuban work force generally remained uncooperative, apathetic, and, at times, openly rebellious.

PHASE THREE

Early 1970 marked a major turning point in the Revolution. The government had singlemindedly focused on efforts to mobilize labor brigades, reward productive workers with moral incentives, and reach the ten-million-ton mark in the sugar harvest. While the 1970 sugar harvest was the largest in Cuban history, it fell substantially short of the government's exalted goal. More important, the leadership carried out the harvest with complete disregard for the rest of Cuba's suffering economy. The failure to reach the 1970 *zafra* target, along with severe shortages, negative growth rates, continual labor resistance, and Soviet pressure to rationalize economic policy, forced Cuban leaders to reassess their labor program. Indeed, Castro and his associates paused to rethink the relationship between *conciencia* and economic and political realities. Che's theory of the "new man" and his notion that a state might simultaneously construct communism and socialism had to be discarded, or at least postponed. The Cuban economy, the state's productive base, desperately needed attention. Consciousness and cultural transformation would have to wait.[103]

102. *Bohemia*, September 12, 1969; see also Hugh S. Thomas, *Cuba: The Pursuit of Freedom* (New York: Harper & Row, 1971), n. 10, p. 1448.

103. Sergio Roca, "Cuban Economic Policy in the 1970s: The Trodden Path," in *Cuban Communism*, ed. Irving Louis Horowitz, 4th ed. (New Brunswick, N.J.: Transaction, 1981), p. 89.

Castro Acknowledges Defeat

In a stunning concession Fidel Castro openly acknowledged that the failure to reach the 1970 *zafra* target resulted directly from foolish idealism and unrealistic policies. On May 20, 1970, while nearly a million citizens stood listening in Havana's Plaza of the Revolution, Castro humbly conceded: "The people aren't the ones who have lost the battle for the ten million.... We—we alone—are the ones who lost the battle ... the administrative apparatus and the leaders."[104] In August, in another public speech, the Cuban leader again stressed that the government had used poor judgment: the "economic developments are much more difficult than we had imagined, the problems are much more complex."

In December Castro admitted that the government had been foolish to believe that policies would succeed as a "result of some sort of magic." The leadership had discovered that in reality economic problems could not "be whisked away very easily." Castro continued: "Let's not do as we have done so often.... [W]hen we get an idea, ... [it] is taken directly from the brain that hatched it to the world of reality where it died for lack of minimal [objective] conditions.... Some try to impose their ideas on reality, rather than reality on their ideas."[105] A September 1970 *Granma* article developed the same line of argument: "Perhaps our major idealism has been to believe that a society which has scarcely left the shell of capitalism could enter, in one bound, into a society in which everyone would behave in an ethical and moral manner."[106] The leadership now insisted that Cuba must "slow down" its transition to communism. Castro solemnly informed his citizens that the Revolution was now "entering a new phase; a much more serious, mature, profound stage."[107]

As part of this new approach the government reexamined the insubordinate and unsupportive attitudes and behavior of Cuban laborers. After concluding that the government and workers were simply not communicating sufficiently, Cuban officials took pains to listen to workers and strove to understand their grievances. The government encouraged laborers to participate in workplace discussions regarding absenteeism, working conditions, productivity, and other such issues. The leadership also signaled to workers that in the future it would improve working conditions, would take seriously their rights and concerns, would give unions more

104. Karl, pp. 27–37.
105. *GWR*, December 20, 1970, p. 3.
106. *Granma*, September 8, 1970.
107. *GWR*, December 20, 1970, pp. 3–7; see also Mesa-Lago, *Cuba in the 1970s*, pp. 25–26.

authority, and would give all laborers more participation in decision-making.[108]

Despite these measures, by September 1970 the government had detected little progress in labor behavior and attitudes. Rather than taking steps to improve working conditions, Fidel Castro once again reproached the workers, blaming them for "lingering prerevolutionary labor attitudes." Castro lamented:

> Some people, without morals and without a sense of their social duty, today take the liberty to scorn their work, remain idle, let the weight of the productive effort fall on the shoulders of others, cheat, and do a million and one other things . . . absolutely insensitive and lazy, without an iota of proletarian spirit. . . . There is no doubt that this antiworker spirit, this scorn for the workers . . . exists.[109]

Castro believed that absenteeism presented the leadership with its most serious labor problem. In fact, he estimated that in 1970 absenteeism had reached 20 percent or higher. In August 1970, for example, 52 percent of agricultural laborers were absent from work in Oriente Province. Lack of incentives and disenchantment among workers further increased the rate of absenteeism. Indeed, many workers found they had the ability to skip work and still be able to buy the few goods available with money already earned. One study concluded that by 1970 workers in many enterprises wasted from one-fourth to one-half of the workday.[110]

That same year a study of the small Cuban village of Buena Ventura concluded that the rate of absenteeism had reached an all-time high. The study noted that in 1970 at a time when Cuban citizens were "emotionally and economically geared" to reach Castro's goal of harvesting ten million tons of sugar cane, "only a scattering of individuals from the [town] turned out sporadically for voluntary labor." The study also concluded that more than 61 percent of the town's citizens never did voluntary labor and 33 percent only participated voluntarily one time during the first revolutionary decade.[111] In a similar study of the first ten years of the Revolution, Lowry Nelson concluded that the "major incidence of absenteeism

108. *GWR*, May 16, 1971, p. 1. See also Salas, p. 341; Domínguez, pp. 275–279.

109. *GWR*, September 20, 1970, p. 2.

110. *Granma*, September 8, 1970, p. 5; cited in Domínguez, pp. 275–276; see also Mesa-Lago, *Cuba in the 1970s*, p. 27; Salas, p. 340.

111. Douglas Butterworth, *The People of Buena Ventura* (Urbana: University of Illinois Press, 1980), pp. 134–135.

during the 1970 *zafra* raises serious questions about worker attitudes."
There can be no doubt, Nelson argued, that "worker morale [was] the
basic cause of the battered Cuban economy."[112] Some Cuban workers were
openly shunning voluntary labor. Others seemed to be refusing to go to
work at all. Few were behaving as the leadership had hoped.

The "Carrot and Stick" Policy

To help to eradicate unacceptable labor attitudes and behavior, the government reintroduced material stimuli. Castro announced that the leadership
would begin using wage differentials in order to raise production. Individual salaries would be based to a substantial degree on the quality and
quantity of goods produced. In despair Castro had turned back to a tactic
that he had earlier renounced forever: material rewards and bonuses designed to induce Cubans to work.

This time, however, the leaders paired the carrot with the stick. Castro
announced that all benefits would be distributed on the basis of worker
production. While officials would reward "exemplary" laborers with better wages and bonuses, they would also punish nonproductive or "bad,"
"lazy," "freeloading," and "shiftless" workers by depriving them of
goods.[113] Castro explained:

> As far as the absentees go, they know they haven't got a chance of
> getting a refrigerator, everybody knows they'll never be able to get
> one, no matter what.... [T]heir right to purchase durable goods
> is taken away.... We are going to give priority to ... a better
> worker, who does his job right and is always on time.... To the
> poor worker, look, you're getting to be a little lazier.... We can go
> even further and deprive him of his clothing ration card.[114]

Castro warned that when deciding who gets special goods, preference
would always go "to the worker who is ... good, conscientious." If you
get "a little lazy, a little less conscientious, we are going to deprive you of
your quota in [the] workers' dining room."

112. Nelson, p. 116. In 1970 another scholar wrote: "It is quite certain that absenteeism,
poor discipline ... have for years been recognized as the real evils of the Cuban economy,
neither appeals nor fines have been able to eradicate them. It is said in Havana that if there
were a way of making every Cuban work the full eight-hour-day the law demands of him,
the situation would improve rapidly" (Karol, p. 426).

113. See Moore, p. 318.

114. Fidel Castro, speech delivered to the Central Organization of Cuban Trade Unions,
September 3, 1970, published in *GWR*, September 20, 1970, p. 4; see also Nelson, p. 119.

This carrot-and-stick strategy, designed to accommodate the material-istic desires of labor and coerce its slackers, signaled an important policy change. On the one hand, the government had clearly subordinated its original goal of creating proper *conciencia* to the new objective of raising productivity. Indeed, expanding production levels became the govern-ment's supreme objective. Accordingly, the leaders moved to improve la-bor performance by providing productive workers with the very material rewards that had previously been scorned as mere capitalist incentives.

Such a policy, reflecting an official effort to cooperate and accommodate disgruntled workers, might be viewed as a small victory for Cuban labor. The government would now reward productive workers with tangible benefits. At the same time, however, the leaders withheld material rewards from workers whose performance continued to lag. By treating productive workers well and punishing the unproductive, the government made quite clear that the leadership, and ultimately Fidel Castro, would continue to try to control Cuban labor.

Coercion Intensifies

The new decade brought forth a renewed emphasis on strict coercion to bring about behavioral change. In September 1970, for example, in a vig-orous effort to increase labor productivity, the state enacted another series of labor laws. Castro argued that a "rational and just society" has the "right to adopt measures of a coercive type" against "exploiters." He warned that these laws would put "pressure" on those "who want to live like parasites off the work of others, refusing to fulfill their most elemen-tary social and human duty." He justified the new laws against indolence by explaining that they "will express the will of the working people of Cuba. . . . The capitalists would never enact laws against indolence, be-cause they themselves are the parasites in the society in which they live."

Castro went on to berate the "corrosive, demoralizing and disorganiz-ing action of laggards."[115] Where man works for society, he pronounced, "laziness must become a crime—a crime similar to stealing. . . . The lazy person robs the people daily."[116] In May 1970 government officials an-nounced that Cubans who had applied for exit visas before May 21, 1970,

115. *GWR*, September 20, 1970, p. 9; see also Fidel Castro's September 28, 1970, speech in Nelson, p. 119. See *Bohemia*, July 31, 1970.

116. *GWR*, September 20, 1970; see also Fidel Castro's September 28, 1970, speech in Nelson, p. 119; see Fidel Castro's speech of July 26, 1970, in *Bohemia*, July 31, 1970. For an interesting discussion of these laws and this phase of the Revolution, see Moore, p. 318.

would henceforth not be allowed to leave the country.[117] These Cubans, Castro explained, owed their labor to the Revolution.

A few months later Minister of Labor Jorge Risquet introduced work quotas, or work "norms."[118] Quotas required a specific amount of work from each laborer as well as from each production unit. Authorities denied various goods, or imposed salary cuts, upon workers who did not reach their quota. By May 1971, this new quota system affected more than three thousand enterprises, and seven hundred thousand workers were operating under this new quota system.[119] And by the end of 1973, 70 percent of all state workers labored under the pressure of work quotas. Among others, President Osvaldo Dórticos hailed the quotas as a positive step toward increased productivity.[120]

The Cuban leadership also called on the unions to accept the responsibility of enforcing labor laws and worker discipline to ensure optimal production. The unions became "vigilance" organizations, similar to the Committees for the Defense of the Revolution, with the task of "watching over" and "reporting trouble[some] workers." In August 1970 Jorge Risquet explained that the unions were to work closely with government officials to lead and oversee Cuban labor.[121] As Raúl Castro later emphasized, the unions "are the instruments that organize and lead the working masses. . . . The principal tasks are productivity and work discipline." The government also employed the CDRs to assist in social vigilance, that is, to keep the government informed of resistant and recalcitrant workers. Castro announced that the function of the CDRs would be to watch over the workers and to report "criminal activity."[122]

The Law Against Laziness

Throughout the last several months of 1970 the government encouraged workers to hold local meetings to determine how the absenteeism problem should be handled. The leadership, which extensively publicized these meetings, claimed that angry workers were themselves demanding harsher laws. That Cuban workers would actually propose a law that would harshly punish their own absenteeism will strike many as dubious. Indeed,

117. Moore, p. 318.
118. *GWR*, May 16, 1971, pp. 1–8.
119. Ibid.
120. *Granma*, September 16, 1970, p. 1; see also *GWR*, March 28, 1971, p. 2.
121. *GWR*, October 9, 1970, p. 10; October 24, 1971, pp. 4–5.
122. Ibid., October 4, 1970; December 10, 1970; for a vivid description of this new role for the CDRs, see Karol, p. 457.

according to a 1971 survey carried out by the Ministry of Food Industry, most workers showed little or no concern for absenteeism. In fact, the survey reveals that more than 40 percent of the workers did not even mention it as a concern.[123]

Castro, disingenuously perhaps, assured the workers that the leadership would "bend" to their wishes, would respond to the "nationwide clamor for a law against loafers," and would reluctantly enact even stricter laws.[124] In September Risquet declared: "To tell the truth, the working masses have, for years, demanded that the revolutionary government adopt rigorous laws against laggards and loafers. Nevertheless we didn't want to be too hasty in enacting a law."[125]

On October 15, 1970, Risquet proposed the first antiloafing or vagrancy law, Resolution No. 425. Under this sweeping measure disobedient workers would be placed in labor camps. Such a regime appealed to Cuban leaders for several reasons. Forced labor, unlike incarceration, did not deplete the work force, yet placing guilty laborers in labor camps effectively removed them from the national labor culture. The troublesome and the nonproductive, who were thought to infect or contaminate other workers, could be separated, stigmatized, and supervised closely.[126]

Debating the law for more than a year, supposedly in order to get the workers' opinion, may have been largely a propaganda ploy. The government is likely to have introduced a harsher antiloafing law precisely because the leaders themselves viewed it as the best means to improve the dismal level of economic productivity. Imposing penal sanctions for loafing suggests that Cuban leaders recognized that, since the moral incentives system had failed, compulsory measures had to be enacted to attain acceptable production levels. By December 1970 a draft of the "Law against Laziness" had been prepared, and the newspapers published it the following month. Thereafter, the leadership launched a massive campaign to encourage worker "discussions" of the new law, and *Granma* published various articles praising its objectives.

The preamble to the new law stated that Cuba had many parasitic citizens who did not work, caused problems in the workplace, and set unwor-

123. Domínguez, p. 488; see also Salas, p. 342; *Verde Olivo*, January 31, 1971, p. 4. According to the survey, concerns of workers from most important to least important were better tools, better health standards, personal on-the-job protection, quality of production, and, finally, absenteeism.

124. *Bohemia*, September 18, 1970; see also *GWR*, September 20, 1970, p. 11; Salas, pp. 342–343.

125. *GWR*, September 20, 1970, pp. 10–12; see also Salas, p. 342.

126. Salas, p. 343.

thy examples for youth. Consequently, the law obligated all men between the ages of seventeen and sixty to put in a full work day. The government considered liable for punishment anyone who missed or left work fifteen days without reasonable justification or who had been reprimanded by their work council at least twice. Sanctions for the "predelinquents" ranged from internment in a reeducation and rehabilitation labor camp to imprisonment from twelve to twenty-four months.

Under the law workers convicted of more serious crimes, such as "economic sabotage," would be sent to prison for life or, in rare cases, for eventual execution before a firing squad. The particular punishment accorded various offenses depended upon such factors as age, number of dependents, length of employment, labor and social records including voluntary participation, and personal or family reasons that might have affected the performance and motivation of the offender.[127] In most cases sanctions could be doubled or tripled at the court's discretion. To assist the government in enforcing the law, Cuban leaders called on the CDRs, the unions, the police, and all citizens to report "crimes of loafing."[128]

The degree of security that Cuban workers felt during the discussions of this harsh law is questionable. Did citizens feel free to speak out against the new law? Were workers assured that they might openly oppose the leadership's initiative without suffering retribution? The evident human rights violations engaged in by the Castro government over the years must have led many workers to conclude that open opposition would pose dangerous risks. In March *Granma* claimed that more than 76 percent of the workers had discussed and approved the law without change.[129] At the same time a front-page article in *Granma Weekly Review* exclaimed: "[Cubans are] joyous over the new anti-loafing law!"[130] Having deftly manufactured public support in this manner, the government on March 15, 1971, enacted the "Law against Laziness."[131]

Thereafter, Cuban leaders tried to justify the antiloafing law by arguing that workers had been sleeping on their jobs, feigning incompetence, and producing little. Indeed, in mid-1971 Fidel Castro went so far as to accuse Cuban sugar *macheteros* of producing less than their slave ancestors. This type of "laziness," he declared, required harsh measures to raise productivity:

127. Ibid., p. 345.
128. Nelson, p. 122.
129. *Granma*, March 9, 1971, p. 1; see also editions of *Bohemia*. The complete text of the law is in *GWR*, March 28, 1971.
130. *GWR*, March 28, 1971, p. 1.
131. Published in the U.S. *Foreign Broadcast Information Service* (*FBIS*), March 15, 1971.

This Revolution will only attain its moral zenith when men who are free will be capable of equaling the production of those who were forced to [produce] as slaves. . . . Slavery has disappeared, but there is no proof that a rational free man is capable of surpassing the production of a slave society without being coerced to! In the final analysis, that's the problem we're debating now. . . . I am personally convinced that you still have people about the place who need a certain degree of coercion.[132]

A *Granma* editorial reiterated this view:

We must make a free man produce more than when he was a slave. . . . We're fighting to extirpate from out of society the ideological left-overs of our past . . . delinquency, laziness and absenteeism. . . . It is not enough to be free men who enjoy these advantages. . . . We must strengthen our ideological work to make the masses understand what their freedom means. Perhaps, then, we will obtain from a free, non-alienated man more labor, more production than when he was still a slave.[133]

Castro thus made perfectly clear that Cuban workers, like their slave ancestors, lacked an acceptable labor *conciencia* and needed "a certain degree of coercion" to motivate them to labor in the sugar fields.[134]

The "Law against Laziness," as sweeping in its provisions as it was vague in its proscribed conduct, afforded the state vast discretion to limit individual rights.[135] Cuban courts, lacking any tradition of judicial review or independence from the Castro government, failed either to strike down the law as overly broad or to protect citizens from arbitrary enforcement. Nevertheless, the law applied only to citizens already in the labor force. It did not affect the many who needed recruiting, including about 400,000 teenagers who were neither in school nor working. To remedy this shortcoming, Castro introduced yet another labor law—one that required all persons over fourteen years of age to register with the authorities.[136] Predictably, perhaps, Cuban youth reacted in fear. On the eve of promulgat-

132. Fidel Castro June 12, 1971, speech, *Granma,* September 7, 1972, p. 2; quoted and discussed in Moore, p. 319.
133. *Granma,* September 7, 1972, p. 2; quoted in Moore, p. 319.
134. Moore, p. 320.
135. Domínguez, pp. 251–252; see also Ian McColl Kennedy, "Cuba's *Ley Contra la Vagrancia*—The Law on Loafing," *UCLA Law Review* 20, no. 6 (August 1973): 1203–1219.
136. Nelson, p. 123.

ing the registration law the government was pleased to find that more than 101,000 persons had registered for work, half of them new workers.[137]

A New Objective: Higher Productivity

The Cuban government turned to forced labor in other contexts as well. In the early 1970s the leadership began to establish rehabilitation "work armies," often with compulsory participation. These groups became yet another form of punishment for absenteeism, truancy, inefficiency, theft, or gambling.[138] At the same time the regular Armed Forces trained its Army of Working Youth only for production, not for combat. Raúl Castro stated that this army's objectives were "quantity and quality." The government paid participants accordingly and further encouraged production with humiliation tactics designed to motivate cooperation. Leaders denounced individual problem workers in the newspaper, over the radio, and in front of their peers. Indeed, authorities forced the most troublesome workers to sleep at the work center, often on the floor.[139]

By 1971 the leadership had openly shifted its priority from developing *conciencia* to increasing production and strengthening the economy. We must eradicate "certain idealisms," Castro warned in January 1971, idealisms such as overestimating worker "*conciencia*." Jorge Risquet asserted that "we have fallen into idealism and . . . our apprenticeship has cost a great deal."[140] On May Day 1971 Castro stressed the need to adopt policies that would immediately alleviate Cuba's economic crises:

> The way to communism is not a question of consciousness alone. It also has to do with the development of the forces of production and the material base. . . . We cannot fall into the idealism of thinking [that] . . . consciousness has been developed and that we already have the necessary material foundation. . . . This really is not the case. . . . If . . . we idealistically go further ahead than is possible, we will have to retreat sooner or later.[141]

137. *GWR,* March 28, 1971, pp. 2–4; May 16, 1971, p. 2; see also *Olivo Verde,* May 9, 1971, p. 6; Nelson, p. 123.

138. See Domínguez, pp. 359–360; also see Matthews, p. 301.

139. Nelson, pp. 123–124.

140. *GWR,* October 24, 1971, pp. 4–5.

141. Ibid., May 16, 1971, p. 7. In another speech Castro said: "We have to commit ourselves to the search for a way of developing *conciencia* which will take us to communism. But the road to communism is not only a road of *conciencia,* but also a road of development

In November 1971 Castro admitted that he had overestimated the government's ability to create *conciencia:* "Let us not forget one thing, and that is that spontaneity does not solve any problems. . . . It is easier to change structure than to change the conscientiousness of man."[142]

Accordingly, the government deemphasized considerably its reliance on "voluntary" labor. Castro conceded that, since Cuban citizens typically refused to volunteer their time, voluntary labor projects would be scaled down to a subsidiary concern. He observed: "Voluntary labor should be carried out [only] to overcome backlogs in the fulfillment of production plans." The leadership came to adopt the view that voluntarism would no longer amount to a vital contribution.[143] Now Cubans would work because the state forced them to do so.

New approaches notwithstanding, the intractable problems of labor resistance, particularly absenteeism, continued to vex the Cuban leadership. In late 1971 a Havana radio program reported: "Due to absenteeism of transportation workers, 554,000 persons were unable to travel during the month of September. A total of 1,847 trips were cancelled due to absentee workers."[144] In December Castro complained to a group of workers about waste, absenteeism, equipment misuse, and poor maintenance. During the same month President Dórticos charged that Cuba's railroad workers mistreated equipment and worked inefficiently.[145]

In May 1972 Castro responded by further tightening work quotas and reemphasizing the incentives program.[146] He reiterated that the government would double its efforts to distribute goods on the basis of worker behavior.[147] In July 1972 he announced that authorities would distribute thousands of radios, stoves, refrigerators, television sets, and pressure cookers depending upon how workers had performed. By May 1973 the unions had distributed to "meritorious workers" more than two million durable consumer goods valued at 237 million pesos.[148]

As part of this ongoing campaign the government also established a system of merits and demerits to be carried out and enforced by union leaders.[149] In this system the union publicly discussed the work record of

---

of the productive forces and of the material base." Entire text of speech in ibid., November 28, 1971.

142. Ibid., December 19, 1971, pp. 12–13.
143. Matthews, p. 296.
144. Nelson, p. 119.
145. Mesa-Lago, *Cuba in the 1970s,* pp. 33–34.
146. *New York Times,* May 15, 1972, p. 12.
147. *GWR,* October 10, 1971, pp. 2–5.
148. *Bohemia,* May 4, 1973, p. 6; see also Roca, p. 106.
149. See *GWR,* September 20, 1970, pp. 4–5.

each laborer. Workers earned merits by doing voluntary labor, attending classes, producing quality products, and saving money, materials, and time. When distributing extra benefits—promotions, transfers, appliances, and housing—government officials relied on the information in these files. At the same time wastefulness, disrespect, lack of discipline, repeated punishments, or poor quality performance brought demerits to the worker's record.[150]

The Economy Grows

Throughout the 1970s the Castro government's policies remained focused on the foremost goal of bringing about sustained economic growth. The results were generally quite positive: for a time the Cuban economy boomed. Aside from the new rhetorical emphasis on economics over politics and ideology, various factors contributed to a swift and impressive economic upswing. With the economy being critically scrutinized by the leadership, government officials improved management and planning. The more efficiently organized economic strategy allocated and used capital effectively. At the same time sugar prices soared on the international market and various states chose to relax the hemispheric embargo against Cuba. All this helped to bring about a significant flow of credit from market economies. The Soviets also contributed substantially to the economic boom on the island by increasing credits and postponing Cuban debt obligations.[151]

In addition, Cuban leaders invigorated the economy by instituting several concrete measures. First, they partially decentralized control over state enterprises. Hence, the leadership gave managers of these enterprises more independence to hire, dismiss, and transfer workers and to deal with internal problem areas. Second, to raise productivity further, Cuban officials continued to deemphasize voluntary labor and emphasize material incentives and wage differentials. The government began paying workers for overtime and distributing housing, vacation time, and durable consumer goods to skilled laborers who overfulfilled work quotas. In addition, it allowed certain market practices and restored the value of money as a buying tool.[152]

150. *Granma*, December 15, 1977. An April 25, 1971, *GWR* article stressed that only workers with strong records would receive new house units. Priority, the article said, would go to those with the best job performance. Need was a secondary consideration.

151. Mesa-Lago, *The Economy of Socialist Cuba*, pp. 176–177.

152. Ibid., pp. 29–32, 176–177; see also Fidel Castro speech, *GWR*, December 20, 1970, p. 6; Fidel Castro speech, *GWR*, December 17, 1987, pp. 6–9; *Granma*, November 30, 1978, p. 3.

Economic Crisis Once Again

Although all worked as planned for a time, at the end of the 1970s and into the early 1980s the Cuban economy took a decided turn for the worse. Several factors triggered this economic crisis. Sugar prices on the international market dropped precipitously. The Cuban leadership faced grave problems in the fishing and nickel industries as well as near disasters in health and agriculture, such as an epidemic of porcine cholera. Rapidly increasing dependence on the Soviet Union weakened Cuba's economic autonomy. The heavy burden of military involvement in Africa proved to be further debilitating.[153] Perhaps most significant, in the first half of the 1980s Cuba's hard-currency trade deficit and Western foreign debt rose dramatically.[154] When the Cuban government responded to these difficulties ineffectively, even lower levels of production followed.

Struggling with these problems in the early 1980s, the Castro leadership initiated economic liberalization. The government allowed private farmers to sell their surplus in free markets, and it permitted citizens to carry out private sales of housing. The government also issued Cubans self-employment licenses that allowed them to drive taxis and carry out minor repair and construction services. These reforms, however, failed to bring about much improvement. By early 1983 the extent to which Cuba's economy had deteriorated alarmed government officials.[155]

These worries only intensified in 1985 when Mikhail Gorbachev, the new General Secretary of the Soviet Communist Party, initiated sweeping policies of economic and political reform. Cuban leaders believed these reforms directly threatened the economic and political security of the Revolution. To worsen the crisis, attitude problems among workers surfaced once again. Officials complained that signs of laziness, mismanagement, corruption, inefficiency, materialism, negligence, and even rebellion appeared throughout society. The government blamed these vices and bourgeois attitudes on the liberal economic policies of the 1970s and early 1980s.[156]

153. Mesa-Lago, *The Economy of Socialist Cuba*, p. 36.

154. See Susan Eckstein, "The Rectification of Errors Or the Errors of the Rectification Process in Cuba?" *Cuban Studies* 20, no. 1 (Fall/Winter 1990): 73. According to Eckstein, this occurred basically because hard-currency exports did not keep pace with imports and because the cost of servicing money previously borrowed from Western sources soared in the mid-1980s.

155. Mesa-Lago, *The Economy of Socialist Cuba*, pp. 28–36.

156. *FBIS*, December 8, 1986, p. Q1.

PHASE FOUR

In February 1986, responding to these problems, Fidel Castro introduced the "Rectification" at the Third Party Congress. The leadership hoped this would amount to a decisive phase in the Cuban Revolution's efforts to create a new Cuban citizen. Certainly the Rectification marked an abrupt and dramatic break from policies of the 1970s and early 1980s. The officially sanctioned materialistic policies of these years, the leadership believed, had openly encouraged and strengthened latent capitalist attitudes—materialism and selfishness—and had undermined the development of proper *conciencia*.

In many respects the Rectification starkly rejected the official thinking of the previous decade. Cuban leaders designed this "strategic counteroffensive" to avert what they viewed as pervasive social and economic deterioration.[157] In a December 1986 speech in Havana, Fidel Castro criticized the widespread decadence of Cuban citizens. He complained that the country contained far too many "opportunists, populists, irresponsible, weak and paternalistic people."[158] "The lack of controls," Castro noted, had allowed "some to grow rich."[159] All this had to end. Those involved in "all kinds of shady business in order to make money" had to be stopped.[160] Castro accused many citizens—workers, students, professionals, and Party members—of lacking *conciencia* and falling under the spell of immoral materialism.

The Rectification's Attack on Labor

Once again the government singled out the Cuban worker for blame. Negative capitalist attitudes, Castro insisted in August 1986, had surfaced in the workplace. The decadent attitudes of the 1970s most clearly "manifest themselves in the labor sector."[161] After twenty-five years of Revolution, the Cuban leader lamented, labor attitudes and the consequent levels of worker productivity remained abysmally low.[162] Government officials reported that labor resistance and decadence amounted to the most telling

157. Jorge I. Domínguez, "Leadership Changes in Cuba since 1960," in *Leadership Change in Communist States,* ed. Raymond C. Taras (Boston: Unwin Hyman, 1989). See also *GWR,* June 15, 1986, p. 3.

158. *GWR,* December 7, 1986, Special Section, p. 3.

159. Ibid., June 15, 1986, pp. 3–4.

160. Ibid., July 13, 1986, p. 9.

161. Ibid., August 3, 1986, p. 1.

162. Ibid., August 2, 1987, p. 3.

economic crisis since the Revolution's inception. Creating proper attitudes toward labor once again became the government's leading priority. In late 1986 Castro declared: "Industrial know-how and a work ethic are nobody's whim. They are a requisite of modern life. . . . They are a must if we are to narrow the gap . . . between an underdeveloped country . . . and the industrialized nations." And Castro concluded, "We need industry— an industrial ethic not just to eat, dress and live decently, but to survive!"[163]

As part of the new campaign the leadership berated the apparent inefficiency in Cuban enterprises. In December 1986 a Havana television announcer commented that unacceptably poor plant efficiency in Cuba's sugar mills amounted to the country's greatest problem. The announcer contended that during the January to November 1986 period twenty-nine industrial, sugar, construction, and people's government enterprises had failed to fulfill production plans.[164] In that same month Fidel Castro himself chided construction workers for moving too slowly in their efforts to construct badly needed medical facilities.[165] He also attacked widespread inefficiency and absenteeism among nurses and repairmen. These, he claimed, were signs of "terrible national selfishness." Authorities levied much the same criticisms at agricultural workers. One leader, Julian Rizo Alvarez, commented that the Cuban agricultural and livestock sectors needed increased efficiency.[166] And Fidel Castro demanded stricter labor requirements within the agricultural sector of society.[167]

The Cuban leadership also criticized workers for their inability to fulfill daily work hours. At the Third Party Congress Castro insisted: "[S]ocialism cannot be constructed if there are problems with the fulfillment of work hours in the field . . . and if people work between 4 to 5 hours in the fields. Socialism cannot be constructed if only . . . 80 percent, 75 percent, or 70 percent of work hours are fulfilled."[168] Castro complained about the misuse of work hours in "sugarcane and general agriculture, in construction, in factories, in dozens of places. . . . Those negative trends must be eradicated." He continued: "No one has . . . seen it ever, anywhere, that a country can develop, advance and be enriched without labor. We must learn how to create an honorable concept of labor. All our honor . . . must be gathered together to increase the value . . . the importance of labor."[169]

163. A Fidel Castro speech on December 19, 1986, in ibid., January 11, 1987, p. 7.
164. *FBIS*, December 19, 1986, p. Q6.
165. Ibid., December 23, 1986, p. Q10.
166. Ibid., December 24, 1986, p. Q7.
167. Ibid., December 8, 1986, p. Q13.
168. Ibid., December 5, 1986, p. Q22.
169. Ibid.

In early 1987 the Cuban government carried out a study of 471 enterprises and found more than 20,000 violations of labor regulations.[170] Castro reminded his people that the labor laws required Cubans to use the workday wisely. He announced that the leadership intended to enforce the laws and to eradicate "all that nonsense and foolishness that we have been examining" because it has led everywhere to "lack of discipline." Discipline, the Cuban leader maintained, "is basic in production. . . . [I]t must be dealt with through effective political, social and ideological education. . . . We must master . . . the science of organization and management."[171] In a 1987 speech Castro complained that too many people were "tinkering around and wasting time . . . people only working fifty percent of capacity."[172]

Cuban officials scolded workers, enterprise managers, and supervisors for negligence and materialism. "Some of our enterprise heads," Castro bitterly concluded, "have also become capitalist-like entrepreneurs."[173] The Revolution's leader also attacked managers for unnecessary hiring: "There is nothing more expensive, more useless, than overstaffing."[174] Castro worried that "enterprises were asking constantly for more men instead of controlling . . . their work."[175] He called on work centers to stop "inflating their payrolls" and praised those, such as the National Science Center and two power plants, that complied. He chastised others, such as enterprises in the tourism industry, that failed to cut workers' salaries.

Within several years the government had slashed administrative jobs by 6,300 workers and managerial jobs by 16,400.[176] Still, Castro declared that certain "elements" should be "ashamed of themselves for having . . . taken advantage of the state's magnanimity."[177] The "bourgeois enemy," he warned, still exists.[178] In June 1991 Politburo member Jaime Crombet told managers that "those who can be easily tricked, are crooks or fools. . . . Beware . . . you cannot continue."[179] With such repeated rhetorical warnings the Rectification Campaign initiated another official effort to transform Cuban labor attitudes.

170. *GWR,* February 8, 1987, p. 3.

171. Ibid., July 5, 1987, p. 5.

172. Fidel Castro Speech at an information meeting of the Provincial Committee of the Party in Havana, January 7, 1987, in ibid., January 25, 1987, p. 2.

173. Ibid., April 27, 1986, p. 9.

174. Ibid., October 18, 1987, p. 6.

175. Ibid., April 27, 1986, p. 10 (supplement); also quoted in Eckstein, p. 77.

176. Eckstein, p. 84; cited from *GWR,* February 21, 1988, p. 3; December 25, 1988, p. 9.

177. *GWR,* January 13, 1986, p. 9.

178. Ibid., May 25, 1986, p. 4.

179. *FBIS,* June 21, 1991, p. 1.

Abandoning Material Incentives and Encouraging Voluntarism

In response to the decadent materialism and negligent attitudes that characterized Cuban labor, the leadership during the Rectification suddenly abandoned the economic liberalization policies of the early 1980s. The revolutionary government limited private enterprise and immediately eliminated the use of prices and some material incentives. The leaders claimed that doing away with material incentives would work to eradicate Cuba's "lack of discipline" and "fetish for money."[180] Indeed, Castro reminded his listeners that "a consciousness, a communist spirit, a revolutionary will ... will always be a thousand times more powerful than money."[181] For both ideological and economic purposes, the government also announced that moral incentives would once again replace material incentives as the primary means to motivate workers. As in the late 1960s, another period of severe scarcity of resources, *conciencia* became the leadership's all-encompassing obsession.

As part of the renewed focus on moral incentives, the government began to press citizens—for the first time in more than ten years—to volunteer their labor. As the government focused its attention elsewhere, voluntary labor had steadily declined over the intervening years. The minibrigade movement, Fidel Castro complained, had completely died out, and in Cuba "there are even people who ignore and combat them."[182] A year later he recalled:

> The ... view that voluntary work was neither basic nor essential gained more and more ground. . . . The idea was that voluntary work was kind of silly, a waste of time, that problems had to be solved with overtime, with more and more overtime, and this while the regular workday was not even being used efficiently. We had fallen into the bog of bureaucracy, of overstaffing, of work norms that were out of date, the bog of deceit, of untruth. We'd fallen into a whole load of bad habits that Che would have been really appalled at.[183]

180. Fidel Castro's speech, *GWR*, January 12, 1986, p. 6. See also May 7, 1989, p. 4.
181. Ibid., December 14, 1986, p. 2 (supplement); quoted in Rhoda Rabkin, "Cuba: The Aging of a Revolution," in *Socialist Cuba: Past Interpretations and Future Challenges,* ed. Sergio G. Roca (Boulder: Westview Press, 1988), p. 35.
182. *GWR*, June 15, 1986, p. 3.
183. Ibid., October 18, 1987, p. 4.

"Voluntary work," the Cuban leader announced three months later, has "languished" and has become "something of a pastime for adults and youngsters, a formality."

In 1987, in his annual 26th of July speech, Castro told Cubans that the state had re-created the construction minibrigades cast aside earlier in the Revolution. Since much construction needed to be done, he pointed to voluntary labor as the only sensible answer. The leaders called upon these brigades, comprised of workers temporarily released from their work centers and people who were not otherwise employed, such as students, housewives, and jobless members of the labor force, to build housing and social facilities, such as doctors' offices, schools, and day-care centers. These minibrigades, Castro claimed, would help to create the "communist work spirit" and, in line with Marxist thought, help to break down the barriers between manual and intellectual labor.[184]

"What will all of this cost?" Castro asked. And he answered, "The incredible thing is that it won't cost in terms of wages." The Cuban leader called on citizens to volunteer their labor in order to "rebuild" Havana by constructing 225,000 homes by the year 2000.[185] Cubans must volunteer their labor in order to create the proper "communist work spirit" and to preserve the Revolution.[186] During the Rectification the Cuban government thus began to insist anew that voluntarism would be fundamental to the ongoing effort to create *conciencia*. Voluntarism was supposed to provide a telling blow against the selfish materialism of the past decade.

Officials then began to encourage all Cuban citizens—children as well as senior citizens—to contribute to this nationwide labor effort. A December 1987 *Granma* article rallied the elderly to join voluntary labor groups, claiming that it would improve their health and make them "feel useful."[187] Children, Castro insisted, must also participate in constructing homes and schools. In a January 1988 speech he noted that Cuban children were helping to build day-care centers.[188] The government also claimed that Cuba had six hundred schools in the countryside, including senior high schools and vocational schools. In total, more than three hundred thousand students worked the land to supply the country with food. Castro noted enthusiastically, "[This] relationship between

184. Eckstein, p. 69.

185. See *GWR,* January 12, 1986, p. 4; see also August 2, 1987, p. 11; September 13, 1987, pp. 3–4.

186. Fidel Castro, quoted in ibid., August 3, 1986, p. 5; December 13, 1987, pp. 8–9.

187. *Granma,* December 31, 1987, p. 1; also see *GWR,* December 13, 1987, p. 9.

188. *GWR,* January 12, 1988, p. 3.

intellectuals and manual labor contributes to the students' overall education."[189]

Moral Incentives

In 1987, in rhetoric reminiscent of the Revolutionary Offensive, the Party announced that it would reinitiate the ritual of honoring outstanding workers with awards and distinctions. In January 1988 the government presented thousands of citizens with voluntary work certificates.[190] In early 1990 Fidel Castro awarded the title of "Labor Hero of the Republic of Cuba" to a group of workers and presented revolutionary flags to seventeen outstanding cooperatives.[191] In June Castro gave the National Vanguard Flag to the Blas Roca Construction Contingent.[192] The following September the leaders rewarded three hundred civilians and military comrades with medals.[193] In May 1991 Fidel Castro again presented Labor Hero titles to numerous workers who had demonstrated exceptional attitudes and behavior.[194]

To motivate workers and raise productivity, the Cuban Confederation of Labor created new "moral" incentives as well. It resurrected the 1968 Guevarist concept of emulation. In order to save textiles the authorities selected as awards ceramic, wood, or glass objects over flags.[195] Cuban officials also announced a set of new rules regarding emulation. Unlike in the late 1960s awards would go only to those who surpassed their quotas; those who merely reached their quotas would not be honored.[196]

To inculcate better labor attitudes, the leaders, particularly Fidel Castro, began to lecture with renewed vigor about the virtues of hard work. They encouraged citizens to adopt a proper revolutionary *conciencia* and beseeched workers to think as true revolutionaries. Invoking military rhetoric, Castro declared: "For all revolutionaries today, ideological struggle is the front line of combat, the first revolutionary trench."[197] In July 1986 Castro reminded citizens that "the Revolution doesn't mean economic

189. Ibid., March 2, 1986, p. 8.
190. Ibid., January 10, 1988, p. 3.
191. Ibid., February 4, 1990, p. 8.
192. Ibid., June 10, 1990, p. 9.
193. *FBIS*, September 11, 1990, p. 2.
194. Fidel described these workers as dedicated, modest, humble, and selfless. In addition, he presented Jesús Menéndez medals to five additional outstanding workers. See ibid., May 3, 1991, p. 1.
195. Ibid., October 4, 1990, p. 7.
196. Announced on Radio Rebelde, August 29, 1987; see also ibid., August 31, 1987, p. 1.
197. *Bohemia*, December 26, 1980, p. 59.

development alone.... [I]t also means defending an ideology ... and a whole series of values that must be promoted."[198] In January 1987 Castro told Party members that "there is only one way" for Cuba to develop—"serious, intelligent and responsible work."[199] He continued: "We are under an obligation to be more serious in our work, to work harder than ever before."

One week later Castro again echoed the words of Che: Cubans must "double their efforts" and work "in a communist manner with a communist spirit and a communist awareness."[200] The following month a *Granma* article called on workers and managers to "have a revolutionary, socialist concept and a communist attitude."[201] Two months later Castro stated that "socialism is based fundamentally on conscience."[202] And in January 1988 the Cuban leader remarked, "We must push negative tendencies and mistakes and shoddy workmanship to one side.... [I]f we work well,... we'll be making more correct use of freedom."[203]

During this period the government not only implored citizens to change their attitudes and behavior, it also sternly criticized them. In a December 1987 speech, for example, Fidel Castro criticized "shoddy work, lack of discipline, bureaucratic-technocratic attitudes and laxness."[204] Several months later he reprimanded workers for the poor quality of their performance. "Quality," he explained, "is an even larger problem than quantity. One hundred well-laid bricks are better than 120 or 130 poorly laid ones." A few weeks later, speaking on the thirty-fifth anniversary of the Moncada Barracks attack, Castro scolded his listeners and reminded them that if Cubans continued to work at the current levels, the country would never develop. "We ... have some bad habits," Castro conceded. "It would be demogogical and irresponsible to tell the people or any citizen that a country can develop and obtain everything it needs [while] working deficiently or working little."[205]

In December 1988 at the celebration of the thirty-second anniversary of the *Granma* landing, an irritated Castro rebuked the masses for the "manifestation of indiscipline, ... wrongdoing, sloppiness, social indisci-

198. Fidel Castro, *GWR*, July 13, 1986, p. 9.

199. Fidel Castro speech at an information meeting of the Provincial Committee of the Party in Havana, January 7, 1987, ibid., January 25, 1987, p. 2.

200. Ibid., January 11, 1987, p. 7; January 25, 1987, p. 4.

201. Ibid., February 1, 1987, p. 1.

202. Fidel Castro, ibid., April 19, 1987, p. 12. In late 1987 Castro implored workers to adopt a "spirit of working" (ibid., December 13, 1987, p. 8). "Worker consciousness must be raised," a *GWR* article stated (ibid., September 25, 1988, supplement).

203. Ibid., January 10, 1988, p. 3.

204. *Granma*, December 31, 1987, p. 1.

205. *GWR*, August 7, 1988, p. 3.

pline, and delinquency."[206] He demanded that they "work better and more efficiently." In a speech to the National Union of Construction Workers, Castro went so far as to contend that all Cubans were guilty: "In the future we will have to change the notion of enterprise. . . . The worst crime committed . . . and all are guilty . . . is to have millions and millions of people dedicated to useless activity."[207] Cuba required an entirely "new mentality, a new culture, and new values."[208]

Cuban officials also called on citizens to view work in honorable terms. In November 1987, for example, Castro criticized citizens for scorning work and demanded that labor be viewed with respect and reverence. He reprimanded Cuba's high-salaried professionals for not carrying out "a difficult chore" alongside the agricultural worker. A professional, he explained, must "create with his hands and not only with his intelligence."[209]

"Well-being can't come before work," Castro declared, "for work leads to well-being and only work can produce well-being." The Cuban leader continued: "We live in a time when . . . work can't be viewed as punishment but rather as a means for progress. . . . We must make a supreme effort in economizing and achieving efficiency."[210] In early 1989 Castro delivered another speech, bitterly complaining: "It is terrible that people should shirk manual labor."[211] After defining professionals in curious fashion as surgeons and Party members, Castro made quite clear that they too would be required to contribute to the national labor effort.[212]

Creating Construction Brigades

To its chagrin, the government speedily discovered that Cuban productivity had grown immune to rhetorical appeals. Only two years after their revival, the minibrigades had still failed to construct their quota. Although the officials had planned to have the minibrigades construct 50,000 houses between 1987 and 1989, the leaders ultimately reduced that target number to 35,000. By November 1989, however, only 15,515 houses had been built in the prior three-year period, 44 percent of the target. In October 1989,

206. Ibid., December 18, 1988, pp. 2–5.

207. Ibid., July 17, 1988, p. 5.

208. Ibid., January 10, 1988, p. 2.

209. Fidel Castro, speech at Havana Provincial Party Meeting, November 29, 1987, ibid., December 13, 1987, p. 8.

210. Ibid., July 24, 1988, p. 4.

211. Ibid., January 22, 1989, p. 4.

212. Fidel Castro, speech at Havana Provincial Party Meeting, November 29, 1987, ibid., December 13, 1987, p. 8.

on the third anniversary of the revival of the minibrigades, Castro harshly criticized their inefficiency: "The brigades," he complained, are "disorganized," careless with equipment, waste resources, and "lack control of costs."[213]

In view of such failures Cuban leaders decided that construction contingents might be a better means to tackle the problem. Authorities thus carefully selected workers, paid them well, and gave them comfortable, air-conditioned living quarters, first-rate food, special health care, and other amenities. Although the contingents worked long and hard, often twelve to fifteen hours a day, authorities did not pay overtime.

In October 1987 the government created one such construction group called the Blas Roca Labor Contingent. While it initially consisted of one brigade of 167 men, the Contingent slowly expanded and by 1990 included thirty brigades with more than 4,000 workers. By late 1990 more than 35,000 Cubans throughout the country labored in either a minibrigade or a labor contingent.[214] While these labor organizations raised productivity to some degree, they still continued to be hampered by shortages in fuel and construction material.[215]

Augmenting the Role of the Party

In its attempt to raise Cuban consciousness further, the government carried out measures to strengthen considerably the role of the Cuban Communist Party in monitoring worker behavior and enforcing labor laws. In December, at the Third Party Congress, Castro insisted that during this difficult period of struggle the Party must be at the "center of the battle to correct errors."[216] He called on Party leaders to be more rigorous, strict, disciplined, and demanding. Their objectives should be to destroy capitalist work habits and to guide laborers to "rectify their actions" and adopt "truly communist" behavior in the workplace.[217] The Party must generate virtues such as a "passion for creative work, a spirit of solidarity, noble patriotism ... [and it must] continue to fight [the] corruption of capitalist society."[218]

213. Ibid., October 15, 1989, pp. 2–4; also cited in Carmelo Mesa-Lago, "On Rectifying Errors of a Courteous Dissenter," *Cuban Studies* 20, no. 1 (Fall/Winter 1990): 104–105.

214. *GWR*, August 20, 1989; July 8, 1988, p. 3; February 9, 1986, p. 4; see also *FBIS*, October 4, 1990, p. 1; *GWR*, February 4, 1990, p. 8.

215. Mesa-Lago, "On Rectifying Errors of a Courteous Dissenter," p. 105.

216. *FBIS*, December 8, 1986, p. Q1. Also *GWR*, January 25, 1987, p. 3.

217. *FBIS*, December 5, 1986, p. Q16.

218. *GWR*, February 16, 1986, p. 16.

In July 1988 Castro underscored the vital importance to the Revolution of an unchallenged, highly centralized party: "In our rectification process . . . the role of the party is made stronger, . . . the role of our party becomes increasingly essential. There will be nothing to weaken the party's authority. . . . We need just one party. . . . [S]ocialism must be built and the basic builder is the party."[219] Henceforth, the government would centralize under Party supervision all sectors of the Cuban state's skeletal economy. The Party had "to be everywhere," to "see everything that is going on," and to "fight against things that we see being done wrong everywhere."[220]

In October 1990 the commission meeting to plan the Fourth Party Congress released a report that approved new Politburo proposals to increase the Party's authority. It proposed centralizing and concentrating the Party's decision-making functions in the hands of considerably fewer cadres. The commission advocated significantly curtailing the power of grass-roots-level Party entities. The text of the report stated: "[The] party will fulfill its role of orientation and control."[221] At the close of the October 1991 Party Congress, Castro again reiterated that the Party's role would expand further: "The Cuban Revolution is inconceivable without the Party, power is inconceivable without the Party, socialism is inconceivable without the Party."[222]

By late 1991, however, the government faced mounting economic crises. Soviet and East European subsidies and imports of fuel and other needed products continued to dwindle, as did Cuba's hard-currency reserves. At the same time the leadership publicly lamented that moral suasion had failed once more to motivate citizens to volunteer their labor. With few citizens volunteering, the agricultural sector continued to suffer from a decided shortage of able workers.

Worker Reassignments and Salary Cuts

To strengthen basic production units, Cuban leaders introduced labor regulations that allowed the government to reassign to agricultural work laborers in nonessential sectors or in sectors lacking fuel and other necessities. Castro informed Cubans that much effort would go toward ensur-

219. Ibid., August 7, 1988, p. 3; see also *Granma*, December 31, 1987, p. 1.
220. *GWR*, January 25, 1987, p. 4; quoted in Rabkin, p. 35.
221. See *GWR*, February 10, 1991, p. 1; October 14, 1990, p. 9; see also *FBIS*, October 9, 1990, p. 3; *GWR*, January 25, 1987, p. 3. In addition, the Party carried out a kind of purge in which many negligent cadres were replaced.
222. *Miami Herald*, International Edition, October 14, 1991, p. 4A.

ing the success of the island's newly introduced "food program," which sought to enhance agricultural self-sufficiency through increasing domestic production of fruits and vegetables.[223] In October 1990 Castro declared that "no more social projects will be started . . . no schools, day-care centers, hospitals."[224] And the government immediately reassigned workers to agriculture, including at least twenty thousand from Havana at the peak of the sugar harvest.

The government initiated the labor reassignment process by confiscating many Havana taxis and sending the drivers off to agricultural work. Cuban authorities required these drivers to divide each month between fifteen days of taxi driving and fifteen days of agricultural labor.[225] Two months later the leadership permanently assigned a group of construction workers to agricultural activities. To house these roving workers, the government created more than fifty agricultural labor camps scattered throughout the country.[226] The leadership simply informed the workers that they would remain in the camps and at their new jobs for a minimum of two years.[227] By late 1991 the government had started to construct small towns in rural areas to enable laborers to live and work in the agricultural sector on a more permanent basis.[228]

During this period of closing unnecessary, expensive, or inefficient enterprises and relocating workers to the agricultural sector, many laborers found themselves unemployed and discontent. To ease their concerns, the government assured these "available" workers that jobless persons waiting for a new assignment would continue to receive 60 percent of their salaries. The state would not, however, allow them to continue eating their meals in the workers' cafeterias.[229] At the same time those who were offered a new job, but displayed a "bad attitude" and refused to accept it, would receive one month's pay and no more.[230] In July 1991 the Castro government announced that nearly 87 percent of Cuba's surplus workers had been reassigned, mostly to the agricultural sector.[231] The leadership also pruned workers from the overgrown bureaucracy and transplanted

223. The Food Program is explained in *FBIS*, February 7, 1991, p. 2.

224. Ibid., October 1, 1990, p. 12; see also January 2, 1991, p. 4.

225. Ibid., October 24, 1990, p. 3.

226. Ibid., September 26, 1990, p. 4; October 12, 1990, p. 3; October 26, 1990, pp. 4–5; January 2, 1991, p. 4; February 7, 1991, p. 6; February 26, 1991, p. 15.

227. Ibid., December 13, 1990, p. 3.

228. Susan Kaufman Purcell, "Collapsing Cuba," *Foreign Affairs* 71 (1992): 134.

229. *Miami Herald,* International Edition, February 14, 1992, p. 3A.

230. See *GWR*, December 9, 1990, p. 5; see also *FBIS*, September 26, 1990, p. 4; October 5, 1990, p. 1; October 10, 1990, p. 2; February 4, 1991, p. 1; April 1, 1991, p. 11; *Granma International (GI)*, April 28, 1991, p. 2.

231. *FBIS,* July 23, 1991, p. 4.

them to agricultural work. In February 1992, for example, the government announced that the work force in the Agriculture Ministry's central offices had been cut by 52 percent and that more than forty-six thousand employees had been relocated from the Construction Ministry to state farms.[232]

In addition to reducing employment security the government sought to reduce unemployment and seniority rights as well. The leaders announced that industrial jobs were to be filled on the basis of qualification and skill, not years of service as before.[233] In some sectors, such as construction, the government abandoned its traditional revolutionary policy of guaranteeing a basic wage. The authorities allowed State enterprises to hire on a piecework basis. As their labor needs changed, managers could take on and dismiss workers. They could also pay employees less than a full-time wage.[234] In some cases the government also cut salaries, an effective cost-saving measure in a time of economic despair.

In July 1988 *Granma Weekly Review* ran a series of articles, the first of which was entitled "In Praise of Work."[235] The second article explained that the most difficult aspect of Rectification was the official requirement that wage disparities be eliminated. Those making more money would be forced to give up the excess, the article explained, since their salaries were "based on obsolete norms and mistaken production criteria."[236] Not only did the government cut dramatically certain selected salaries but the salary of nearly every Cuban fell slightly throughout the late 1980s. At the same time prices of consumer goods increased. Although these policies encouraged labor efficiency and minimized nonproductive expenditures, they substantially diminished the quality of life for the average Cuban worker.

Finally, the government moved, once again, to crack down on vagrancy, mismanagement, corruption, noncompliance, and lack of discipline in the workplace. Castro reminded Cuban citizens that now, more than ever before in the thirty years of Revolution, the Cuban state could not and would not tolerate laziness. In September 1989, for example, the leadership severely penalized railroad workers for negligence, poor discipline, and unacceptable work habits.[237] Government officials assured their listeners that uncooperative workers would be sent forthwith to the sugar fields. Henceforth, hard agricultural labor would punish such offenses as absenteeism and vagrancy.

---

232. *Miami Herald*, International Edition, February 14, 1992, p. 3A.
233. *GWR*, August 3, 1986, p. 5; see also Eckstein, p. 72; *GWR*, February 12, 1988, p. 3; *GWR*, December 25, 1988, p. 9.
234. Eckstein, pp. 72–73.
235. Ibid., September 17, 1988, p. 3
236. Ibid., September 18, 1988, p. 3.
237. Ibid., September 17, 1989, p. 3.

These new policies toward labor—voluntarism, reassignment, and salary cuts—represented a throwback to past policies.[238] The government reverted to Che's tactics of moral suasion and coercion in order to change attitudes and raise productivity. Given the prevailing economic climate, however, the leaders had few carrots to offer. They significantly reduced tangible benefits such as material incentives for exemplary worker performance.[239] Instead, government measures forced workers to perform specific jobs, to live in labor camps, to accept cuts in already low salaries, and to disrupt their personal life by leaving their home and family. Fidel Castro had effectively stripped the Cuban labor force of the few choices it had formerly retained. Should a laborer refuse to cooperate, the officials simply denied him a salary. Life under Castro's Rectification Campaign could be quite brutal for the nonconformist.

How did the workers respond? In July 1990 *Bohemia* ran a lengthy article on the "serious problem" of frequent and abrupt job changes among Cuban workers. The article contended that most Cubans avoided agricultural work when possible: "Social conditions cause very few to want to be farm workers. . . . That idea has still not changed." The article cited a survey, conducted by the Union of Young Communists, that sought to discover the degree to which Cuban laborers were satisfied. According to the survey results, only about one-third of the workers interviewed expressed happiness with their jobs. Most were unhappy in their new assignments because family and friends did not consider their work respectable. Moreover, the survey concluded, parents were encouraging their children to avoid agricultural labor and to remain at home until a more respectable job became available. The *Bohemia* article concluded by urging citizens to view manual labor as a meaningful and valuable form of work.[240]

The UJC survey reveals the degree to which the Cuban state forced its workers to perform labor they neither enjoyed nor respected and from which they gained very little. Even more important, however, given the obvious links of the pollsters to the government and the possible repercussions of speaking out against official policies, is the startling fact that so many workers admitted to dissatisfaction. The survey suggests that after more than thirty years of rigorous official attempts to transform culture the people's attitudes toward manual labor had changed very little.

The performance of workers reflected their unhappiness. Indeed, despite the threat of being fired or transferred, workers continued to labor

238. See Rabkin, p. 35.
239. See, for example, *GWR*, February 6, 1986, p. 4.
240. *Bohemia*, July 27, 1990, pp. 42–45.

ineffectively. The government's constant and inefficient system of transferring workers from one work site to another only worsened the problem. In January 1991 an article in *Trabajadores,* the CTC's official newspaper, discussed the high degree of labor turnover in Havana City Port. According to Guillermo Aguiar, Assistant Director of Post Operations, new workers often barely finished the training period before moving on: "People . . . desert their jobs every day by the dozens. . . . Today one group is starting and another is leaving with no explanation."[241] Despite the new official labor policies, levels of productivity failed to improve.

Increased Vigilance

In yet another effort to counter these intractable labor difficulties, the government called on mass organizations, such as the CTC and the CDRs, to increase vigilance and pressure in the work sites to create proper revolutionary work attitudes. In early 1987 Fidel Castro told union leaders that the CTC's primary role during the process of Rectification was to construct labor socialism and communism throughout the workplace.[242] At the closing session of the CTC Congress, Castro called on the union to strive for efficient management and leadership of the workers and insisted that the unions require "good work," "labor discipline," and "economic efficiency."[243] In September 1990 *Trabajadores* published an article calling on the CTC to "reinforce, more than ever, our collective vigilance against waste, hoarding, speculation and cronyism."[244] A month later Pedro Ross Leal, the Secretary General of the CTC, stated that the union should guard against poor worker performance. It needed to respond with "great severity to social undiscipline and violations of rules."[245]

A meeting of the CTC National Secretariat concluded that "social deformities" must be fought and the CTC must "not tolerate poor work."[246] In February 1991 Leal told a group of workers: "[Since] many labor centers are encountering production problems, [the role of the union is] to lead [and] guide [the workers]."[247] In March 1991 the CTC hinted that it would revitalize "worker guards" as militia-type labor organizations designed to enforce labor laws and to report offenders.[248]

241. *Trabajadores,* January 26, 1991, p. 3.
242. *GWR,* January 25, 1987, p. 7.
243. Ibid., February 4, 1990, p. 8.
244. *Trabajadores,* September 1, 1990, p. 1.
245. *FBIS,* October 18, 1990, p. 4.
246. Ibid., October 17, 1990, p. 1.
247. Ibid., February 15, 1991, p. 11.
248. *Bohemia,* March 22, 1991, pp. 26–29.

Cuban leaders also created a new government organ, the People's Councils, to minimize the bureaucracy within work sites and to guard more closely the behavior of workers and citizens. The government assigned to the PCs the role of investigating and removing troublesome workers or managers from their posts. As Jorge Lezcano Pérez, First Secretary of the Party in Havana Province, explained, the leaders created the PCs to control crime, waste of resources, and labor problems: "We expect that these councils will be able to have a more adequate control of state resources."[249] A few days later Castro explained that presidents of the People's Councils "will be poking around" in butcher shops, restaurants, salons, and elsewhere, looking for possible problems, and "they will know what is going on." The PCs, he stated, will "help us in this battle" to "fight the vices . . . [and] forms of corruption." Castro reminded his listeners that Cuba was experiencing great difficulties and fighting "a battle for efficiency." He continued: "We must be proud soldiers of this era, this hour, this struggle, this mission."[250] The Councils, Castro claimed, "will be watching everything, . . . imposing and demanding order."[251]

Meanwhile, the President of the National Assembly of People's Power, Juan Escalona Reguera, praised the People's Councils as important means for the Council of State to improve worker efficiency and to supervise vigilantly all that occurred within their jurisdiction.[252] In October 1990 Fidel Castro met with the presidents of the People's Councils and predicted that the PCs would "establish more discipline, more order, more efficiency, more authority."[253] To assist in the vigilance campaign against social "vices," Cuban leaders called on the "combative virtues" of the CDRs.[254]

The government also turned to the masses themselves and insisted that they, too, should pressure, publicly and privately, all those workers who were loafing or otherwise resisting government policies. In late 1990 Castro insisted:

> [Cubans should] create a climate of condemnation for the scoundrels, the loafers, the idlers, and parasites. . . . It is a moral climate that should pressure. . . . I am referring to those who abandon the ship of the Revolution. . . . There are some around, I can see them

249. *FBIS*, September 26, 1990, pp. 7–8.
250. Ibid., October 1, 1990, p. 16.
251. Ibid., pp. 15–16.
252. Ibid., October 11, 1990, p. 3.
253. Ibid., October 12, 1990, p. 2.
254. *GWR*, October 14, 1990, p. 5; see also October 21, 1990, p. 9.

here . . . those who lose their morality and try to spread their demoralization. We must confront them.[255]

The Cuban leader continued: "In difficult times the *gusanos* want to rear their heads and they must be told *gusanos* back to your hole! *Gusanos* to your filth! to your garbage! *Gusanos* to your rot and shut up!"[256] In January 1990 Castro implored Cuban citizens to continue "slugging against the unbelievers and shutting their mouths, struggling against those who are attempting to divide us."[257]

During the early 1990s the leadership, increasingly irritated, intolerant, and embittered, continued to harangue the masses about their unacceptable production performance and their dismal labor *conciencia*. In late 1990, invoking military language, Castro appealed to his workers to be "disciplined, efficient, productive" like "soldiers at the foot of the cannon."[258] In another speech Fidel Castro complained that "much disorganization, much unproductiveness, many delays" plagued the workplace. These problems "must be rectified."[259] Indeed, throughout this period Castro and his colleagues singled out one industry after another for criticism.

For instance, in March 1990 the Cuban leader reprimanded sugar workers, reminding them to increase production and decrease the negligence that was causing breakdowns on the job.[260] Five months later, Castro criticized workers for lacking discipline. He insisted, "Vices must be swept aside."[261] In late 1989 Castro excoriated the steelworkers for laziness, inefficiency, and mismanagement: "How can a country move ahead amid such disorder, amid such laziness . . . due to undiscipline?" Blaming both managers and workers, he exclaimed, "[These enterprises will] have to improve, improve, improve. . . . Here laziness was institutionalized."[262] In December 1990 Castro called for discipline in agricultural labor where "vices" abound.[263] During the same month the Eighth Plenary Session of the National Association of Small Farmers called for increased discipline, efficiency, and labor sacrifice in agriculture.[264] In mid-1992 the official

255. *FBIS*, October 1, 1990, p. 15.
256. *GWR*, October 4, 1990, p. 5.
257. *FBIS*, January 1, 1990, p. 2.
258. Ibid., October 4, 1990, p. 6.
259. Fidel Castro speech, ibid., p. 1.
260. Ibid., March 15, 1990, p. 5.
261. Ibid., October 1, 1990, p. 8.
262. Ibid., December 28, 1989, pp. 15–17.
263. Ibid., December 27, 1990, p. 1. In another speech he verbally attacked workers' "lack of discipline . . . lack of motivation." Ibid., December 31, 1991, p. 13.
264. Ibid., December 14, 1990, p. 3.

trade union publication *Trabajadores,* which usually boasted of the triumphs of Cuban workers, published a series of articles criticizing the "passive" work ethic of Cuban managers and workers.[265]

In fact, throughout 1991 the Cuban economy had worsened for reasons far apart from Cuban labor. The Soviets had cut oil exports to Cuba from thirteen million tons in 1989 to only ten million in 1990. That oil arrived slowly: by the end of 1991 only seven million tons had come.[266] The same year the Soviets significantly cut credits, military sales, and grain shipments to Cuba. They also reduced Cuban sugar imports from 4.4 million tons in 1990 to less than 3.5 million tons in 1991.[267]

After the failed Soviet coup in August 1991, economic relations between Moscow and Havana quickly deteriorated. The Soviet Union began to require Cuba to pay for its imports with hard currency at market prices. By September 1991 Cuba had still not received its promised supply of Soviet rice. In addition, only 16 percent of the expected vegetable oil and about one-half of the expected butter had actually materialized on the island. Moreover, struggling with their own problems, the Soviets never delivered supplies of fertilizers and chemicals, imperative for sugar production. Nor did long-awaited spare parts, wood, glass, paper, and sheet metal appear.[268]

Consequently, by August 1991 the Castro government had to close hundreds of factories, cut bus routes by one-half, curtail newspaper publications, reduce train and air services, curb television and radio broadcasting, and shut down many of the country's restaurants and movie theaters. The state even went so far as to replace garbage trucks with pushcarts and 10,000 tractors with more than 80,000 beasts of burden.[269] The leadership also imported hundreds of thousands of bicycles from China to replace automobiles on the streets of Havana.[270] In addition, the authorities strictly rationed most consumer goods, including medicine, canned goods, gasoline, tobacco, clothing, shoes, soap, oil, and nearly all foodstuffs.[271]

To make matters worse, when the Soviet Union finally dissolved itself, the Cuban government lost the last remnants of the economic alliance it

265. Cited in *Christian Science Monitor,* August 19, 1992, p. 18.

266. *Miami Herald,* International Edition, November 8, 1991, p. 3A.

267. Ibid., September 26, 1991, p. 5A.

268. Purcell, pp. 131–132.

269. *Miami Herald,* International Edition, November 8, 1991, p. 3A; December 1, 1991, p. 3A; December 6, 1991, p. 3A; December 28, 1991, p. 3A; also see *Granma,* November 29, 1991; Purcell, p. 132.

270. John Newhouse, "A Reporter at Large: Socialism or Death," in *The New Yorker,* April 27, 1992, p. 57. See also *Washington Post,* July 13, 1992, p. A15.

271. *Miami Herald,* International Edition, October 6, 1991, p. 1A.

had once depended upon so heavily. Indeed, by the end of 1991 the virtual disappearance of trade with former Eastern bloc allies forced Cuba to cut its imports by nearly one-half.[272] In October 1991 the government slashed the number of working hours in many of the factories still operating. In some cases salaries, also, were reduced by one-half.[273] In early 1992 the government cut electricity use by 12 percent.[274]

Meanwhile, to offset the rising farm costs of fertilizer, pesticides, herbicides, and imported seeds, the state doubled the prices of vegetables and fruit. This placed an even greater burden on Cuban citizens already painfully squeezed by rationing and the scarcity of most foods and consumer goods.[275] In February 1992 Castro remarked that the economic crisis facing Cuba was the most severe since the triumph of the Revolution. Castro asked: "What is the October [Missile] Crisis in comparison with the situation in which we find ourselves following the disintegration of the Soviet Union?"[276]

Given these dire economic conditions, the morale of workers plummeted. Labor apathy, inefficiency, materialism, and low productivity plagued the government. In early 1991 the Vice Minister of Communications blamed the state's poor telephone service on "high absenteeism among operators."[277] On March 26, 1991, Carlos Aldana, then the Party's chief ideological spokesman, complained that Cubans have "lacked daring . . . lacked courage . . . [unwilling to confront] difficulties and complexities."[278] Once again, the Cuban economy had derailed.

CONCLUSION

A society's ability and willingness to labor is explained not merely by the temporary structures of the economic system but also, and much more vitally, by that society's culture. The experience of revolutionary Cuba suggests that deeply ingrained manifestations of historical, religious, political, economic, and social phenomena do not yield readily to government policies. The essence of a society's collective will is not often malleable through schemes of social engineering.

272. Ibid., October 19, 1991, p. 4A.
273. Ibid., November 2, 1991, p. 3A.
274. Ibid., January 4, 1992, p. 4A; *Washington Post*, July 13, 1992, p. A15.
275. *Miami Herald*, International Edition, February 16, 1992, p. 4A.
276. Ibid., February 23, 1992, p. 3A; see also Newhouse, p. 57.
277. *Bohemia*, January 25, 1991, pp. 30–33.
278. *FBIS*, March 26, 1991, p. 1.

When the Castro government took power in the late 1950s, the leaders viewed Cuban labor attitudes as reflecting a history of aristocracy and hierarchy, of slavery and capitalist domination. Once Castro declared his Marxist-Leninist faith, he and his colleagues sought to eradicate this troublesome traditional work ethic and to impose a socialist labor mentality that would be more appropriate for the Marxist-Leninist structures.

Castro and his small coterie of *barbudos* set out with a task that Lenin long ago assigned to the Communist Party. Lenin instructed Party officials to infuse the lost masses with a consciousness from without. Dutifully, the Castro government sought to inculcate a different work ethic, a new *conciencia*, by virtually every conceivable strategy from militarizing society to controlling the distribution of resources. During the early postrevolutionary era the government experimented with combining moral suasion, material incentives, and coercion in an attempt to transform labor attitudes. Cuban workers, however, refused to cooperate, and these official efforts ultimately failed.

The second decade of the Revolution witnessed several trends. First, the revolutionary leaders changed their principal goal. The early failure to transform culture, along with the impending economic crisis, forced the leadership to subordinate the goal of cultural change to a more urgent objective: increasing production levels. The leaders sought to control the behavior of workers in order to raise the abysmally low levels of production.

The government also, in large part, rejected the use of moral rewards as a means to motivate workers; instead, it initiated the use of material incentives. This policy initiative suggests that the government bent to the demands of Cuban workers: laborers might work harder if the government rewarded them with tangible benefits. Yet, in fact, even material incentives failed to elicit proper behavior among Cuban workers. Hence, the government came to rely overwhelmingly on coercive methods to force appropriate work behavior. This combination of material incentives and coercion succeeded, at least temporarily, in improving productivity and placating Cuban labor.

The economic and political successes of the 1970s ended abruptly. By the mid-1980s the Cuban government confronted a frightening series of crises. To make matters worse, labor performances remained dismal. In response, the government shifted its policies and drew once again on the Guevarist notions of the late 1960s. It harshly criticized Cuban consumerism and abruptly eliminated most material incentives. To change labor attitudes and behavior, the leaders reinstated moral incentives and again attempted to cajole, harass, scold, and persuade the masses. As always, the Castro government did not hesitate to rely on coercion when necessary.

Yet the evidence indicates that even these attempts failed to transform the Cuban labor culture.

By the early 1990s the frustrated Castro government had seemingly tried everything. From suasion to coercion, all the official policies had failed to sway the workers. Labor attitudes continued to present the government with a debilitating, and perhaps insoluble, cultural and economic problem. In fact, the evidence reveals that, much to the Cuban government's disillusionment, labor attitudes and production levels actually worsened over time. Apparently, Cuban citizens were less productive and less willing to work in the 1990s than before the Revolution.

The record thus suggests that most Cuban workers rejected many of the revolutionary requirements of the Castro government. In some cases workers apathetically ignored or shunned the government's demands. In other cases workers actively resisted official measures. Certainly, for the most part, the acts of resistance by Cuban workers were neither organized nor directly confrontational. Rather, resistance tended to be subtle, at times covert, and often anonymous. In their antiestablishment activities, individual Cuban workers employed different tactics to counter the government's requirements. Laborers in various industries performed carelessly, loafed on the job, damaged property, departed work early, and in numerous instances refused to go to work at all. In a few isolated cases workers openly rebelled. These informal, disorganized methods of resistance created for the Castro government obstacles that proved to be insuperable. The leadership severely overestimated its ability to force workers to think and behave in a manner that the laborers did not perceive as serving their interests. Consequently, the dearth of support from Cuban labor repeatedly forced the Castro government to recast its policies, either by lowering its expectations and asking less of workers or by offering material incentives to those laborers who cooperated with official policy.

Unquestionably, Cuba's labor culture in the early 1990s bore little, if any, resemblance to the ideal "socialist" culture that the government had long sought to create. The traditions of a people die hard. Institutions can be quickly reformed or abolished; cultural patterns are not so readily altered. The Castro government, despite its control of virtually all resources in society and all the instruments of formal power, found that it could not control its own workers. The country's labor force clung tenaciously to their own limited forms of informal and quiet, yet nonetheless formidable, power.[279]

279. For an insightful study of a similar example of popular resistance, see James C. Scott, *Weapons of the Weak: Everyday Forms of Peasant Resistance* (New Haven: Yale University Press, 1985).

5

Revolutionary Sports
A Genuine Success

> Sports for us is to serve as an instrument of
> recreation as well as ideological and physical training
> for the coming generations.
> —*Granma Weekly Review*

> We encourage sports activities . . . as an
> instrument for forging the new man of the
> Communist society.
> —Luis Orlando Domínguez

The Cuban government's inability to accomplish sweeping cultural change is particularly evident in several aspects of society. Even though the government targeted youth as the major instigator of change and expended substantial resources to create a proper "youth consciousness," the leaders' difficulties with drugs, apathy, disrespect, defiance, and juvenile delinquency among young Cubans continued apace. In addition, for many years Fidel Castro championed equality among the sexes and urged Cuban men and women to eliminate undesirable prerevolutionary attitudes toward women. Here, too, attempting to change Cuban culture failed. A new gender consciousness never emerged. Similarly, despite relentless efforts to eliminate prerevolutionary traditional attitudes toward manual labor and to create a "revolutionary work ethic," the Cuban leadership continued to struggle with resistant workers and acute labor problems, including apathy, vagrancy, corruption, absenteeism, and misuse of state property and equipment. In these and other areas the Castro government repeatedly fell short in its attempt to transform Cuban culture. Indeed, the leadership consistently met with subtle, yet confounding, resistance.

This chapter is based upon "The Politics of Sports in Revolutionary Cuba" by Julie Marie Bunck in *Cuban Studies* 20, edited by Carmelo Mesa-Lago. Published in 1990 by the University of Pittsburgh Press.

Despite these repeated failures, however, the leaders succeeded in dramatically changing Cuban culture in at least one regard. After much effort the government successfully nurtured a latent prerevolutionary interest in watching sports, particularly baseball, into a flourishing national revolutionary sports consciousness. Promoting new attitudes toward sports was a leading official objective for domestic and international reasons. At home, the Cuban government used mass participation in sports to unify and mobilize citizens, to preoccupy, invigorate, and rally the population. Sports participation also was an obvious means to build healthier, hardier, skilled citizens in order to improve military and labor performances. In addition, Cuban leaders seized upon sports training as an opportunity to regiment and educate the population politically. Through mass sports participation the government effectively controlled much of the leisure time of children, students, and workers.

The leadership also supported and encouraged participation in sports, particularly among the young, for international political reasons. By carefully screening its citizens, then assisting promising youth with sophisticated training, the government sought to create world-class athletes. The leadership, in turn, put these athletes on display as "successes" of the socialist Revolution. They served as Castro's international revolutionary spokesmen, as his example of Cuba's perfect, balanced, "new man."

Small countries with weak economies, such as Cuba, sometimes search for novel ways to display power and prestige in the international arena. With its impressive international athletic performances, an underdeveloped country such as Cuba was able to gain world prestige, status, and respect. Compared to any other country with a broadly similar per capita income (Brazil, Colombia, Mexico, Costa Rica, Ecuador, or Chile), Cuba took an extraordinarily impressive position among the most athletically dominant countries in the world.[1] Cuban leaders also succeeded in taking their country's repeated victories at international sporting events as an opportunity to make political statements. In an attempt to demonstrate solidarity among socialist countries, for example, Cuba made international news by refusing to send athletes to the 1984 and 1988 Olympic Games. Finally, the revolutionary government continually used sports to create nationalist, anti-American, anticapitalist, and antiimperialist sentiments among the Cuban population.

Why did the leaders succeed in fostering new attitudes toward sports when they were utterly unable to do so in various other aspects of society?

1. The 1987 per capita income of Cuba ($US 1,590) was below that of Argentina ($US 2,331), Chile ($US 1,950), Costa Rica ($US 2,238), Mexico ($US 1,800), Paraguay ($US 1,640), Uruguay ($US 1,665), and Venezuela ($US 4,716). The statistics are taken from *The World Almanac and Book of Facts: 1987* (Pharos Books, a Scripps Howard Company, 1987).

What conditions prevent and what conditions promote the creation of new cultural attitudes? What factors contributed to the leadership's impressive athletic successes? Who gained from the new sports ethic? What role does the citizen play and what role does the government play in bringing about successful cultural change? The subject of sports in revolutionary Cuba raises each of the foregoing questions.

SPORTS IN PREREVOLUTIONARY CUBA

For some decades before the 1959 Revolution, Cuba participated in various international sports events. Cuban athletes, however, generally performed quite poorly. As one of twenty teams that gathered to compete in the first international Olympic Games in 1900, Cuba took home its first medal. In the first and second Olympic Games combined, Cuba won twelve medals. All twelve were in the highly specialized sport of fencing. Not until 1948 did Cuba win another Olympic medal—a silver in yachting. The country never again won an Olympic medal until after the 1959 Revolution.

In 1926 Cuba, with two other countries, founded the Central American and Caribbean Games. In 1951 Cuba participated in the first Pan American Games held in Buenos Aires. Despite this early interest in sports, the country never ranked particularly high in such regional sporting events. Although Cuba participated in the Central American Games, the Pan American Games, and the Olympics throughout the 1950s, its athletes were at best average. At the 1955 Pan American Games, for instance, Cuba won one medal. At the 1959 Pan American Games, Cuba placed eleventh out of sixteen teams.[2]

The majority of Cubans participating in prerevolutionary sports were upper-class elites who had access to facilities and to sports clubs. The government provided little or no support for domestic or international competition. Indeed, sports formed "highly professionalized entertainment."[3] Perhaps as a consequence, all classes of Cubans enjoyed sports spectating. Baseball, the national sport, had a particularly keen following and, unsurprisingly, was Cuba's strongest sport. During the 1950s Cuba won several international amateur baseball championships.

Baseball attracted young athletes from all classes, most of whom aspired to play in the American professional leagues. In fact, in the 1940s Fidel

2. See R. J. Pickering, "Cuba," in *Sport under Communism*, ed. James Riordan (London: C. Hurst, 1981), pp. 148–149.
3. Don Anthony, "Introduction," in ibid., p. 5.

Castro, an avid baseball player, was scouted and ultimately rejected by the Washington Senators. Similarly, boxing attracted participants from all classes. Here again, the possibility of turning professional in the United States allured many Cuban athletes.[4] By the late 1950s Cuba boasted the highest number of foreign athletes in the American major leagues.[5] Yet, despite this widespread interest in baseball and boxing, most prerevolutionary lower-class and middle-class Cubans failed to engage actively in a wide range of sports.

SPORTS IN REVOLUTIONARY CUBA

By the early 1990s Cuban athletes and teams were among the best in the world. The country rose from mediocrity in international sporting circles to become a formidable power. Cuba's boxers and baseball players were consistently considered the best such amateurs in the world.[6] Indeed, Cuba's soccer, wrestling, volleyball, weightlifting, water polo, and track and field teams had become world class. Its men's gymnastics, fencing, and softball teams and its women's chess, judo, volleyball, and basketball teams regularly performed in outstanding fashion.[7] In fact, in many events the Cubans routinely defeated teams from much more populous and wealthy countries, including the United States.[8]

In the decade of the 1980s Cubans consistently ranked at the top of most international competitions. They placed eighth at both the 1976 Montreal Olympics and the 1980 Moscow Olympics. Although the Cu-

4. See Pickering, p. 149; see also Trevor Slack, "Cuba's Political Involvement in Sport since the Socialist Revolution," *Journal of Sport and Social Issues* 6 (1982): 35.

5. *USA Today,* July 3, 1992, p. 2B.

6. In July 1992 Cuba's men's baseball team had won sixty-three of sixty-four championship games over the prior five years. By the end of August 1992 the same team had won its last twelve major international tournaments, including the 1992 Olympics at Barcelona. See *USA Today,* July 3, 1992, p. 2B; *Washington Post,* August 4, 1992, p. C9.

7. For example, the Cuban boxing team took titles in feather, light, middle, bantam, and heavyweight at the Belgrade 1987 World Cup Team Competition. See *Granma Weekly Review (GWR),* February 28, 1988, p. 5. Also, the Cuban men's baseball team won the world championship in 1990. See ibid., August 26, 1990, p. 9; April 9, 1989, p. 9. Cuban high-jumper Javier Sotomayer set a world record in September 1988. See ibid., August 20, 1989, p. 8. Cuba's weightlifting team won all golds at the 1986 Pan American Weightlifting Championship. See ibid., May 18, 1986, p. 1.

8. See, for example, ibid., August 10, 1986, p. 1. This article discusses Cuba's world champion men's baseball team. See also ibid., May 15, 1988, p. 5. In the summer of 1992 Cuba's men's baseball team won six out of eight games played with the U.S. amateur team. See *Washington Post,* August 4, 1992, p. C9.

bans boycotted the 1984 Los Angeles Olympic Games and the 1988 Seoul Games, they nonetheless regularly won the Central American and Caribbean (CAC) Games by a wide margin. For example, at the Fifteenth CAC Games in 1986, in which twenty-six teams participated, Cubans won 300 of the 870 medals presented.[9] In the 1987 Pan American Games, Cuba placed second to the United States and earned 175 medals. The larger, wealthier states of Canada and Brazil took third and fourth places with totals of only 162 and 61 medals respectively. In the 1991 Pan American Games, hosted by Cuba for thirty-nine participating countries, Cuban athletes performed splendidly. They earned 140 gold medals, ten more than the United States, which led in overall medals, 352 to Cuba's 265. Canada finished far behind in third with 22 golds and 127 overall. Brazil once again placed fourth with 21 golds and 79 total. At the 1992 Olympic Games in Barcelona, Spain, Cuban athletes performed superbly, placing fifth with 31 medals, 14 of which were golds.[10]

Despite a relatively small population and low per capita income, Cuba was able to develop a truly remarkable sports program. Cuba's per capita income ranked far below its athletic equals. Other countries with comparable per capita incomes could not approach Cuba's sports performances. For example, Cuba placed among the top ten teams at the 1976 Olympics. Cuba's 1976 per capita income ($US 570), however, lagged far behind that of the other nine countries, including Poland ($US 2,000), East Germany ($US 3,300), West Germany ($US 6,029), Romania ($US 1,200), Bulgaria ($US 1,650), Hungary ($US 2,200), and Japan ($US 4,038).[11] Indeed, Cuba built one of the strongest and most impressive national sports programs in the world.

LAYING THE FOUNDATION FOR VICTORY

In 1961, as the Castro government began its ambitious effort to fashion a new communist citizen, sports formed a central target for the leaders' efforts. The prerevolutionary Cuban sports culture squarely represented much that the government sought to eliminate. In order to create a "new man" in a different society, the leadership believed that sports had to take on a social role that would contribute to Marxist-Leninist objectives.

9. *GWR*, July 20, 1986, p. 12.

10. The unified team from the Commonwealth of Independent States took first place (112 medals), the U.S. placed second (108 medals), Germany took third (82 medals), followed by China (54 medals).

11. Statistics taken from the 1976 *Almanac*.

Thus, during the first years of the Revolution the leaders instituted several potent measures. They publicly denounced—through speeches, newspaper articles, billboards, and radio programs—the role of sports in prerevolutionary society. They called for the destruction of old "capitalist" attitudes toward sports. The place occupied by athletics in prerevolutionary society, the leadership explained, was altogether inappropriate for revolutionary Cuba.

Various Cuban officials bitterly attacked the "elitist" role of pre–1959 sports. In 1960 Fidel Castro declared, "At the Olympics, it was shameful to see the position occupied by Cuba because the rich, accustomed to good living, had not the necessary spirit of sacrifice to be good athletes." And Castro concluded, "Good athletes must come from the . . . working classes, from the lower strata, because they are capable of sacrifice."[12] A year later Castro asked, "Sport . . . what had become of sport? Apart from providing entertainment for the children of the rich families in their aristocratic schools and clubs, sport had become a form of business."[13]

Some years later the Director of Cuba's National Institute of Sports, reviewed the need for a revolutionary sports objective: "It is necessary to get rid of old ideas about sports [and] . . . its exclusive and discriminatory nature. . . . [It is] necessary to develop a new conscience and a new attitude" toward sports.[14] Another leader attacked sports elitism by saying: "With the systems of sports participation existing in Cuba previously, [athletic events] gravitated around institutions, around private clubs which were only for the powerful classes, the national bourgeoisie, those who could belong to clubs because they had money and opportunities."[15]

Government officials also stressed the exploitative nature of professional sports in prerevolutionary Cuba. One official observed: "It is necessary to get rid of . . . commercial and mercantile aims and objectives, as seen in professional sports, whose most advanced expression in our country was in baseball and boxing, where top quality human material was purchased at a low price, making our athletes objects that were for sale or exchange."[16] Fidel Castro harshly criticized such professionalism and described prerevolutionary athletics as "a piece of merchandise, an object of exploitation."[17]

12. Fidel Castro, 1960 speech, in *Fidel: Sobre el deporte,* ed. Sonia Castanes (Havana: 1975); cited in Pickering, p. 149.

13. Fidel Castro, 1961 speech, cited in Pickering, p. 152.

14. *GWR,* September 10, 1972, p. 9.

15. Rafael Cambo, ibid., January 26, 1969, p. 8.

16. Ibid., September 10, 1972, p. 9.

17. Fidel Castro, 1961 speech, cited in Pickering, p. 152.

The revolutionary government also viewed traditional Cuban sports as a product of American imperialism. Officials attacked American culture and its influence on athletes in prerevolutionary Cuba. Indeed, anti-Americanism permeated the rhetoric of government leaders. In a 1971 speech Castro declared: "Imperialism has tried . . . to instill a feeling of inferiority. . . . Let us say that it is part of the imperialists' ideology to present themselves as superior, and to develop in other peoples an inferiority complex. Sport has been used to that effect." Another Cuban official explained: "[The Americans] were able to attract young people who excelled in sports throughout the island by promising them jobs or by actually giving them money; by obtaining houses for them, and by offering them membership in an exclusive club where they could rub elbows with . . . the big shots."[18]

THE NATIONAL INSTITUTE OF SPORTS, PHYSICAL EDUCATION, AND RECREATION

The government did more, however, than verbally assail the role of prerevolutionary athletics and publicly encourage the development of a different sports consciousness. The leaders also carried out several measures to hasten the transformation of attitudes. In the early 1960s the government introduced a project to build a number of fields, playgrounds, and athletic schools throughout the country. In February 1961 the leadership created The National Institute of Sports, Physical Education, and Recreation (INDER), whose motto became "Listos para Vencer" (Ready to Win). The Institute would oversee sports education in every school and institution on the island. This agency was to become the guiding force behind the mercurial development of Cuban sports.

Immediately after its founding, the Institute took on the formidable task of creating a new sports consciousness and arousing nationwide interest in participatory sports. It introduced a national "Participation Campaign," a program to educate and activate the masses. Among its principal aims, INDER sought to combat the notion that sports were for the rich and not for all Cubans. In 1967, as part of this campaign, the government abolished all professional athletics and announced that admission to sports events throughout the nation would be free. "Sports today," a March 1967 *Granma Weekly Review* article read, "are the right of the people, an important factor in the integral training of our youth. . . .

18. Fidel Castro, cited in ibid., p. 149; *GWR*, January 26, 1969, p. 8.

Sports are no longer sponsored by those financial interests which formerly controlled professional sports, now abolished in Cuba."[19] Indeed, INDER encouraged all Cubans to participate in athletics.

The Institute's Participation Campaign also implemented a screening process to select the best athletes from across the Cuban state. This process integrated local and national athletic activities through sports schools. Since the process of creating top-rate athletes ideally begins at an early age, the Institute directed and appointed specialists, experts, and coaches drawn from around the world to instruct Cuban children of all ages. Until the late 1980s most of these experts came from the Eastern bloc.

In addition to INDER the Cuban government established the Voluntary Sports Councils (CVDs). These councils organized sports programs, competitions, and athletic activities all across the island. The councils also introduced team games in factories, schools, and community centers. To promote the national sports campaign, the CVDs put up posters and advertised on television and through the newspaper.

The process by which a young Cuban reached a sports school can best be represented by a pyramid. At the base of the pyramid were local competitions. Children of all ages went to local sports centers, which provided weekend athletic camps.[20] In addition, students competed at school and local games called *spartakiades,* providing experts the opportunity to find promising talent. Outstanding athletes were sent on to local physical education centers called Schools for Basic Training in Sports (EIDEs); the winners then moved to more challenging competitions, including local children's olympics and games sponsored by the Armed Forces or the universities. The very best athletes advanced to the municipal or district level. From there, those with extraordinary potential continued on to provincial, then national, and ultimately international competitions.

During this process the state provided to the competitors, free of charge, all meals, uniforms, facilities, transportation, dormitories, coaches, and sporting goods. Throughout these competitions, completely supervised by INDER and the Ministry of Education, government officials searched out "high-yield" athletes and chose the very best for special Schools for Advanced Training of Athletes (ESPRAs).[21] As José Rodrígues, the Institute's commissioner for highly competitive sports, explained: "We have tests for children. . . . Many times we go and search for those we believe have some special talent."[22] It was a rare occasion, perhaps, when the Institute lost or overlooked a particularly talented young-

19. *GWR,* March 19, 1967, p. 3.
20. Ibid., June 14, 1987, p. 2.
21. Ibid., April 9, 1989, p. 9; see also August 20, 1989, p. 8.
22. *Boston Globe,* January 3, 1988, p. 69.

ster. The vast majority of those who would compete internationally for Cuba thus began intensive training at an early age.[23]

The impressive *Ciudad Deportiva* (Sports City) formed the centerpiece of the nation's sports program, housing on the outskirts of Havana the National Institute of Sports along with several other sports institutes. The Sports City contained training and competition facilities (the National Training Center), the Institute of National Medicine, and the National Physical Education Institute. The national sports industry, located nearby, produced gloves, shoes, spikes, bats, basketballs, and other sports equipment. Until the severe economic crisis in the early 1990s, the sports industry had employed one thousand workers. By 1992, however, the industry's work force, as well as its level of production, had significantly decreased.

The Sports City also included a track, an outdoor pool, a modern aquatics complex, a fifteen-thousand-seat indoor arena, and an eighteen-thousand-seat soccer stadium. The Castro government built many more facilities for the 1991 Pan American Games, including a natatorium, a gymnastics compound, a spectacular velodrome, and a village with fifty-five buildings for athletes.[24] The leadership thus created a highly centralized, extremely focused, and exceedingly expensive national sports project.[25] According to Cuban officials, hosting the 1991 Pan American Games cost more than $24 million in hard currency, a shocking figure given Cuba's desperate economic crisis at the time.[26]

In addition to creating INDER to control the selection of athletes, the Cuban government instituted various other significant measures, such as founding advanced physical education schools and training additional coaches, sports instructors, and specialists. The leadership also constructed playgrounds, city arenas, stadiums, and swimming pools. And it hosted numerous national competitions.[27] As a consequence of all of these measures, the government succeeded in bringing a broad range of sports to the Cuban people.

By the end of the first decade of the Revolution, Cuban leaders were lauding the country's accomplishments in international competitions and were attributing them to the Revolution. A January 1969 *Granma Weekly*

23. *GWR*, August 20, 1989, p. 8. See also Paula J. Pettavino, "Novel Revolutionary Forms: The Use of Unconventional Diplomacy in Cuba," in *Cuba: The International Dimension*, ed. Georges Fauriol and Eva Loser (New Brunswick, N.J.: Transaction, 1990), p. 385.

24. *Boston Globe*, January 3, 1988, pp. 55, 69; see also *Granma International (GI)*, May 13, 1991, p. 1; *Washington Post*, July 29, 1991, pp. A1, A14.

25. See Pickering, pp. 156–158; also see *Boston Globe*, January 3, 1988, pp. 55, 69.

26. *Washington Post*, July 29, 1991, p. A14.

27. *GWR*, November 26, 1969, pp. 8–9.

Review article stated: "Ten years after the triumph of the Revolution, Cuban sports are a vanguard force in the Revolution, an uncontested and enduring reality."[28] In 1974 Castro announced: "Nowadays we win medals in Central American, Pan American and even Olympic competitions. . . . We can say that our athletes are the children of the Revolution and, at the same time, the standard-bearers of that same Revolution."[29] In 1976 another Cuban official explained: "We are only seeing the beginning of Cuba's sporting Revolution. Given another four years and the inspiration of being in Mother Russia at the 1980s Olympics, Cuba will have achieved a great deal more."[30]

THE REVOLUTIONARY GOVERNMENT AND SPORTS: A DOMESTIC POLITICAL TOOL

Certainly, the Cuban sports program served to provide the Castro government with legitimacy and support at home and abroad. It assured even the lowliest Cuban citizen access to athletics for recreation and health. What is not so frequently recognized, however, is that the sports program provided the leadership with an instrument of domestic political control. Sports aided the government's efforts to mobilize, educate, and supervise Cuban citizens. To some degree, the emphasis on physical fitness also sought to strengthen the military and enhance production. Finally, athletics provided the government with a means to oversee the free time of Cuban citizens.

A Means to Mobilize Citizens

Immediately after taking power, Fidel Castro and his associates moved to mobilize the population. Whether through voluntary labor programs, mass organizations, the literacy campaign, the threat of an American invasion, or rallies on the Plaza of the Revolution, the government constantly sought to activate the people through nationalist slogans and antiimperialist rhetoric. In a manner eerily reminiscent of the approach taken by Nazi German leaders, the Cuban leadership viewed sports as a way to invigorate the masses, to promote nationalism and patriotism, and to bring its

28. Ibid., January 26, 1969, p. 9.
29. Fidel Castro, 1974 speech, cited in Pickering, p. 150.
30. Pickering, p. 154.

people to fighting trim. A thoroughly mobilized population preoccupied with sports was thought to be a considerable asset for the government. Hence, the leaders declared widespread athletic participation to be a pre-eminent goal for the Cuban people. As the Director of INDER explained, "The main cause, the fundamental objective, is a greater participation by the people, which should reach massive levels."[31] In 1966 the leading official goal for the Cuban sports program was the "development of a widespread, mass movement."[32] As Castro stated proudly:

> Cuba is the first country in the world where all primary and secondary schools, as well as technological schools and universities, include sports as an integral part of their curricula. This assures a widespread sports movement which arises from the masses and is strengthened by the efforts of the people. Sports consciousness has grown and developed extraordinarily among our people.[33]

A Revolutionary Sacrifice and a Battle for Survival

In their official sports campaign, Cuban leaders invoked the concept of struggle, sacrifice, and battle for the survival and eventual victory of the Revolution. In 1987 Castro spoke to the Cuban athletes departing for India to participate in an international competition: "[The] people are bidding [their athletes] . . . farewell like the Spartans did with their soldiers; urging them to return wielding their shields or else dead on their shields which is tantamount to saying *Patria o muerte, venceremos*."[34] A month later Castro praised the members of Cuba's victorious Pan American Games teams. He commended the athletes for their "patriotic, revolutionary, and combative spirit" and boasted that "there was not a single crack, deserter, or traitor" among the members. The imperialists "wanted to get us," Castro declared, "but they encountered the fists of our country's athletes."[35] In July 1991 the Cuban leader reiterated that his country was determined to carry through with its plan to host the Pan American

---

31. *GWR*, September 10, 1972, p. 8.

32. Ibid., June 19, 1966, p. 3.

33. Ibid.

34. Ibid., August 9, 1987, p. 3.

35. *FBIS*, September 4, 1987, p. 1. In September 1990 the Cuban leaders spoke to the country's defeated women's volleyball team and exalted them for their commendable sacrifice and struggle. Ibid., September 7, 1990, p. 5.

Games despite severe economic troubles. In calling the Games Cuba's "sacred commitment," Castro argued that hosting them amounted to an act of courage and honor.[36]

A Means to Improve the Military and Increase Production

The government also viewed participating in athletic activities as fundamental to developing strong, active, healthy, and productive citizens. Karl Marx himself wrote that to raise productivity levels the masses must take part in athletic activities.[37] Cuban leaders consequently believed that sports could be critical to the Revolution's success. A 1967 *Granma Weekly Review* article emphasized the importance of participating in athletics in order to "lay the ground" for including sports "as an indispensable part of education, culture, health, and national defense."[38] In 1972 a Cuban official explained:

> [P]hysical education and sports constitute means for obtaining an integral formation that harmonizes the potentials of human nature in order to develop citizens who are strong physically.... These citizens must always be willing to give the best of themselves for the benefit of society.... [T]he Cuban Government views the systematic practice of sports and physical education as indices for development and biological growth, factors that contribute to the ... physical effectiveness for work in a society of producers, and elements that aid in the formation of ... strong character that is needed to face up to all the obstacles and difficulties involved in overcoming the deficient structure of development.[39]

For the Cuban leaders the sports hero exemplified the ideal disciplined worker, loyal revolutionary, and obedient soldier.

In 1961 the Cuban government established a program for testing the athletic ability of citizens. Officials administered the Test of Physical Education (LPV) to all citizens—the military, workers, farmers, children—to discover their physical abilities. The government, a *Granma* article stated,

36. *Washington Post*, July 29, 1991, p. A1.
37. See Geralyn Pye, "The Ideology of Cuban Sport," *Journal of Sport History* 13, no. 2 (Summer 1986): 124.
38. *GWR*, March 19, 1967, p. 3; see also January 10, 1988, p. 6.
39. Ibid., September 10, 1972, p. 8; the first part of this quote is cited in Pye, p. 121.

would use the test to determine what types of physical education various citizens needed in order to ensure a healthy and highly productive work force. As one official declared:

> The LPV program began in 1961. . . . Immediately the people made an identification with the initials "LPV," converting them into a symbol of their courage and decision to fulfill the tasks of the Revolution; to construct Socialism; to create a new society. . . . The objectives of the tests . . . are to determine the strength, speed, and physical endurance of every citizen and, having once achieved this, to establish . . . plans to cultivate his capacity to the maximum.[40]

In a 1966 speech Fidel Castro observed, "It is important to emphasize how sports in our country have become activities practiced by the masses. . . . [A] broad sports movement has developed in Cuba among workers and members of the Revolutionary Armed Forces." And Castro concluded by noting, "This movement is also being encouraged among the great masses of agricultural workers."[41]

A Form of Political Education

Although the state promoted athletics to encourage mass participation and develop a healthy, productive citizenry, it also viewed sports as a means of politically and ideologically educating the masses. This idea had long interested communist thinkers. In 1917 Lenin emphasized the need to build a High School for Sports and Physical Culture. Lenin believed, as did Marx, that having the masses participate in athletic activities could be a vital step toward creating the new "communist man."[42] In its process of cultural transformation, the Cuban government continually attempted to inculcate its people with the proper revolutionary attitudes: struggle, sacrifice, fortitude, dedication, voluntarism, and hard work.[43] Plainly, these attitudes and values are closely related to those required of successful athletes.

Throughout the course of the Cuban Revolution, the leaders believed that sports would contribute admirably to developing a new national *con-*

40. *Granma*, October 30, 1966, p. 2.
41. *GWR*, June 19, 1966, p. 3.
42. Anthony, p. 6.
43. See Ernesto (Che) Guevara, "On Creating a New Attitude" and "Man and Socialism in Cuba," in *Venceremos! The Speeches and Writings of Ernesto Che Guevara*, ed. John Gerassi (New York: Macmillan, 1968), pp. 336–348; 387–400.

ciencia. A 1966 article explaining the Cuban sports program stated that "strengthening our athletes ideologically" forms one of the program's chief objectives.[44] A popular sports slogan in Cuba read "sport is the source of will, perseverance, physical vigor and mental agility."[45] A 1966 editorial declared: "Sports for us is to serve as an instrument of recreation as well as ideological and physical training for the coming generations."[46] Several years later Luis Orlando Domínguez, then the First Secretary of the National Committee of the Union of Young Communists, stated: "We encourage sports activities . . . as an instrument for forging the new man of the Communist society. . . . [S]ports . . . are . . . an essential component of the communist training of our new generations."[47] At the 1975 First Party Congress, Fidel Castro described Cuban athletes as "an example of discipline, dedication, modesty and courage."[48] In 1987 Dr. Eduardo Bernabe Ordáz, director of a psychiatric hospital in Havana, commented that "sports aren't only necessary from the recreational viewpoint, but also in . . . physical and mental formation."[49]

The leadership also used sports as a means to legitimize control over youngsters through athletic organizations. Boarding schools, country camps, sports schools, student militias, day-care centers, athletic training centers, various mass organizations, special youth Committees for the Defense of the Revolution,[50] and regularly scheduled competitive events, all offered the leaders efficient ways to regiment and educate Cuba's youngsters.

The Castro government proceeded on the belief that "sports education" must begin early, shortly after birth. In the 1960s Cuban officials instructed parents to exercise infants at an extremely young age (forty-five days old) and to massage the limbs of their babies.[51] In a 1961 speech Castro explained:

> All organizations want young people to be vigorous, disciplined and strong in character. . . . The whole nation is interested in hav-

44. *GWR*, June 19, 1966, p. 3.

45. *Boston Globe*, January 3, 1988, p. 55.

46. *GWR*, June 19, 1966, p. 3.

47. Ibid., September 21, 1975; first quoted by Pye, p. 122. Domínguez is now serving a twenty-year prison term for corruption.

48. "Fidel's Main Report to the First Congress," *GWR*, January 4, 1976; see also Marvin Leiner, *Children Are the Revolution: Day Care in Cuba* (New York: Viking Press, 1974), p. 48. Leiner explained that group sports are encouraged among children of all ages to foster a collectivist spirit.

49. *GWR*, July 5, 1987, p. 8.

50. For more information on the youth CDRs, see Richard Fagen, *The Transformation of Political Culture in Cuba* (Stanford: Stanford University Press, 1969), p. 85.

51. Pickering, pp. 166–167.

ing children who are equally healthy.... Every family, every
mother and father is the health and future of children.... Every
Cuban family is therefore interested in physical education and
sport for its children.[52]

If a child showed early signs of athletic ability, the Cuban government
encouraged its parents to have the child tested and to start formal classes
and coaching. The leadership urged parents of particularly talented children to place the youngsters in Schools for Basic Training in Sports, located throughout the provinces and on the Island of Youth. These schools,
completely funded by the government, provided special training grounds
for very young children.[53] The authorities thus offered luxuries to young
Cubans with athletic potential: better food, comfortable living quarters,
modern facilities, and opportunities to travel and compete. Older athletes
sometimes received even greater bonuses such as a car or pocket money.[54]
In return the government was able to exert far greater influence over educating and training the athletes. By the same token the Cuban government
minimized the influence of parents by removing children from the home
for extended periods of time.

The government expected parents, however, to do their part to complement the leaders' efforts. Cuban officials regularly encouraged them to
learn about and to record the physical development of their children
through "instruction and progress cards." Day-care centers offered to children (from less than one year old up to first grade) full-time "education"
and "sports training." Regardless of whether or not the mother worked
outside the home, the government vigorously encouraged parents to place
their children in such day-care centers.

As children participated in sports, the authorities attempted to instill
in them revolutionary attitudes regarding team cooperation. For example,
the government instructed teachers to have the children participate in
group activities to promote selfless, cooperative attitudes. Separating a
child from the group, or team, formed a common mode of punishment
and associated individualism with something undesirable and punitive.[55]
Once the children left the day-care schools, sports education continued.
All primary and secondary schools, most of which were boarding schools,

52. Fidel Castro, 1961 speech, cited in ibid.
53. *GWR*, April 9, 1989, p. 9.
54. *Boston Globe*, January 3, 1988, p. 69.
55. See John Griffiths, "Sport: The People's Right," in *Cuba: The Second Decade*, ed.
John Griffiths and Peter Griffiths (London: Writers and Readers Publishing Cooperative,
1979), p. 252; see also Pye, p. 123.

required students to take physical education classes. University students had to take such classes until after the second year.

A Means to Encourage Cubans to Devote Leisure Time to Creating the "New Man"

The state used mass participation in Party-controlled sports activities to exert some influence over the "free time" of workers and youth. In the leadership's plan to transform Cuban culture, leisure time was to be managed and used in a constructive, educational manner. Officials thus regularly encouraged workers to join various athletic teams and organizations. Once again, this decidedly increased the government's influence in the citizen's daily "private" life.

In 1966 the leadership introduced new labor legislation that redefined "leisure time" and instructed the workers on how to manage their free time. An October 1966 editorial quoted Marx's definition of "leisure time" as "that which man has available for his education, for intellectual development, for the fulfillment of social functions, for social relations and for the free exercise of his physical and intellectual forces."[56] In the Marxist tradition, the Cuban leaders believed that leisure time was another means to be put to efficient and valuable use in creating the new communist citizen. Toward that end the government aimed to manage and monitor the workers' free time. After stating "Whatever a person does during his free time is closely related to his attitude toward work and society," the 1966 article concluded, "Free time will be instrumental in forming the social outlook of the new man: a man capable of living in a communist society."[57]

Free time, the leaders instructed, must be devoted to reading, or to family, sports, and political activities, or other "intellectually valuable" choices as well as to several hours of volunteer work. The government announced that citizens' seminars would be held to teach the value of leisure time in a socialist society.[58] These seminars discussed sports, politics, the economy, and other topics.

The Castro government's domestic sports program thus had several objectives. It sought, via official rhetoric and moral suasion, to change opinions and attitudes. To increase production and invigorate the Armed

56. Marx, quoted in *GWR*, October 23, 1966, p. 2; also cited in Pye, p. 122.
57. *GWR*, October 23, 1966, p. 2.
58. Ibid.

Forces, the program also attempted to mobilize the Cuban people and to create a highly active mass movement that would strengthen the population physically and mentally. Through the sports program the leaders substantially augmented their abilities to control the citizenry. Sports institutes, scholastic physical education programs, official management of leisure time, and government regulation and control of day-care schools, all afforded the leaders more extensive influence over youngsters and adults.

THE REVOLUTIONARY GOVERNMENT AND SPORTS: THE INTERNATIONAL ARENA

Coupled with strengthening, mobilizing, educating, and controlling its people through athletics, the Cuban government also attempted to use sports in the international arena for another set of reasons. The leaders consistently employed sports on the world stage to illustrate, domestically and internationally, the successes of socialism and to reinforce Marxism-Leninism at home and abroad. This was accomplished through speeches revelling in Cuban athletic victories, then denouncing American society, and, on occasion, spreading pro-Cuban, anti-American propaganda. Finally, the leadership relied on its athletic successes to bolster international prestige and to gain global respect and status.

Demonstrating the Triumph of Socialism over Capitalism

The leadership claimed that the country's impressive progress in international sports events demonstrated the success of the Revolution and of socialism. After Cuban athletes returned from the 1966 Central American Games, a *Granma* article read: "With ... the development of a healthy sports policy, and also, with the growth of the collective spirit, increasingly heroic and increasingly steadfast, our country will reap great victories." And the article concluded, "We will not look upon this as a triumph of our nation, but rather as the triumph of an idea, a social system, a concept of life."[59]

In a 1962 speech Fidel Castro exclaimed: "One day, when the Yankees accept peaceful coexistence with our own country, we shall beat them at

59. Ibid., July 18, 1966, p. 7.

baseball too and then the advantages of revolutionary over capitalist sports will be shown!"[60] Ten years later Castro reiterated: "We aspire to . . . the triumph of a worthy concept of sports. . . . We have raised the revolutionary concept of sports. . . . [I]n addition to having taught a lesson to the enemy, they have also achieved an extraordinary victory, not for our country, but for an idea."[61]

In a 1975 speech a leading official described Cuba's athletes as the vanguard of the Revolution and exclaimed:

> You are disciplined, can stand up under long days of training to win a people's victory and are full of courage and the kind of morality only possible when representing a people with a triumphant revolution. . . . Today, we would like to acknowledge your achievement and to exhort you to continue advancing with firm steps toward the highest goals along the undefeated way of the Revolution.[62]

"Our athletes," Fidel Castro commented, "are magnificent revolutionaries."[63] Slogans hanging on the walls and from the ceilings of Cuban stadiums and sports schools reminded citizens that their athletes were products and symbols of the Revolution. Castro asserted: "[One] could not conceive of a young revolutionary who would not also be a sportsman."[64]

The government rarely missed an opportunity to attack prerevolutionary "capitalist" (professional) sports and to proclaim the merits of "revolutionary sports." Cuba, the leaders frequently declared, has "clean, pure sports," uncorrupted by capitalist motives and greed.[65] After Cuba's victories at the 1966 Central American Games in Puerto Rico, Castro stated:

> Those who said that sports would fail in Cuba for lack of professionalism, that there would be no stimulus . . . received their reply in Puerto Rico. . . . It was demonstrated that professionalism conspires against sports. . . . [P]rofessionalism destroys sports. . . . [S]ome day our athletes will also beat yankee athletes, and will demonstrate that . . . indeed, there do exist some ideas and con-

60. Fidel Castro, 1962 speech, cited in Pickering, p. 152.

61. GWR, September 10, 1972, p. 9; full text of speech in GWR, July 8, 1966, p. 7.

62. Luis Orlando Domínguez, then First Secretary of the National Committee of the Union of Young Communists, is quoted here. See ibid., September 21, 1975, p. 9.

63. Ibid., July 8, 1966, p. 7.

64. Fidel Castro, cited in Eric Wagner, "Baseball in Cuba," Journal of Popular Culture 18 (Summer 1984): 117. I have changed slightly Wagner's translation of the quote.

65. GWR, June 19, 1966, p. 3; see also September 21, 1975, p. 9.

cepts superior to others and some social systems superior to others.[66]

As one Cuban official explained, sports in Cuba is not a form of business or capitalist profit but is a right: "And that's where our policy of mass participation is reflected, a policy that has eliminated all discrimination and made it possible for us to obtain a number of victories."[67] In his address to the First Party Congress, Castro commented that "[p]rofessionalism, which degraded and ruined sports, was left behind, together with gambling, betting, drugs and other vices."[68]

The Cuban press consistently reiterated this view. A 1987 *Granma Weekly Review* article discussed a Cuban boxer, Niño Valdés, who had fled to the United States. While noting that another Cuban boxer had committed suicide in Miami, the article lamented that "most professional boxers who went to the United States in search of wealth and opportunity now live in poverty or face deplorable situations." The article described Niño Valdés as "a victim of the grips of professionalism that even cost him the loss of his left eye. ... Niño was a promising super heavyweight but the dirty deals in pro boxing prevented him from getting away."[69] Similarly, in May 1987 a *Granma Weekly Review* article discussed the return to Cuba of Angel García, a professional lightweight boxing champion in the 1950s. García, who returned to Cuba for an eye operation, was described as in "dire financial straits ... sleeping and begging in the Paris metro."[70]

Cuban athletes at international competitions also served as spokesmen for the Castro government and often criticized the concept of professional sports. In 1967 one Cuban athlete, who had been incorrectly reported to have defected, stated publicly, "If one day they should say that I have left Cuba, this will only be true if I have become a guerrilla in Latin America."[71] In 1974 when Teófilo Stevenson, Cuba's best world-ranked boxer, was offered US $1 million to fight America's top fighters, he responded: "What is one million US dollars compared to the love of eight million Cubans?"[72] Government officials repeatedly called Stevenson a "symbol" of the Cuban Revolution.[73]

66. Ibid., July 3, 1966, p. 7.
67. Ibid., September 10, 1972, pp. 8–9.
68. Ibid., January 4, 1976.
69. Ibid., January 11, 1987, p. 13.
70. Ibid., May 17, 1987, p. 8.
71. Ibid., August 27, 1967, p. 7; first quoted in Pye, pp. 125–126.
72. *Sports Illustrated,* March 1974.
73. See, for example, *GWR*, May 25, 1986, p. 1.

More recently, at the Pan American Games in Indianapolis in 1987 one athlete from Cuba commented: "[W]e have seen champions in the capitalist countries who have spent all their money end up in misery, drunk and unemployed."[74] At the 1991 Pan American Games a Cuban athlete told foreign reporters, "I have been to many capitalist countries and I know of athletes who were very famous and had much money. When they are finished, they have to turn to begging. . . . We are one of the few countries in the world where a sports person has a fully guaranteed life."[75] At the same time boxer Teófilo Stevenson again reiterated: "I don't think in terms of millions. I have what I need. I wouldn't change for all the gold in the world."[76]

At the 1992 Olympic Games in Barcelona, Spain, Cuban athletes once again served as revolutionary spokespersons, criticizing "capitalist" sports and claiming they performed for the love of Fidel Castro and the Cuban people. At the 1992 Olympics Alberto Juantorena, former Olympic gold medalist and president of the Cuban Sports Institute, declared that Cuban athletes would never perform simply for money. He explained: "Our great athletes prefer to be millionaires in the love [they receive] from the Cuban people than accept the offers of money they receive daily."[77]

Similarly, gold-medal boxer Félix Savon observed that he would reject any offers to box professionally. He explained, "For me, it's an honor to represent my people. To play professionally is bad. It's exploitation of man by man."[78] At the same time Cuban volleyball player Joel Despaigne stated: "I've had offers to play in Italy, but we [athletes] are part of Cuba's national patrimony and we don't agree with [the idea of] playing professionally."[79] Cuba's gold-medal boxer Ariel Hernández Ascuy declared, "I've never liked professional boxing, never. Some people box for the money. I love boxing for the sport."[80] Mireya Luis, the captain of Cuba's Olympic gold-medal women's volleyball team, explained that her team performed well in order to bring "tremendous joy to the people of Cuba."[81]

The government frequently compared revolutionary sports to athletics in prerevolutionary Cuba. A 1980 *Granma* article read:

74. *Boston Globe,* January 3, 1988, p. 69.
75. *Washington Post,* August 18, 1991, p. D7.
76. Ibid.
77. *The Daily Yomiuri* (Tokyo, Japan), August 4, 1992, p. 15.
78. Ibid.
79. Ibid.
80. *Washington Post,* August 10, 1992, p. C7.
81. Ibid., August 8, 1992, p. D7.

The showing of the Cubans at the Moscow Games far surpassed that of the small contingent that represented our country during the pseudorepublic. . . . During 1900 to 1956 Cuba participated in six Games with delegations of barely 60 people. . . . Cuba was represented in Moscow by 237 athletes. . . . [T]he panorama is in stark contrast to the prerevolutionary era.[82]

The Cuban government also aggressively publicized its athletic superiority over capitalist countries. In April 1988 Castro reminded his citizens that their athletes won 175 medals in the 1987 Pan American Games, set eight records, and beat the United States in boxing, fencing, baseball, rhythmic gymnastics, wrestling, weightlifting, and volleyball.[83] Similarly, after the 1991 Pan American Games Castro boasted that the Cubans had finally defeated the Americans: the Cubans won 140 gold medals while the Americans won only 130. When Cuba's Olympic Gold Medal winner, Alberto Juantorena, returned home after the 1976 Montreal Olympics, he publicly offered his medal to Fidel Castro, announcing: "It is necessary to think of the revolution as having created everything including our victories in sport. The revolution created the necessary conditions, health care and facilities. I am proud of the revolution."[84] Finally, at the 1992 Barcelona Olympics, after Cuban boxers had collected 7 gold medals, Alcides Sagarra, Cuba's boxing coach, exclaimed: "This is the best performance in the history of Olympic boxing. Never has anyone done what our team did."[85]

Providing Opportunities to Make Political Statements

In the international arena, along with the leaders of many other countries, Fidel Castro used attention to sports to make political statements. Castro decided to have the Cuban teams forgo both the 1984 Los Angeles Games and the 1988 Seoul Games in order to demonstrate outrage over international affairs. However, having raised interest in sports to a fever pitch, the Cuban government may have been reluctant to pull its teams from too many international competitions. Consequently, Cuba was one of the first

82. *Granma*, August 17, 1980.
83. *GWR*, April 3, 1988, p. 2.
84. *Sports Illustrated*, August 29, 1977; also quoted in Pye, p. 125.
85. *Washington Post*, August 10, 1992, p. C7.

states to announce that its teams would be participating in the 1992 Barcelona Games.

From the early years of the Revolution the government plainly viewed international sports events as an opportunity to rally anti-American sentiment. In a 1966 national speech to congratulate Cuban athletes upon their return from the Central American and Caribbean Games, Castro denounced the United States representatives of the professional baseball leagues for trying to sign Cuban players to professional contracts. Perhaps reflecting his own unhappy experience with the scouts and front office of the Washington Senators, Castro declared: "They wanted to buy [them] because that's their business. And it should be prohibited. It is immoral, corrupt, indecent that . . . a gang of hucksters should appear offering contracts and bribes with obvious disrespect for sports. They did their utmost to intimidate, to frighten, to divide and to weaken our delegation."[86] Castro continued: "The imperialists have been plotting ever since these Olympic Games were announced. They started to hatch all kinds of plots to undermine the success of the Cuban delegates. . . . They embarked upon a series of maneuvers, of violations, of tricks. . . . On many occasions the referees were Yankees, mind you, and possibly a good many of them agents of the CIA."[87] In July 1991 officials once again chastised American major league baseball scouts for contributing to the defection of Cuban baseball star René Arocha.

Over the years Cuban newspapers inundated the population with anti-American sports propaganda. As one newspaper article asserted:

> The imperialists have once again suffered a humiliating defeat. . . .
> The U.S. news agencies have had to admit that the Yankees suffered
> a resounding defeat. . . . [They] have found themselves obliged to
> admit the failure. They have made themselves ridiculous: they have
> been unmasked and have once again shown their true colors as
> hypocrites, as cynics, and as fools.

The article continued: "The anti-sports policy of the imperialists has been brought to light and it has been shown that the U.S. government in pursuit of its miserable political objectives, attempts to violate the rules."[88]

In a 1975 speech publicized across Cuba another official addressed the Cuban delegation returning from the North and Central American Games held in Los Angeles. He excoriated the United States: "The situation to-

---

86. *GWR*, July 8, 1966, p. 7.
87. Ibid., p. 6.
88. Ibid., June 18, 1966, p. 3.

day is very different. It is becoming harder and harder for the United States to continue using sports as a weapon to maintain its domination. It turned sports into an instrument, a tool of its infernal mercantile apparatus with the stress on professionalism, as a means to demonstrate its much-touted superiority and arrogance."[89] To the athletes the official said: "You were able to see the decay of the system in the country. You also received demonstrations of support from the exploited and oppressed in the United States and from those who are discriminated against." After Cuban athletes traveled to the 1970 Central American Games held in Panama, a defector told the U.S. Senate Subcommittee on Internal Security that Cuban authorities had even chosen the ship for propaganda purposes. The *Victoria de Giron* ("Victory of the Bay of Pigs") was selected to transport the team precisely because its name would irritate the North Americans.[90]

The Castro government also used international sports events to associate Cuban victory with revolutionary struggle against imperialism, warfare with the United States, and determination to triumph. A 1966 editorial read:

> Only a few days ago our people answered the imperialist provocation at Guantanamo with the first decision to fight, mobilizing the Revolutionary Armed Forces. . . . Now, once again, our people's firm and determined attitude has paralyzed the Yankee government's maneuvers. We must be ready to fight . . . in every area of political and social activity. We must battle the imperialists at every point, just as we have done in the political, military and ideological arenas—in the field of sports.[91]

A 1975 editorial praised Cuba's sports revolution for having "made it possible for the small nation, which grew in status thanks to its people's moral greatness, to prevail over the capitalist superpowers in eleven of the events of the Pan American Games."[92] A 1986 *Granma Weekly Review* article referred to imperialist "sports aggression against Cuba." Referring to the 1987 Pan American Games, Castro observed that Cuba won the gold and silver medals in the 75-kilogram weightlifting competition. "The defectors," Castro noted acerbically, "had to settle for bronze."[93]

Moreover, the leadership used international sports events as an oppor-

89. Ibid., September 21, 1975, p. 9.
90. See Slack, p. 39.
91. *GWR,* June 19, 1966, p. 3.
92. Ibid., September 21, 1975, p. 9.
93. Ibid., August 23, 1987, p. 5.

tunity for Cuban athletes to distribute pro-Castro, anticapitalist propaganda and deliver anti-American speeches. Not only were the 1970 Central American Games fraught with instances of pro-Castro propagandizing by Cuban athletes but at the 1971 Pan American Games in Colombia the Cuban team marched in at the opening ceremonies and, on a signal from the Cuban President of INDER, threw their red berets into the crowd.[94]

Cuba as an International Sports Power

Most critically, the Cuban government used sports to bolster the country's international prestige, status, and power. In pursuit of a positive international image, Castro hoped to demonstrate how progressive, modern, and well-organized his country had become. In a 1974 speech Castro exclaimed, "I can assure you that one of the things most admired by our Latin American neighbors is our sporting successes."[95]

Throughout the years the Castro government raised as the ultimate ambition for its revolutionary athletes the representation of Cuba in international sports competitions. A September 1972 editorial emphasized the importance of sports activities to develop "more and more qualified athletes" to compete abroad.[96] In his 1975 address to the First Party Congress, the Cuban leader hailed the national sports program as a tremendous success. Castro exalted that Cuba had become the champion of the Central American Games and of the Pan American Games "among the Latin American countries."[97]

To advance its international prestige, the Cuban government also sought bilateral sports exchanges. For instance, in September 1991 Cuba agreed to send 150 coaches, specialists, sports doctors, and athletes to Mexico to help the latter country prepare for the 1992 Olympics in Barcelona, Spain. Before the 1991 Pan American Games, a former Cuban baseball player coached the Venezuelan baseball team.[98] In 1992 a number of countries, including Tanzania, Spain, Mexico, Thailand, India, China, Pakistan, Uganda, and Ireland, sought Cuban assistance in coaching their

---

94. *Bohemia*, August 6, 1971; also discussed by Slack, p. 39: "A group of Cubans was reported to have distributed pro-Castro propaganda and made political speeches in defiance of orders by games' officials prohibiting such action."

95. Fidel Castro. *Fidel: Sobre el deporte*, ed. Sonia Castanes (Havana, 1975).

96. *GWR*, September 10, 1972, p. 9.

97. Ibid., January 4, 1976.

98. *GI*, April 7, 1991, p. 11; *GWR*, March 31, 1991, p. 7.

Olympic boxers. Indeed, the boxers from each of these countries had Cuban instructors at the 1992 Olympics. Cuban coaches assisted Ireland's boxers in receiving the country's first gold medal ever and first silver medal since 1956.[99] Cuba and Mexico also agreed to send teams to eighty bilateral competitions in 1992.[100]

In 1991 the Cuban government launched its most remarkable effort to strengthen its international status through sports by hosting the Pan American Games. Despite dire financial and political difficulties, Castro, in typical go-for-broke style, hosted the Games and enjoyed Cuba's impressive athletic successes. The leadership apparently viewed the Games, perhaps the most ambitious international event in its revolutionary history, as a wise investment of extremely scarce hard currency. The Games were seen as a means to attract tourists and international attention. As part of this sports campaign, the leadership often recounted sophisticated advances in sports medicine on the island. And Cuba hosted various international sports medicine conferences.[101]

Castro's international sports program thus had a number of objectives. The leadership sought to demonstrate to the world the success of the socialist Revolution and the superiority of a socialist consciousness over a prerevolutionary capitalist one. Moreover, the leaders used international sports events as an occasion to criticize American capitalism, individualism, and selfishness, and to distribute anti-American propaganda. Castro repeatedly seized upon the international attention at a major sports event to make international political declarations. Most important, the Cuban government attempted to gain international prestige and status through the triumph of its athletes.

Cuban Athletes: A New Elite

Fidel Castro and the other revolutionary leaders thus took a widespread positive attitude toward athletics and molded it into a remarkable sports consciousness. The government's actions—building playgrounds, creating special sports institutes, constructing Ciudad Deportiva, and implementing physical education programs in nearly all schools and most day-care centers—unquestionably contributed substantially to transforming Cuban sports culture. The leadership's use of propaganda—speeches on erad-

99. *Washington Post,* August 10, 1992, p. C7.

100. *Miami Herald,* International Edition, October 1, 1991, p. 1B.

101. The first such conference was held in 1966. See *GWR,* September 4, 1966, p. 2. See also March 3, 1991, p. 3. This article discusses the then upcoming Pan American Congress for Sports Medicine held in Cuba in May 1991; ibid., November 27, 1988, p. 5.

icating elitism, professionalism, and equality, glorifying the athlete-hero, scorning the United States, and extolling the virtues of socialism—also aided in developing the new sports consciousness. Nevertheless, Castro's chief tactic may well have been that used by most countries to lure athletes to work hard and win: material incentives.

Cuban officials routinely claimed that their athletes trained and competed for the love of Cuba and socialism alone. As noted above, some Cuban athletes echoed these claims. Yet the contention by the leadership that the athletes were amateurs who were paid nothing is untrue. More likely, many Cuban athletes competed because they personally gained from doing so. Authorities offered substantial benefits to them, incentives that proved to be quite difficult to resist in such a limited consumer society. Athletes, unquestionably, lived a significantly higher quality of life than the average Cuban citizen. At the expense of the State athletic teams enjoyed international-standard, luxurious sports facilities, substantially better, more varied, and nutritious foods than the average citizen, and regular opportunities to travel outside the island.

Moreover, the government offered outstanding sports heroes—the new "elites"—special incentives, including pocket money, a lucrative salary after retirement, and other bonuses.[102] In 1991, for example, the Cuban government paid baseball players on the national team 230 pesos a month, roughly $300 at the official exchange rate. While this may not seem like a very good salary by Western standards, it comprised an exceptional income in Cuba. According to Ana Quirot, Cuba's bronze medalist runner at the 1992 Barcelona Olympic Games, top Cuban athletes earned a salary "typical of those with a university degree."[103]

Government officials allowed various athletes, upon their retirement or some other special occasion, to buy cars at significantly reduced prices, opportunities that very few Cubans enjoyed.[104] These luxuries stood out in a society where the government rationed nearly all goods and services. In addition, successful hero-athletes often became Party members, serving as spokespersons for the government and its policies. Both Alberto Juantorena and Teófilo Stevenson, perhaps the Revolution's two finest athletes, were members of the Cuban Communist Party. Juantorena also served as Vice-President of INDER and Cuba's representative on the Council of the International Track and Field Federation.[105]

102. *Boston Globe,* January 3, 1988, p. 69. Certain government officials have openly acknowledged that the sports program in Cuba has created undesirable elitism among Cuban athletes. See, for example, *GWR,* January 10, 1988, p. 6. See also *Washington Post,* August 8, 1991, p. D7.

103. *Washington Post,* August 18, 1991, p. D7.

104. Ibid., August 4, 1991, p. D10.

105. See *GWR,* June 12, 1988, p. 5; June 14, 1987, p. 3.

Thus, although Castro never ceased attacking capitalist, professional sports, in certain respects the Cuban system paralleled that in Western sports powers. The revolutionary leaders offered their outstanding athletes higher salaries, material bonuses, travel opportunities, and other benefits rarely available to the average Cuban citizen.

CONCLUSION

This chapter has discussed the goals and successes of Cuba's official revolutionary sports program. Clearly, both the revolutionary government and the island's best athletes gained considerably from Cuba's sports victories. But what did the ordinary citizen gain? Sports are, of course, fun and invigorating, a form of recreation. Athletics promote good health and physical strength. Although Cuban citizens always enjoyed watching sports events, the Castro government provided them with the ability to participate freely themselves. This perhaps sheds light on why the population willingly, even enthusiastically, supported the leadership's sports program.

In all societies athletics provide mental and physical release from the stress and frustrations of daily life. This is particularly true in a country such as Cuba where freedom of movement is curtailed, goods are generally of poor quality and tightly rationed, and individuals have few opportunities to express dissatisfaction. Cuban citizens, in particular, must have immensely valued the chance to join in vigorous athletic activities.

Sports also offered the people a means to individual expression, a way to compete, to achieve, and to accomplish. In any society the opportunity to achieve individual fulfillment is highly valued. In a noncapitalist, anti-individualistic society such as revolutionary Cuba, such an opportunity is particularly coveted. This, perhaps, also helps to explain why Cuban citizens placed such high value on sports participation.

Finally, sports brought to Cuban youngsters the chance to perform well athletically and thus to earn the status of Cuban athlete, which guaranteed a higher quality of life than the average citizen. Sports also provided some citizens with repeated, and cherished, trips abroad to countries outside of the Communist bloc. International sports events granted to many Cuban athletes the long-awaited moment to defect. During the 1971 Pan American Games, for instance, four Cuban athletes defected to the United States.[106] After a string of defections in the intervening decades, in July

106. Slack, p. 39.

1991 a widely popular Cuban baseball player defected to the United States.[107]

The leadership's success in developing a revolutionary "sports consciousness" can be attributed, in part, to the goals and aspirations of the government and the citizens. Since athletics offered so much to the Cuban people, sports provided unusually fertile ground on which Fidel Castro could plant a new culture. Indeed, the sports program provided something for everyone, in essence a quid pro quo. Most official attempts to create social attitudes in other areas of Cuban life failed to accomplish their objectives precisely because this balance, this "something for everyone," was missing. For example, the government's attempt to create new work attitudes failed because the people could see no tangible benefits in changing their traditional way of life. In calling for volunteer work, moral incentives, and nonmaterialism, the leadership offered nothing to citizens in return except long, hot days in the cane fields and lengthy lines that led to a few poor-quality goods. In the case of sports, however, Cuban citizens willingly accepted the government's program because personal gains could be realized from modifying their behavior. This suggests that new cultural attitudes may be created when the government's aspirations and those of its subjects prove complementary.

In addition, in the case of sports the Cuban leadership's assault on prerevolutionary attitudes was more selective than in other areas targeted for revolutionary change. In its efforts to transform popular attitudes toward labor, for instance, the government tried to eliminate many prerevolutionary attitudes and create new, radically different attitudes. While the leadership sought to destroy some aspects of Cuba's prerevolutionary sports attitudes, such as views toward professional sports and the notion that sports participation should be reserved for the upper class, it preserved other aspects, such as the widespread popularity of sports. The government's revolutionary sports program, while sweeping and radical in many respects, relied to some degree on prerevolutionary attitudes to gain popular support. Sports in prerevolutionary Cuba were widely popular. While most citizens did not participate, many enthusiastically spectated. The foundation upon which the government built its phenomenal sports programs had already been laid: Cubans enjoyed watching sports, particularly baseball. Thus the leaders could seize on the substantial popularity of sports and refocus this interest to promote different attitudes toward Cuban sports, including views toward mass participation in sporting events, the political significance of sports competition, the revolutionary importance of international sporting events, and the shame of professionalism.

107. *Washington Post*, August 4, 1991, p. D10.

The government's success in creating a sports *conciencia* suggests that attempts to promote cultural change work best when the government relies, however marginally, on some attitudes and values already widely held by much of the population. In the case of sports an element of continuity existed between the culture the leadership sought to eliminate and that which it aimed to create. The leaders urged Cuban citizens to adopt new attitudes and values as well as preserve old ones. Thus, citizens likely did not view this program as a threatening and radical break from the past.

6

The Successes and Failures
of the Quest for
a Revolutionary Culture

> Che wanted to make other Ches. He tried—perhaps
> unconsciously—to impregnate nine million Cubans
> with his seed. . . . To the plump little man who goes
> and returns to work, to the city bureaucrat, to the
> man who sings in the shower, Guevara was asking
> for the moon.
>
> —Carlos Alberto Montaner

Fidel Castro's quest to establish a revolutionary culture in Cuba largely
failed. The revolutionary government's attempt to destroy or transform
certain aspects of prerevolutionary Cuban culture and to create a culture
appropriate for the ideal Marxist society typically met insuperable obstacles. So, too, did the government's efforts to alter behavior often fail.
The leadership seems to have erred in holding firmly to the Marxist conviction that the thought processes and behavior of citizens are essentially
malleable. What lesson might be drawn from this study of Fidel Castro's
quest, over more than three decades, to transform Cuban culture?

ASSESSING THE GOVERNMENT'S
CULTURAL PROJECT

The various campaigns to alter Cuban culture made Fidel Castro the
leader of one of history's most radical experiments in cultural transformation. As the preceding chapters have illustrated, in their efforts to transform culture the Cuban leaders employed an array of strategies: moral
persuasion, material rewards, public humiliation, and others. Indeed, once
Cuban leaders realized that moral suasion failed to change the attitudes
of people on the island, they regularly resorted to harsher methods. As
time passed, and culture proved unbending, most of these coercive mea-

sures became more directly oppressive. If the government could not change culture, it would attempt to take the initial step of changing behavior. Thus, while the leadership retreated from excesses of coercion during the late 1970s and allowed some freedom of action, the 1980s and the early 1990s brought renewed repression: political harassment, incarceration, forced labor, work transfers, and the deprivation of basic goods. In trying to ensure mass cooperation and proper behavior, the government punished scores of individuals.

But, whichever methods the state implemented, the entire project resulted in a steady increase in state intervention in the lives of its citizens. In its efforts to realize extensive cultural change, the government exerted unprecedented authority in the schools, the workplace, the home, and in all official organizations. In its attempts to change behavior through further social discipline, the Castro leadership established a far-ranging network aimed at maintaining order and control. Over time, the *círculos*, the military, the mass organizations, the People's Councils, and the Committees for the Defense of the Revolution extended their tentacles around the moral, academic, and political lives of Cuban citizens from early childhood on. Authorities noted deviant behavior and strictly penalized offenders. While the government was not able to force cooperation, the uncooperative were not able to live for long without being detected and harassed.

The Cuban attempt at cultural transformation thus fell into cycles of repression. While policies passed through phases of suasion and coercion, the leaders repeatedly became frustrated that cultural transformation was not occurring as smoothly as their guiding doctrine had predicted, or as rapidly as they had anticipated. This brought on redoubled efforts, and redoubled efforts often meant coercion. When carrots proved to be ineffective, Fidel Castro grasped the stick more firmly and wielded it more recklessly.

EXPLAINING THE RESPONSE OF CITIZENS

If this study had discovered sweeping changes in the way Cuban people behaved thirty years after the Revolution as compared to their behavior prior to the Revolution, explaining the cause of those changes would have been an extremely formidable task. It would have been necessary to try to disentangle true changes in culture from mere changes in behavior. However, what is most striking about Cuba under the Castro government is that even the behavioral changes that the leadership sought did not generally occur. Even when confronted with substantial direct and indirect coercion, many citizens failed to change their behavior. If behavior remained unchanged, then the official project to change culture, to change the values, beliefs, and attitudes of citizens, certainly failed as well.

How then do we explain the noncompliant and uncooperative response of most Cuban citizens—youth, workers, women—when confronted with official efforts to change their traditional attitudes and beliefs? Resistance to the revolutionary government's efforts to transform culture may be attributed, on the one hand, to the unwillingness of Cubans to change radically their traditional views. On the other hand, aside from their efforts to change sports culture, the Cuban leadership selected quite difficult—indeed, perhaps implausible—targets for cultural change and embarked on its ambitious programs without effective strategies.

Consequently, some citizens in revolutionary Cuba willfully resisted official policies to change behavior or to transform culture. This resistance, however, tended to be quiet and informal, though ultimately effective. Because Cuban citizens possessed little access to resources, limited influence over official decision making, and virtually no formal instruments of power, they waged neither an open battle nor a selective guerrilla campaign against the leadership. The uncooperative generally did not directly confront the formal power structure. Such a frontal attack on the official political hierarchy would doubtless have been interpreted by the government as a direct threat to its security. A merciless response would almost certainly have followed.

Instead, some Cuban citizens tended to employ subtle, individual, undeclared, and often discreet forms of everyday resistance.[1] They did not make explicit demands but simply demonstrated their unhappiness with official policy through repeated minor acts of irritating, but nonthreatening, disobedience, such as loafing on the job or feigning incompetence. Many workers displayed their dissatisfaction with the government by refusing to go to work or by abusing state property, even when it was not materially in their interest to do so. Many more chose to ignore the government's relatively lenient work quotas, even when doing so meant forfeiting badly needed material goods. Although such daily acts of resistance may have occurred more frequently in response to official attempts to change the behavior of Cuban citizens, they most likely occurred as well in response to government policies aimed at transforming culture. For instance, Cuban husbands who pressured their wives to remain at

---

1. James C. Scott provides a valuable study of everyday forms of resistance by powerless groups. I found his work particularly helpful in my analysis here. See Scott, *Weapons of the Weak: Everyday Forms of Peasant Resistance* (New Haven: Yale University Press, 1985).

home may have been resisting not just the Cuban government's efforts to change behavior but its efforts to change the island's culture as well.

Perhaps more important, the response of many Cuban citizens to the cultural policies and objectives of their government reflected not so much a mere lack of cooperation as a very human inertia, a refusal to change deep-seated attitudes and beliefs. While the Cuban government could, in some cases, force changes in behavior, it did not know how to reach and alter culture. Here, perhaps, the leaders were exploring wellsprings of human nature much deeper and far less accessible to official policies. Indeed, some aspects of the cultural change proposed by the Cuban government were wholly implausible. The government may have attempted to change aspects of Cuban culture that no official policy could affect so readily, or at least so rapidly.

THE OFFICIAL RESPONSE TO WIDESPREAD NONCOMPLIANCE

The widespread, though low-intensity, resistance of Cuban citizens, paired with the inertia associated with attitudes developed over many centuries, made a shambles of the government's most carefully plotted policies. After thirty years of attempting to transform culture, the leaders found that they were incapable of eradicating unacceptable attitudes and behavior and of devising policies to convince citizens to think and act differently. Fidel Castro and his revolutionary associates gravely underestimated the difficulty of the task they had taken on. While the government could crush the open disobedience of a few, foot-dragging and inertia combined to amount to a much more formidable problem, one that proved quite difficult to overcome.

Unsupportive Cuban citizens often forced the leadership to modify its strategy, to test another approach, in further attempts to realize its behavioral and cultural objectives. In this sense citizens influenced the policy decisions of the Cuban government. In fact, at times the leaders actually accommodated the quiet demands of Cuban citizens. For instance, during the Revolutionary Offensive Fidel Castro encouraged laborers to produce efficiently by offering moral rewards. Workers, however, were not satisfied. They wanted to be materially rewarded for their efforts. Consequently, production levels dropped precipitously, and rates of absenteeism skyrocketed. The leadership responded to this crisis by reintroducing material incentives to induce workers to produce.

At other times the noncompliance of citizens convinced the leadership to abandon its objectives altogether. The government's willingness to recognize the religious beliefs of Cuban citizens and to open the Party to religious believers illustrates not only that the State accommodated popular demands but that it actually abandoned an earlier, widely touted, official objective: creating an atheist state. Nevertheless, while in some instances the government did accommodate the uncooperative masses, or abandon objectives altogether, it more typically tried to coerce citizens to change their behavior, if not their attitudes.

SUCCEEDING AT CULTURAL CHANGE

While the evidence suggests that the Castro government failed in its bid to create revolutionary new attitudes toward women and labor and among youth, Cuban leaders impressively succeeded in their attempt to create different popular attitudes toward sports. Why did the leadership succeed in creating a new sports *conciencia* when it failed in so many other respects? Why in this case did the government meet less popular resistance?

First, the leadership's success in creating a sports *conciencia* may illustrate that culture can be altered more readily when, rather than attempting to eliminate a preexisting cultural attitude entirely, the government finds important elements of preexisting culture that can be preserved and nurtured. One might say it is easier to graft a hybrid culture than to create an altogether new one. In its attempt to inculcate sweeping cultural changes in the area of labor, for example, the Castro government vigorously attacked virtually every aspect of traditional culture. Had the leadership relied more heavily on traditional symbols, words, and values, it might have provided citizens with some continuity and familiarity that could have made cultural transformation more palatable and less threatening.

In the case of sports, while the government assaulted most aspects of Cuba's prerevolutionary sports culture, including popular views toward professional athletics and elite participation, it preserved some significant aspects that could develop into the foundation for Cuba's revolutionary sports ethic. That the government could form the basis of its new sports culture by adopting certain aspects of prerevolutionary culture may explain why this effort succeeded while others failed.

Second, citizens in most human societies tend to be inherently self-interested. They tend to support policies that improve their well-being. The success in developing a revolutionary sports consciousness can be attributed, in part, to the fact that both Cuban citizens and the Castro government clearly benefited from the sports *conciencia*. The leadership gained substantial international prestige and recognition. The citizens gained the opportunity to improve their mental and physical health by participating freely in sports activities. Moreover, Cuban officials offered many outstanding athletes lucrative salaries, a significantly improved quality of life, and an opportunity to travel abroad to noncommunist countries.

In any society cultural change may be possible when the interests of citizens and leaders converge and complement one another. Most of the Cuban government's attempts to create new social attitudes failed precisely because this balance, this "something for everyone," was missing. For example, despite thirty years of promises and demands for sacrifice by the leaders, the average Cuban citizen gained very few tangible benefits from the labor *conciencia* the leaders long advocated.

Of course, in part Castro may have been the victim of a vicious circle. The meager returns may have been the consequence of a failed effort to create a new labor culture; in turn, a new labor culture may have failed to develop because economic rewards had been so meager. To escape this circle, Cuba's Marxist economy would have had to work so well that the country's standard of living increased dramatically. Such a turn of events might have produced the necessary incentives for a new labor *conciencia* to take effect. In fact, of course, the Cuban economy faltered repeatedly, and the people lost whatever faith they might once have had in the ability of a new labor *conciencia* to improve their lot in life.

Much the same argument holds true for Cuban women. During the Revolution's first thirty years, traditional Cuban attitudes toward women did not significantly change. Cuban attitudes toward female occupations, sexual mores, women in politics, and women's responsibilities in the home remained surprisingly traditional. Why? One important reason is that the revolutionary leaders, who themselves harbored some traditional views of women's social role, never adopted in practice the revolutionary attitudes espoused in their rhetoric. The Castro government enjoyed the benefits of labor by Cuban women. It demanded the unflinching support of women for government policies. However, the government failed to offer much in return for their labor and support. The leadership never vigorously implemented the kinds of broad, progressive, and noncoercive measures that might have provided women with concrete results. For instance, the Cuban leadership was unwilling to appoint women to powerful political and economic posts. Such policies would have given women a voice in the political and economic decisions made on their behalf, and given them the opportunity to gain the respect of men and women in Cuban society. Such a course of action might have made the people more inclined to change their social attitudes. Instead, no one gained much from the Castro government's policies toward women, and cultural change was extremely limited.

The success of cultural change in Cuban sports and the failures of cultural change regarding labor, youth, and women suggest that a mutually beneficial outcome might be a precondition for cultural change. If the leaders and the people see their interests being served, the chance for successful cultural change improves exponentially. However, when citizens do not believe that their interests will be served, their attitudes tend to remain steadfast and unyielding.

CULTURAL RESISTANCE IN REVOLUTIONARY SOCIETIES

This study thus argues that the Castro government's attempt to transform culture met with substantial human obstacles. Indeed, the Cuban leadership has not been alone in finding that tinkering with society's traditional values, attitudes, and beliefs can be an exceptionally uncertain endeavor. In past years a broad range of Marxist regimes have struggled, often at great lengths and without much success, against the remarkable persistence of traditional culture. The inherent difficulties in attempting to create new cultural attitudes and beliefs antithetical to well-established value systems have long been apparent around the world.[2]

Today, amidst the debris of the collapse of communism within the Soviet Union and Eastern Europe, many traditional attitudes and values are reemerging. While many decades of communism as well as the inexorable process of modernization altered some aspects of culture, many traditional values and attitudes survived. In their efforts to destroy and create culture, many Marxist governments eventually succumbed to a vibrant and powerful civil society willing to employ subtle, yet effective, forms of human resistance. In fact, throughout much of Eastern Europe, certain fundamental views, such as those toward nationhood, ethnicity, and religion, emerged from the revolutionary period intact, in some cases nearly unscathed, and occasionally perhaps even strengthened.

Ultimately, then, this study of the Cuban Revolution and its effects on traditional culture raises a series of far broader questions. What is the

2. David Paul's work on cultural change in communist Czechoslovakia offers perhaps the most interesting study of culture in these former communist Eastern European nations. See Paul, *The Cultural Limits of Revolutionary Politics: Change and Continuity in Socialist Czechoslovakia* (New York: Columbia University Press, 1979).

relationship between cultural and institutional change in revolutionary societies? To what extent have communist regimes been able to transform traditional culture? In what respects have citizens resisted and frustrated the government's programs to bring about cultural change? How and under what circumstances are governments able to change culture? To what extent do communist leaders ultimately rely on coercion to attempt to impose on their people changes in behavior or actual changes in culture? Finally, why have Marxist governments in Africa, Asia, Latin America, Eastern Europe, and the Soviet Union so profoundly failed to transform their country's culture?

The collapse of communism and the revival of traditional culture throughout the former Soviet Union and the Eastern bloc suggest that, even after many decades, traditional culture can remain quite vibrant. What has taken place in these countries reminds us that while the human spirit may at times lapse into a state of apathy and despair, it may also survive, endure, and, at length, triumph. The daily acts of resistance by Cuban citizens illustrate that, despite thirty years of government manipulation, a willful, persistent, and independent civil society lived on in revolutionary Cuba.

Bibliography

Books

Almond, Gabriel A., and Verbe, Sidney. *The Civic Culture.* Princeton: Princeton University Press, 1963.

Barnett, Clifford R. *Cuba: Its People, Its Society, Its Culture.* New Haven: Human Relations Area Files Press, 1962.

Bernardo, Robert M. *The Theory of Moral Incentives in Cuba.* University: University of Alabama Press, 1971.

Bonachea, Rolando E., and Valdés, Nelson P., eds. *Che: Selected Works of Ernesto Guevara.* Garden City, N.Y.: Anchor Books, 1968.

———. *Cuba in Revolution.* Garden City, N.Y.: Doubleday, 1972.

Butterworth, Douglas. *The People of Buena Ventura.* Urbana: University of Illinois Press, 1980.

Castro, Fidel. *Fidel: Sobre el deporte.* Edited by Sonia Castanes. Havana, 1975.

Conesa Martínez, José. *Ocho Amigos.* Miami: Noya Printing, 1978.

del Aguila, Juan M. *Cuba: Dilemmas of a Revolution.* Boulder: Westview Press, 1984.

del Mar, Marcia. *A Cuban Story.* Winston-Salem: John F. Blair, 1979.

Dolgoff, Sam. *The Cuban Revolution: A Critical Perspective.* Montreal: Black Rose Books, 1976.

Domínguez, Jorge I. *Cuba: Order and Revolution.* Cambridge: Harvard University Press, 1978.

———. *To Make a World Safe for Revolution.* Cambridge: Harvard University Press, 1989.

Draper, Theodore. *Castroism: Theory and Practice.* New York: Praeger, 1965.

———. *Castro's Revolution: Myth and Realities.* New York: Praeger, 1962.

Dubois, Jules. *Fidel Castro: Rebel-Liberator or Dictator?* Indianapolis: Bobbs-Merrill, 1959.

Fagen, Richard. *The Transformation of Political Culture in Cuba.* Stanford: Stanford University Press, 1969.

Fidel Castro. Havana: Campamento 5 de Mayo, 1968.

Fromm, Erich. *Marx's Concept of Man.* New York: Frederick Ungar, 1961.

Geertz, Clifford. *The Interpretation of Cultures: Selected Essays.* New York: Basic Books, 1973.

Gerassi, John, ed. *Venceremos! The Speeches and Writings of Ernesto Che Guevara.* New York: Macmillan, 1968.

Geyer, Georgie Anne. *Guerrilla Prince: The Untold Story of Fidel Castro.* Boston: Little, Brown, 1991.

Gilly, Adolfo. *Inside the Cuban Revolution.* New York: Monthly Review Press, 1964.

Ginsburg, Norton Sydney. *Atlas of Economic Development.* Chicago: University of Chicago Press, 1961.

Goodsell, James Nelson, ed. *Fidel Castro's Personal Revolution in Cuba: 1959–1973.* New York: Knopf, 1975.

Green, Gil. *Revolution Cuban Style: Impressions of a Recent Visit.* New York: International Publishers, 1970.

Gurley, John G. *Challengers to Capitalism: Marx, Lenin, Stalin, and Mao.* New York: Norton, 1979.

Halebsky, Sandor, and Kirk, John M., eds. *Cuba, Twenty-Five Years of Revolution, 1959–1984.* New York: Praeger, 1985.

———. *Transformation and Struggle: Cuba Faces the 1990s.* New York: Praeger, 1990.

Halperin, Maurice. *The Taming of Fidel Castro.* Berkeley and Los Angeles: University of California Press, 1981.

Hook, Sidney. *Marx and the Marxists: The Ambiguous Legacy.* Malabar, Fla.: Robert E. Krieger, 1982.

Horowitz, Irving Louis. *Cuban Communism.* 4th and 7th eds. New Brunswick, N.J.: Transaction, 1981, 1989.

Huberman, Leo, and Sweezy, Paul M. *Socialism in Cuba.* New York: Monthly Review Press, 1969.

Illan, José M. *Cuba: Facts and Figures of an Economy in Ruins.* Miami: Editorial ATP, 1964.

Karol, K. S. *Guerrillas in Power: The Course of the Cuban Revolution.* New York: Hill and Wang, 1970.

Kenner, Martin, and Petras, James, eds. *Fidel Castro Speaks.* New York: Grove Press, 1969.

Larguia, Isabel, and DuMoulin, John. *Hacía una concepción científica de la emancipación de la mujer.* Havana: Editorial de Ciencias Socialistas, 1983.

Leiner, Marvin. *Children Are the Revolution: Day Care in Cuba.* New York: Viking Press, 1974.

Lewis, Oscar; Lewis, Ruth M.; and Rigdon, Susan M. *Four Women Living the Revolution: An Oral History of Contemporary Cuba.* Urbana: University of Illinois Press, 1977.

Lipset, Seymour Martin. *The First New Nation.* Garden City, N.Y.: Anchor Books, 1967.

———. *Revolution and Counterrevolution: Change and Resistance in Social Structures.* New York: Basic Books, 1968.

McMurtry, John. *The Structure of Marx's World-View.* Princeton: Princeton University Press, 1978.

Mankiewicz, Frank, and Jones, Kirby. *With Fidel.* New York: Ballantine Books, 1975.

Marx, Karl. *Capital.* Edited by Frederick Engels and translated by Samuel Moore and Edward Aveling. 2 vols. Moscow: Progress Publishers, 1965.

———. *Grundrisse: Introduction to the Critique of Political Economy.* Translated and edited by Martin Nicolaus. New York: Vintage Books, 1973.

————. *The Poverty of Philosophy.* Edited by Frederick Engels. Moscow: Progress Publishers, 1966.

Matthews, Herbert L. *Revolution in Cuba.* New York: Charles Scribner's Sons, 1975.

Medin, Tzvi. *Cuba: The Shaping of Revolutionary Consciousness.* Boulder: Lynne Rienner Publishers, 1990.

Mesa-Lago, Carmelo. *Cuba in the 1970s: Pragmatism and Institutionalization.* Albuquerque: University of New Mexico Press, 1978.

————. *The Economy of Socialist Cuba: A Two-Decade Appraisal.* Albuquerque: University of New Mexico Press, 1981.

————, ed. *Revolutionary Change in Cuba.* Pittsburgh: University of Pittsburgh Press, 1971.

Montaner, Carlos Alberto. *Secret Report on the Cuban Revolution.* London: Transaction Books, 1981.

Moore, Carlos. *Castro, the Blacks, and Africa.* Los Angeles: The Regents of the University of California, 1988.

Neill, Stephen Charles. *Christian Missions.* Middlesex, Eng.: Penguin Books, 1964.

Nelson, Lowry. *Cuba: The Measure of a Revolution.* Minneapolis: University of Minnesota Press, 1972.

————. *Rural Cuba.* Minneapolis: University of Minnesota Press, 1950.

Nicholson, Joe, Jr. *Inside Cuba.* New York: Sheed and Ward, 1974.

Our Power Is That of the Working People. New York: Pathfinder Press, 1970.

Paul, David. *The Cultural Limits of Revolutionary Politics: Change and Continuity in Socialist Czechoslovakia.* New York: Columbia University Press, 1979.

Pye, Lucian W., and Verba, Sidney. *Political Culture and Political Development.* Princeton: Princeton University Press, 1965.

Rauf, Mohammed A., Jr. *Cuban Journal: Castro's Cuba As It Really Is.* New York: Crowell, 1964.

Ruiz, Ramón. *Cuba: The Making of the Revolution.* New York: Norton, 1968.

Russett, Bruce M.; Alker, Hayward R., Jr.; Deutsch, Karl W.; and Lasswell, Harold D. *World Handbook of Political and Social Indicators.* New Haven: Yale University Press, 1964.

Salas, Luis P. *Social Control and Deviance in Cuba.* New York: Praeger, 1979.

Scott, James C. *Weapons of the Weak: Everyday Forms of Peasant Resistance.* New Haven: Yale University Press, 1985.

Seers, Dudley, ed. *Cuba: The Economic and Social Revolution.* Chapel Hill: University of North Carolina Press, 1964.

Silverman, Bertram, ed. *Man and Socialism in Cuba: The Great Debate.* New York: Atheneum, 1971.

Statistical Abstract of Latin America. Los Angeles: Center for Latin American Studies, University of California at Los Angeles, 1961.

Stone, Elizabeth, ed. *Women and the Cuban Revolution.* New York: Pathfinder Press, 1981.

Stoner, Lynn. *From the Houses to the Streets: The Cuban Women's Movement for Legal Reform, 1898-1940.* Durham: Duke University Press, 1991.

Suárez, Andrés. *Cuba: Castroism and Communism, 1959–1966.* Cambridge: M.I.T. Press, 1967.

Sutherland, Elizabeth. *The Youngest Revolution.* New York: Dial Press, 1969.

Thomas, Hugh S. *Cuba: The Pursuit of Freedom.* New York: Harper & Row, 1971.
———; Fauriol, Georges A.; and Weiss, Juan Carlos. *The Cuban Revolution: Twenty-Five Years Later.* Boulder: Westview Press, 1984.
Urrutia Lleo, Manuel. *Fidel Castro and Company, Inc.* New York: Praeger, 1964.
Wald, Karen. *Children of Che: Childcare and Education in Cuba.* Palo Alto: Ramparts Press, 1978.
Ward, Fred. *Inside Cuba Today.* New York: Crown Publishers, 1978.
Yglesias, José. *In the Fist of the Revolution: Life in a Cuban Country Town.* New York: Pantheon Books, 1968.
Zeitlin, Maurice. *Revolutionary Politics and the Cuban Working Class.* New York: Harper Torchbooks, 1970.

Articles

Almond, Gabriel. "Communism and Political Culture Theory." *Comparative Politics* 15, no. 2 (January 1983).
Anthony, Don. "Introduction." In *Sport under Communism,* edited by James Riordan. London: C. Hurst, 1981.
Baloyra, Enrique A. "Political Control and Cuban Youth." In *Cuban Communism,* edited by Irving Louis Horowitz. 7th ed. New Brunswick, N.J.: Transaction, 1989.
Camarano, Chris. "On Cuban Women." *Science and Society* (Spring 1971).
Cockburn, Cynthia. "Women and Family in Cuba." In *Cuba: The Second Decade,* edited by John Griffiths and Peter Griffiths. London: Writers and Readers Publishing Cooperative, 1979.
Cropsey, Joseph. "Karl Marx." In *History of Political Philosophy,* edited by Leo Strauss and Joseph Cropsey. Chicago: University of Chicago Press, 1987.
"Cuba: Behind a Sporting Facade, Stepped-Up Repression." *Americas Watch* 3, no. 9 (August 11, 1991).
Cuba Socialista 3 (February 1964), Havana.
Domínguez, Jorge I. "Blaming Itself, Not Himself: Cuba's Political Regime after the Third Party Congress." In *Socialist Cuba: Past Interpretations and Future Challenges,* edited by Sergio G. Roca. Boulder: Westview Press, 1988.
———. "Leadership Change in Cuba since 1960." In *Leadership Change in Communist States,* edited by Raymond C. Taras. Boston: Unwin Hyman, 1989.
Dumont, René. "The Militarization of Fidelismo." *Dissent* 17 (September-October 1970).
Eckstein, Susan. "The Rectification of Errors Or the Errors of the Rectification Process in Cuba?" *Cuban Studies* 20, no. 1 (Fall/Winter 1990).
Ellisen, K. W. "Succeeding Castro." *The Atlantic* 265 (June 1990).
Evenson, Debra. "The Changing Role of the Law." In *Transformation and Struggle: Cuba Faces the 1990s,* edited by Sandor Halebsky and John M. Kirk. New York: Praeger, 1990.
"The Federation of Cuban Women Is Five Years Old." *Women of the Whole World* 12 (1965).
Friedenberg, Daniel M. "Notes on the Cuban Revolution." *The New Republic,* February 17, 1958.

Geertz, Clifford. "A Study of National Character." *Economic Development and Cultural Change* 12 (January 1964).

González, Edward. "The Limits of Charisma." In *Fidel Castro's Personal Revolution in Cuba: 1959–1973*, edited by James Nelson Goodsell. New York: Knopf, 1975.

Griffiths, John. "Sports: The People's Right." In *Cuba: The Second Decade*, edited by John Griffiths and Peter Griffiths. London: Writers and Readers Publishing Cooperative, 1979.

Gunn, Gillian. "Will Castro Fall?" *Foreign Policy* 79 (Summer 1990).

Harris, Olivia. "An Overview." In *Latin American Women*, edited by Olivia Harris. London: Minority Rights Group, 1983.

Hernández, Roberto E., and Mesa-Lago, Carmelo. "Labor Organization and Wages." In *Revolutionary Change in Cuba*, edited by Carmelo Mesa-Lago. Pittsburgh: University of Pittsburgh Press, 1971.

Jolly, Richard. "Education: The Prerevolutionary Background." In *Cuba: The Economic and Social Revolution*, edited by Dudley Seers. Chapel Hill: University of North Carolina Press, 1964.

———. "The Educational Aims and Program of the Revolutionary Government." In *Cuba: The Economic and Social Revolution*, edited by Dudley Seers. Chapel Hill: University of North Carolina Press, 1964.

Jowitt, Kenneth. "An Organizational Approach to the Study of Political Culture." *American Political Science Review* 68, no. 3 (September 1974).

Karl, Terry. "Work Incentives in Cuba." *Latin American Perspectives* 7 (Supplement 1975).

Kennedy, Ian McColl. "Cuba's *Ley Contra la Vagrancia*—The Law on Loafing," *UCLA Law Review* 20, no. 6 (August 1973).

Machado Ventura, José Ramón. "Boundlessly Confident in Our Youth." *World Marxist Review* (September 1985).

Mesa-Lago, Carmelo. "Economic Policies and Growth." In *Revolutionary Change in Cuba*, edited by Carmelo Mesa-Lago. Pittsburgh: University of Pittsburgh Press, 1971.

———. "On Rectifying Errors of a Courteous Dissenter." *Cuban Studies* 20, no. 1 (Fall/Winter 1990).

———. "Unpaid Labor in Cuba." In *Fidel Castro's Personal Revolution in Cuba: 1959-1973*, edited by James Nelson Goodsell. New York: Knopf, 1975.

Moreno, José. "From Traditional to Modern Values." In *Revolutionary Change in Cuba*, edited by Carmelo Mesa-Lago. Pittsburgh: University of Pittsburgh Press, 1971.

Murray, Nicola. *Feminist Review* 2 (1969).

Newhouse, John. "A Reporter at Large: Socialism or Death." *The New Yorker*, April 27, 1992.

Orozco, Ramón. "Fidel Holds Out against Reform." *World Press Review* (May 1990).

Padula, Alfred, and Smith, Lois. "Women in Socialist Cuba." In *Cuba: Twenty-Five Years of Revolution: 1959-1984*, edited by Sandor Halebsky and John M. Kirk. New York: Praeger, 1985.

Paulston, Rolland G. "Education." In *Revolutionary Change in Cuba*, edited by Carmelo Mesa-Lago. Pittsburgh: University of Pittsburgh Press, 1971.

Pérez-López, Jorge F. "Bringing the Cuban Economy into Focus: Conceptual and Empirical Challenges." *Latin American Research Review* 26, no. 3 (1991).

Pettavino, Paula J. "Novel Revolutionary Forms: The Use of Unconventional Diplomacy in Cuba." In *Cuba: The International Dimension,* edited by Georges Fauriol and Eva Loser. New Brunswick, N.J.: Transaction, 1990.

Pickering, R. J. "Cuba." In *Sport under Communism,* edited by James Riordan. London: C. Hurst, 1981.

Purcell, Susan Kaufman. "Collapsing Cuba." *Foreign Affairs* 71 (1992).

———. "Cuba's Cloudy Future." *Foreign Affairs* 69 (Summer 1990).

———. "Modernizing Women for a Modern Society: The Cuban Case." In *Female and Male in Latin America,* edited by Ann Pescatello. Pittsburgh: University of Pittsburgh Press, 1973.

Pye, Geralyn. "The Ideology of Cuban Sport." *Journal of Sport History* 13, no. 2 (Summer 1986).

Queralt, Magaly. "Understanding Cuban Immigrants: A Cultural Perspective." *Social Work* 29, no. 2 (March-April 1984).

Rabkin, Rhoda. "Cuba: The Aging of a Revolution." In *Socialist Cuba: Past Interpretations and Future Challenges,* edited by Sergio G. Roca. Boulder: Westview Press, 1988.

Reed, Gerald H. "The Revolutionary Offensive in Education." In *Fidel Castro's Personal Revolution in Cuba: 1959-1973,* edited by James Nelson Goodsell. New York: Knopf, 1975.

Robinson, Joan. "Cuba–1965." *Monthly Review* 17 (February 1966).

Roca, Sergio. "Cuban Economic Policy in the 1970s: The Trodden Path." In *Cuban Communism,* edited by Irving Louis Horowitz. New Brunswick, N.J.: Transaction, 1981.

Salas, Luis P. "Juvenile Delinquency in Postrevolutionary Cuba: Characteristics and Cuban Explanations." In *Cuban Communism,* edited by Irving Louis Horowitz. New Brunswick, N.J.: Transaction, 1981.

Schlesinger, Arthur, Jr. "Four Days with Fidel: A Havana Diary." *The New York Review of Books,* March 26, 1992.

Schmid, Peter. "Letter from Havana." *Commentary* 40, no. 3 (September 1965).

Serra, Clementina. "Report on the *Circulos Infantiles.*" Distributed in Cuba on July 13, 1969.

Slack, Trevor. "Cuba's Political Involvement in Sport since the Socialist Revolution." *Journal of Sport and Social Issues* 6 (1982).

Smith, Lois M., and Padula, Alfred. "The Cuban Family in the 1980s." In *Transformation and Struggle: Cuba Faces the 1990s,* edited by Sandor Halebsky and John M. Kirk. New York: Praeger, 1990.

Stubbs, Jean. "Cuba: The Sexual Revolution." In *Latin American Women,* edited by Olivia Harris. London: Minority Rights Group, 1983.

Szulc, Tad. "Can Castro Last?" *New York Times Magazine,* May 31, 1990.

"Tightening the Grip: Human Rights Abuses in Cuba." *Americas Watch* 4, no. 1 (February 24, 1992).

Tucker, Robert C. "Communism and Political Culture." *Newsletter on Comparative Studies on Communism* 4, no. 3 (May 1971).

———. "Culture, Political Culture, and Communist Society." *Political Science Quarterly* 78, no. 2 (June 1973).

Wagner, Eric. "Baseball in Cuba." *Journal of Popular Culture* 18 (Summer 1984).

"Women's Access to Education." *Women of the Whole World* 1 (1968).

Zeitlin, Maurice. "Inside Cuba: Workers and Revolution." *Ramparts* 8 (March 1970).

Cuban Publications

Bohemia
Con la Guardia en Alto
Cuba Internacional
Cuba Socialista
Granma
Granma International (GI)
Granma Weekly Review (GWR)
Hoy
Juventud Rebelde
Mujeres
El Mundo
Revolucíon
Trabajadores
Verde Olivo

Cuban Documents

Boletin Demanda
Gaceta Oficial de la República de Cuba
1976 Constitution
1976 Cuban Family Code

U.S. Publications

Baltimore Sun
Boston Globe
Christian Science Monitor
Foreign Broadcast Information Service (FBIS)
Miami Herald
Miami Herald (International Edition)
Miami Radio Monitoring Service
New York Review of Books
New York Times
Sports Illustrated
Topeka Capital-Journal
USA Today
U.S. News & World Report
Washington Post

Other Publications

Daily Yomiuri (Tokyo, Japan)
Este y Oeste (Caracas)
Excelsior (Mexico City)
La Hora (Guatemala City)
Latin America Weekly Report
La Nación (San José, Costa Rica)
La Prensa (Panama City, Panama)

Index

abortion, 100
Advanced Guard Movement, 147
Africa, 86, 222
Aguiar, Guillermo, 178
alcoholism, 86
Aldana Escalante, Carlos, 62, 67, 182
  on dissidents, 79
Amaro Salup, Raúl, 75, 80
American professional sports leagues,
  187
Angola, 70, 114
Argentina, 88–89, 114
Aristotle, 128
Armed Forces National Defense College,
  68
Army of Working Youth (EJT), 54, 161
Arocha, René, 206
Asia, 222
Association of Rebel Youth (AJR), 30

Barcelona (1992 Olympics), 189, 204–6,
  208–10
Barral, Fernando, 61
Batabano (Havana Province), 112
Batista, Fulgencio, 125
Batista Santana, Sixto (General), 69
Bay of Pigs, 67
Bernabe Ordáz, Eduardo, 198
Blas Roca Construction Contingent, 170,
  173
Bohemia (magazine), 45, 56, 148, 151, 177
Brazil, 89, 186, 189
Brigades of Militant Mothers for Education
  (Mothers' Movement for Education),
  104–5, 118
Buena Ventura, 154
Buenos Aires, 187
Bulgaria, 189

Camaguey province, 42, 144, 148, 151–52
Canada, 83, 189
Castilla Mas, Belarmino, 46
Castro, Fidel
  on Afro-Cuban religions, 47
  on the armed forces and juvenile delin-
    quency, 32–33
  on cheating in school, 58
  on Che Guevara, 64, 168, 171
  on Cuba's international sporting suc-
    cesses, 194
  on the dangers of idealism, 161–62, 168
  declares Marxist-Leninist faith, 9, 183
  on developing good athletes, 198
  early institutional reforms of government
    of, 9–10
  on the failure of 1970 sugar harvest,
    153
  government's response to Soviet political
    and economic reforms, 15–19
  on *gusanos,* 146, 180
  on "hippies," 44
  on lack of consciousness, 165–68
  on literacy, 23–24
  on material incentives for laborers, 155–
    56, 162
  measures and strategies employed to
    transform culture, 8–14
  on poor labor performances, 156–57,
    166–67, 171–72, 180
  on prerevolutionary attitudes toward la-
    bor, 128–30, 141–42
  on prerevolutionary (capitalist) sports,
    190–91, 202–3, 206–7
  on prostitution, 119
  purges the University of Havana, 34, 36
  on the Rectification, 19, 65, 165–66
  on revolutionary attitudes toward labor,

125–29, 131–32, 140–44, 147–48, 153–
55, 169, 170–72
revolutionary objectives of government
of, xi, 2–4, 7–8, 143
on role of the Party during Rectification,
173–74
on role of the Party in youth education,
62, 64
on role of unions in promoting increased
production, 146
on schools of revolutionary instruction,
27
on Soviet political reforms, 18
on sports consciousness, 195, 197
on union vigilance, 68
on university education, 35, 40–41, 43,
50, 56, 62, 73–75
on U.S. (sports) imperialism, 195, 201–2,
206–7
on vigilance role of CDRs, 69
on women and the Revolution, 87, 89,
99, 104–7, 109, 115–17, 120–21, 124
on work-study education, 50–51, 71–75
on youth and youth problems, 21–22,
41–42, 45, 52–53, 56–58, 61–65, 71
on youth attitudes toward the FAR, 68
Castro, Raúl, 32, 83, 92, 122
on Army of Working Youth, 161
on crime, 78
on drop-out rates, 52
on the FAR and levels of production, 32,
145
on the FMC, 92
on the role of labor unions, 132, 157
on the role of UJC, 65
on Territorial Troop Militia, 68
on youth problems, 63
Catholic Church, 2, 5
in prerevolutionary Cuba, 90, 128
Cedeño, Jorge, 72
Central American and Caribbean (CAC)
Games, 187, 189, 201–2, 206–8
Central Preparatory Commission of the
First Party Congress, 109
Che Guevara Trailblazers Brigade, 145
Chile, 89, 186
China, 181, 189n.10, 208
Colombia, 114, 186, 208
Colomé Ibarra, Abelardo, 69–70
Comecon (Council for Mutual Economic
Assistance), 16

Committees for the Defense of the Revolution (CDRs), 2, 8–9, 12–13, 45–46, 53,
85, 101, 135, 198, 216
CDRs infantiles, 31
restructuring of, 69
vigilance role, 71, 79, 157, 178–79
women's role in, 100, 108–9
Commonwealth of Independent States,
189n.10
Conciencia (revolutionary conscience), xi,
xiii, 4, 9, 11, 14, 17–19, 40, 42, 45, 56,
64, 66, 72, 86, 115, 125, 127, 129, 139–
42, 147, 156, 160–62, 165, 168–70, 183,
197–98, 213, 219–20
Conrado Benito Brigades, 24
Constitution of 1940, 90
Constitution of 1976, 107–8, 124
Article 41, 107
Article 43, 107–8
Council of the International Track and
Field Federation, 210
Costa Rica, 83–84, 186
Crombet, Jaime, 36, 53, 167
Cuba (magazine), 44
Cuban Academy of Science, 104
Cuban Air Force, 83
Cuban American National Foundation, 84
Cuban Commission for Human Rights and
National Reconciliation, 79
Cuban Communist Party, 5, 17, 183
Central Committee of, 66–67, 109, 121
Christians allowed membership in, 59–
60, 86
in crime control, 79
Party Congress (1975), 109, 112–13, 198,
203, 208
Party Congress (1986), 18, 56, 165–66,
173–74
Party Congress (1991), 6
Politburo, 62, 67, 122
role in education of youth, 62
role of expands, 20
Secretariat, 109, 122
successful athletes as members, 210
and women, 92, 121
Cuban National Ballet, 83
culture
definition of, xi, 1–2

day-care centers (círculos infantiles), 9, 31,
97–100, 198, 216

government redefines purpose of, 36–37
government seizes total control of, 36
program expanded, 71–72, 105, 113, 116
role in sports education, 198–99
training teachers for, 48–49
defections, 82–83
de la Cruz Ochoa, Ramón, 61
del Aguila, Juan, 150
Department of Education (FAR), 30
Department of Revolutionary Orientation
(ideology), 66–67
Department of State Security, 70
Despaigne, Joel, 204
Domínguez, Jorge, xii.n.3
Domínguez, Luis Orlando, 185, 198
Dórticos, Osvaldo, 133, 142, 157, 162
drugs, 52, 86
strict laws enacted, 55, 80
Dumont, René, 145
DuMoulin, John, 121

Eastern bloc, 3, 15–17, 27, 174, 182, 192,
221–22
East Germany, 189
Ecuador, 89, 186
education, 21–86
boarding schools (internados), 9, 28
day-care. See day-care centers
drop-out rates, 41, 52
on eve of revolution, 23
exchange programs in Soviet-bloc countries, 27
Ministry of, 29, 46–47, 58, 94, 98, 192
polytechnic programs, 35, 51, 84
in prerevolutionary Cuba, 22
role of schools in sports training, 198–
200, 209
universities. See University of Havana
work-study programs, 12, 48–51, 85
elections (1974 People's Power, Mantanzas),
109, 111–12
emulation, 64, 130–31, 170
Escalona Reguera, Juan, 69, 75
Espín Guilloys, Vilma, 67, 70, 83, 92–93,
116–17, 120–23
Ethiopia, 70
Europe, 86
Exemplary Parenthood Program, 46

Fagen, Richard, xi–xii
Family Code, 110–13

Federation of Cuban Women (FMC), 32,
36, 47, 69, 92–97, 101–2, 106, 109, 120–
21, 123–24
Congress (1990), 115, 124
Constituent Congress (1965), 94
membership, 94, 101
Federation of Secondary School Students
(FEEM), 39, 66
Federation of University Students (FEU),
33, 43, 66, 74
Fernández, José Ramón, 67
Figueros, Max, 42
Film Art Institute, 83
France, 83
Frank País Brigade, 30

García, Angel, 203
García, Gaspar Jorge, 28–29
García Pampin, Ricardo, 37–39
Germany (united), 189
Giron 92, 79
glasnost, 15
Gorbachev, Mikhail, 14, 164
grievance committees (comisiones de recla-
maciones), 130
Guanahacabibes, 134
Guantanamo Bay, 83
Guevara, Ernesto "Che," 2, 19, 64, 152
death of, 10, 142
on production levels, 133
on revolutionary labor attitudes, 125–31,
138–40, 141, 152
on the role of labor unions, 136
socialist emulation, 130–31
views in essay, "Man and Socialism in
Cuba," 35, 140
on women's role in the Revolution, 99
Guevarists, 126–27, 129, 140
gusanos, 38, 146, 180

Hacienda system, 90
Harmony Movement, 79
Hart, Armando
develops polytechnical educational system, 35
on Marxism-Leninism and the universities, 34
removed from Politburo, 67
stresses new ideological direction,
35–36
Hernández Ascuy, Ariel, 204

Higher Council of Universities (Ministry of Education), 43
Huberman, Leo, 148
Hungary, 189

India, 208
Industrial Development in Cuba (report), 141–42
Ireland, 208–9
Isle of Pines (Isle of Youth), 11, 40, 45, 199
Italy, 138

Japan, 189
José Antonio Echeverría Higher Polytechnical Institute (ISPJAE), 60
Juantorena, Alberto, 204–5, 210
juvenile delinquency, 39
    age of criminal responsibility reduced, 54–55
    Castro's view of, 62
    increasing rates of, 44, 52–55, 60–61, 75–82, 85
Juventud Rebelde, 59

Key West, 83

labor, 125–84, 220, 238
    Cuban Confederation of Labor (CTC), 68, 105, 132–33, 150, 170, 178
    Declaration of Principles and Union Statutes, 137–38
    Labor Hero of the Republic (award), 170
    Law Against Laziness (1971), 158–61
    Law of Labor Justice (1964), 136–38
    Ministry of, 130, 134, 137, 148
    National Congress (Twelfth), 137, 141
    National Vanguard Flag (award), 170
    Resolution 1225 (1969), 149–50
    Resolution 5798 (1962), 134
    unions, 136–38, 157
Lage Dávila, Carlos, 67
Latin America, 87–90, 114–15, 117
Lauguia, Isabel, 121
Law Study Commission, 109
Lenin, V. I.
    on the role of the party, 6, 183
    on the role of sports in revolutionary societies, 197
Leontief, Wassily, 151

Lewis, Ruth and Oscar, 101
Lezcano Pérez, Jorge, 179
Lipset, Seymour Martin, 1
literacy (prerevolutionary), 22
literacy campaign, 23–27, 94–95
Llanusa, José, 41
López Moreno, José, 67
Los Angeles (1984 Olympics), 189, 205
Luis, Mireya, 204

Machado Ventura, José Ramón, 76
Machismo, 3, 91, 97, 115
Madrid, 83
Mariel boatlift, 57
Martí, José, 34, 62, 67
Martín, Miguel, 138, 150
Martínez Sánchez, Augusto, 134, 136
Marx, Karl, 3–4, 138
    on cultural transformation, 5–6
    on revolutionary attitudes toward labor, 125–26
    on role of sports in revolutionary societies, 196–97
    on use of leisure of time, 200
Marxism-Leninism, 43, 50, 85, 125, 129, 137, 183, 189, 201, 221–22
Matanzas Province, 109
maternity law (1974), 105
Medin, Tzvi, xiin.3
Mesa-Lago, Carmelo, 148–51
Mexico, 88, 114, 186
    athletic exchanges with Cuba, 208–9
Miami, 203
Mikoyan, Anastas, 34
Military Units to Aid Production (UMAP), 135
Millar Barrueco, José M., 50–51
Ministry of Agriculture, 176
Ministry of Communication, 182
Ministry of Construction, 176
Ministry of Food Industry, 158
Ministry of Foreign Relations, 133
Ministry of the Interior, 38, 76
    role in education, 46
Missile Crisis, 182
Moncada army barracks, 23, 171
Montane, Jesús, 38
Montaner, Carlos Alberto, 87, 123, 215
Montreal (1976 Olympics), 188, 205
Moscow (1980 Olympics), 188

Mujeres (magazine), 93, 99
Mussolini, Benito, 138

National Assembly of the People's Government, 58, 69
National Association of Small Farmers, 180
National Congress of Education and Culture, 53
National Directorate of Police, 60
National Institute of Agrarian Reform (INRA), 27, 136–37
National Institute of Medicine, 193
National Institute of Sports, Physical Education, and Recreation (INDER), 190–95, 204, 208, 210
National Revolutionary Police (PNR), 70
National Revolutionary Police Auxiliary Forces, 70
National Social Prevention and Attention Commission (NSPAC), 70
National Training Center, 193
National Union of Construction Workers, 172
National Union of Writers and Artists, 135
Nelson, Lowry, 154–55
Nicaragua, 83, 86

Office of Military Centers for Intermediate Education, 46
Olympic Games, 186–89
Oriente province, 144, 154

Pakistan, 208
Panama, 207
Pan American Games, 71, 116, 187, 189, 193, 195–96, 204–9, 211
Paris, 203
Participation Campaign (sports), 191–92
peasant produce markets,
   closing of, 18
   opening of, 14
Peasant Vigilance Detachments (*destacamentos campesinos de vigilancia*), 70
Peña, Antonio, 80–81
Peña, Lázaro, 132–33
People's Councils (PCs), 69, 179, 216
perestroika, 14–15
Pérez, Humberto, 67
Pérez Roque, Felipe, 74
Pionero (magazine), 54

Plan de Titulación Maestros, 48
Plan for Technological Instruction, 46
Plaza of the Revolution, 153, 194
Poland, 189
posadas, 96
pragmatists, 127, 142
prostitution, 11, 81, 85, 96–97, 104, 115, 119
Puerto Rico (1966 Central American Games), 202
Purcell, Susan Kaufman, 88, 90

Quirot, Ana, 210

rapid action detachments, 71
rapid response brigades, 72
Rauf, Mohammad, 136
Rectification Campaign, 17–20, 56–57, 63–85, 115–16, 124, 165–82
religion, 47, 59–60, 86
Reserve Officer Training Corps (ROTC), 55
Revolución, 133
Revolutionary Armed Forces (FAR), 38, 115
   attitudes of youth toward, 59, 67–68
   compulsory draft, 10, 32–33, 105
   expanding role of, 11, 19–20, 69–70, 83
   role in crime control, 79
   role in education, 12, 46, 55
   role in sports education, 192, 200–201
   role in sugar harvest (1970), 144–47, 150
   women in, 113
   and youth, 32–33, 54, 83
Revolutionary Offensive, 10, 20, 42, 44, 94, 102–3, 142–44, 148
   objectives and policies of, 10
Risquet, Jorge, 67
   on labor, 148, 157, 161
   on Law Against Laziness (1971), 158
   on women's exclusion from the 1971 anti-loafing law, 105–6
Rizo Alvarez, Julian, 166
Robaina, Roberto, 64–66
   elected to Politburo, 67
Robinson, Joan, 138
Rodrígues, José, 192
Rodríguez, Carlos Rafael, 127, 137
Roca, Blas, 36, 132
   on the Family Code, 111
Romania, 189

Rome, 83
Ross Leal, Pedro, 68, 178

Sagarra, Alcides, 205
Salas, Luis, xiin.3
Savon, Félix, 204
School Goes to the Countryside, 39–40,
    42–43, 146
    popular views of, 42
Schools for Advanced Training of Athletes
    (ESPRAs), 192
Schools for Basic Training in Sports
    (EIDEs), 192, 199
Schools of Revolutionary Instruction (*Es-
    cuelas de Instrucción Revolucionaria*
    or EIRs), 27–28, 54
semiboarding schools (*Semiinternados*),
    49
Seoul (1988 Olympics), 189, 205
Serra, Clementina, 37, 97
Seventh National Assembly of the People's
    Organization in Education, 48
Show Tropicana, 83
Simientes, 97
slavery, 128
Society for Patriotic Military Education
    (SEPMI), 67, 85
Soviet Union, 3, 142, 152, 221–22
    Communist Party, 164
    economic and political relations with
        Cuba, 14–17, 164, 174, 181
    economic and social reforms of, 14–16
Spain, 83, 127–28, 208
spartakiades, 192
sports, 185–213, 219–20
    in prerevolutionary Cuba, 187–88,
        190–91
Sports City (*Ciudad Deportiva*), 193, 209
Stevenson, Teófilo, 203–4, 210
Suárez Campos, María Luisa, 69
Suárez Vega, Ramón, 66
sugar industry, 14
    1970 harvest, 104, 144–55
Superior Institute of Education (*Insti-
    tuto Superior de Educación*),
    27
Superior Pedagogical Institute, 75
Superior Polytechnic Institute, 75
Supreme People's Tribunal, 75
Sweezy, Paul M., 148

Tanzania, 208
teacher training program, 29–30, 48
    at La Plata, 30
    at Minas del Frio, 29
    Soviet and Czechoslovakian contribution
        to, 29
    at Topes de Collantes, 30
    at Varadero, 30
Teladrid, Raúl, 82
Territorial Troop Militia (TTM), 68–69, 85
Test of Physical Education (LPV), 196–97
Thailand, 208
Trabajadores, 178, 181

Uganda, 208
Unified Vigilance and Protection System,
    71
Union of Artists and Writers, 83
Union of Young Communists (UJC), 30–
    31, 39, 43, 53–54, 58, 63, 84, 177,
    198
    Congress (1987), 64, 117
    revitalization of, 63–66
    women in, 121
Union of (Young) Pioneers (UPC), 12, 31,
    37–39, 54, 66, 72
United States, 83, 87–88, 90, 210
    Cuban athletes defect to, 211–12
    sports teams of, 188–89, 205
United States Subcommittee on Internal Se-
    curity, 207
University of Havana
    drug use at, 52
    increasing absenteeism and apathy, 34
    official curbing of autonomy of, 33–34,
        43, 74–75
    purge of, 12, 34, 36, 43
    purge of Department of Political Science,
        34
    work-study program, 50, 74–75
University Student Militias, 33
Uruguay, 89

Valdés, Niño, 203
Vanguard Worker, 108
Varadero International Airport, 78
Venezuela baseball team, 208
Verde Olivo, 44
Victoria de Giron (Victory of the Bay of
    Pigs), 207

Vigilance Brigades, 70
Voluntary Sports Councils (CVDs),
   192

Washington Senators, 187, 206
West Germany, 189
women, 87–124, 220
  in the CDRs, 108–9
  in politics, 108–9, 120–22
  role in prerevolutionary Cuba, 89–92
  in sports, 118

Youth, 11, 21–86
  Centennial Column, 54, 146
  and Christianity, 59–60
  Computer Clubs, 65
  organizations, 30
  policies toward, 11
  Re-education Center, 39
  resistance of, 44–45, 56–62

Zeitlin, Maurice, 135, 138